COMPLETE COACHING GUIDE TO BASKETBALL'S MATCH-UP ZONE

Also by the Author:

The Winning Power of Pressure Defense in Basketball, Parker 1974

Secrets of the Passing-Dribbling Game Offense, Parker 1976

Coaching the Full Court Man-to-Man Press, Parker 1978

COMPLETE COACHING GUIDE TO BASKETBALL'S MATCH-UP ZONE

BURRALL PAYE

PARKER PUBLISHING COMPANY, INC.
WEST NYACK, NEW YORK

Parker Publishing Company, Inc.
West Nyack, N.Y.

Library of Congress Cataloging in Publication Data

Paye, Burrall, 1938-
Complete coaching guide to basketball's match-up zone.
Includes index.
1. Basketball—Defense. 2. Basketball coaching.
I. Title.
GV888.P38 796.32'32 80-12355
ISBN 0-13-159285-8

Printed in the United States of America

HOW THIS BOOK WILL HELP YOU

Man-to-man guarding, most coaches agree, is the best defense in basketball. So if you are blessed with quick, agile players of adequate size, you should play man-to-man variations entirely. But too often you have a few players who cannot master man-to-man techniques. Adding to the difficulty of playing man-to-man exclusively is the knowledge that all attacking teams know their man-to-man offenses better than their other offenses. It is usually the first thing they learn each year, and it is often the first thing they practice each practice session.

You reason that superior opponents will play you man to man. You must also conclude that your team, if it is inferior in personnel, cannot play man-to-man consistently and win. So you resort to a zone or a combination or the match-up.

Modern shooters will bombard the holes and the seams of whichever zone defense you choose. Combination defenses often confuse the defenders as much as the attackers. But the match-up, when played correctly, has no holes or seams. Your opponent's zone offense will always be matched man for man. Their man-to-man offense will always be zoned.

A standard zone defense can offer a temporary change of pace from your man-to-man defense, forcing a strong attacking team to momentarily adjust. However, it will take that strong attacking team only a few possessions to adapt completely. But the match-up is not a secondary or an auxiliary defense, although it can certainly be used as one. The match-up is a primary defense capable of stopping a strong opponent all night.

This book is a complete coaching guide to the match-up zone. Its scope is not limited to one mere match-up formation, an alignment you may not be able to use because of the players you have on hand. Instead, the match-up is shown from the three major zone formations: the 1-3-1, the 2-1-2, and the 1-2-2. Four chapters are devoted to each array. Each section reveals what personnel it is best suited for. Their strengths and their weaknesses are divulged. The drills aid in teaching the concepts. Guidelines are fully illustrated so they will be more easily understood. And all the material is presented in a logical, sequential order so that the text can be used as a quick reference work.

And the book does not stop there. There are entire sections addressed to how you can expand the containing match-up into a laning one, how you can pressure out of the match-up, and how you can adjust and stunt from the match-up. Hybrid defenses that either developed before the match-up or have become offsprings since the match-up have been explored and explained. What these hybrids were designed to stop—and their strengths and their weaknesses—have been disclosed.

All you need to know to teach the match-up—including all the little details—is here. You may even use the fundamental match-up's drills outlined in this book to make your own match-up stronger.

BURRALL PAYE

CONTENTS

PART II

THE 1-3-1 MATCH-UP

PART IV

THE 1-2-2 OR 3-2 MATCH-UP

PART V

ADJUSTMENTS AND PRESSURE FROM THE MATCH-UPS

COMPLETE COACHING GUIDE
TO
BASKETBALL'S MATCH-UP ZONE

PART ONE

DEVELOPMENTAL ASPECTS OF THE MATCH-UP

1 DEFINING THE MATCH-UP

Each coach must find his own defensive system. If your plan includes the match-up, or even if it does not incorporate the match-up, you will surely face it many times. In either case, a full knowledge of the match-up is essential.

This book develops the match-up completely. This chapter presents the beginnings: defining the terms, discussing the whys, disclosing the types, and postulating the rules.

Naming the Match-Up

The match-up is not a man-to-man. It is not a zone. Yet it is both. These three sentences describe the match-up perfectly.

In a man-to-man, every defender is responsible for a man even though the defender might sluff and appear to play some zone. In a basic zone, every defender is responsible for an area as he plays his zone. But in the match-up, every defender is responsible for a man as he plays a zone. The match-up, therefore, is a zone with man-to-man principles.

Match-ups start man-to-man because they match the offensive alignment the opposition uses to attack the match-up zone. As long as the attackers remain content to move only the ball, the defense stays man-to-man. But when the attackers commence cutting through, the rules of the match-up allow the defense to release the cutters (a zone movement) yet stay matched up (man-to-man defense).

Justifying the Match-Up

It is difficult to keep modern offensive continuities in check, because offensive continuities against zones permit the attackers to control the ball until they get the shot they want. Passing games, as well as patterned man-to-man attacks, work havoc against the man-to-man defense. But neither team attack is efficient against the match-up. Opponents must drill on a specially prepared offense if they wish to operate at maximum efficiency against the match-up. Often those teams do not have time to become so specialized. And, naturally, those teams will not have developed their special invasion to the degree that they have cultivated their man-to-man and zone attacks. This alone is sufficient reason to have the match-up in your defensive repertoire.

Varied and complex offensive patterns force the man-to-man defensive coach to adjust his defense, however minutely. The same situation exists for the zone defensive coach. These adjustments keep the defense off-balance and on the defensive. But the match-up zone puts the offense on the defensive. It keeps the attackers off-balance.

Should you have an excellent offensive player whose defense is suspect, you can hide him in the match-up. Or should a player get into foul trouble, the match-up will protect him.

Superior opponents cannot be defeated with the basic defenses: man-to-man or standard zone. So you must devise a defense to keep you in the game. The match-up permits you to concentrate your defense on the superior athletes, yet yield little to the inferior. Plus, you will have drilled on your match-up more than you could practice a defense designed for only one opponent.

You may deploy your personnel where you will get the most from them. Your better defenders can operate in the area of your opponents' greatest offensive efficiency. Your rebounders can stay near the rebounding areas. And your interceptors can cheat into passing lanes, knowing they have zone help behind them.

Match-up defenses can dictate the offensive formations that their opponents will use. Most two guard defensive fronts, for example, will see a one guard offensive attack. Most odd-front zones face an even-front offensive alignment. Much pre-game strategy comes from this knowledge.

A good scouting report on your opposition will tell you what your opponents will do under certain circumstances. If their point offense is weak, then employ an even zone front. If their two guard front is less effective than their point offense, then engage the 1-3-1 or the 1-2-2 match-up. Or if you feel you can break on your opponent, then work from the 2-1-2 match-up. This defense usually faces the one guard front: they have only one man back to stop your fast break.

Some teams read the match-up as a zone. When they attack with a zone offense, you counter by emphasizing the man principles of the match-up. Other teams will use their man-to-man tactics against your match-up. You oppose their man techniques by accentuating the zone principles of the match-up.

You can use your match-up against the individual strengths of your opponents. You can exploit their weaknesses. The defense, for example, can sag on the good big pivot man to prevent him from playing his game. Nearby teammates can offer assistance, even double-teaming the excellent outside shooter.

The defense can lane the teams who use reverse action continuities as their primary attack. If the defenders are located in the outside passing lanes, a team cannot easily reverse the ball. They must spread their attack further outside, slowing down their passing and reducing their precision timing or they will risk an interception by the laning defenders.

Controlling Game Tempo with the Match-Up

It takes time to effectively attack the match-up. There are no holes or seams, leaving little or no penetration. Teams must over pass to find a man who can get off an unhurried shot. Consequently, the offense is slowed down. Those who attack hastily rapidly fall behind. Those who pass and pass and pass commit more and more violations. Those violations put the attackers further and further behind. Playing catch-up against the match-up is extremely difficult.

Because the match-up has one defender guarding each attacker and zone help nearby, driving is minimal, eliminating the great penetrator. Because of this zone help, very few one-on-one situations exist. Because of the zone qualities, screen and rolls are practically non-existent. The offense becomes defensive, moving further out on the court, shooting the longer shots, and reducing their offensive rebounding game.

Match-ups constantly realign their perimeter positioning, matching the positioning of the attackers. Due to being matched, the offense will switch their options and alignments frequently, depositing in the minds of their players the negative thought, "Our offenses will not work."

When offenses become negative, they become defensive. When they become defensive, they lose confidence, become confused, and spread. Those spreads limit rebounding, reduce penetration, nullify movement. In essence, the offense slows down. Add to this your ability to break swiftly from your match-up positioning and you have near perfect game tempo control.

If you prefer to speed up your opponent's offense, you could play pressure man-to-man. Or you could lane the match-up coverage, utilize the match-up traps, or employ the match-up stunts of Chapter 18.

Types of Match-Ups

Teams can play their match-up three ways: They can contain; they can lane; or they can pressure. All three types will be discussed fully. They are defined here.

A team permits perimeter passing while *containing*, but they gain greater coverage inside. Diagram 1-1 displays proper containing coverage. This will be discussed first, then expanded into laning and pressure.

To *lane*, a team merely places its defenders between the potential receivers and the ball. This eliminates the rapid reversal of the ball from one side of the court to the other. Teams that employ reverse action as a method to hurt the match-up can be laned. But the defensive team must not allow itself to become spread so wide while laning that it opens seams inside. Diagram 1-2 shows a typical laning defense. Any babied or misthrown pass will be intercepted. Both 1 and 4 must spread to receive a pass. This slows down the passing, a direct result of laning.

Pressure and stunts offer the third method. Traps and stunts are used to force turnovers, to speed up the game. Every coach will experience a need for this type of defensive attack. One example: you are behind several points late in a game and the opposition begins to stall.

Match-ups, therefore, can be extended or contracted. Containment exemplifies contraction while laning requires some extension of the zone. Trapping might require further extension. If the match-up is your primary defense, all of these are needed to combat all the offenses and all the strategies you will face.

The Three Basic Offenses Versus Match-Ups

For coaching purposes you can divide all offensive alignments into three categories: five perimeter, four perimeter, three perimeter. Dividing the offense into these three categories simplifies the teaching of the match-up rules. Diagram 1-3 shows the only area designated as post coverage. All the rest, including the side and low post, count as perimeter. So a point, two wings,and two low post players (a 1-2-2 formation) would fall under the five perimeter division. But a 1-4 alignment (point, two wings, and two high posts) would represent the three perimeter classification. And a 2-1-2 (two guards, two cornermen, and a high post) would count in the four perimeter category.

Diagram 1-4 shows how we divide the perimeter areas into points, guards, wings, and cornermen. This enables us to discuss cutters from each of these four positions without confusion.

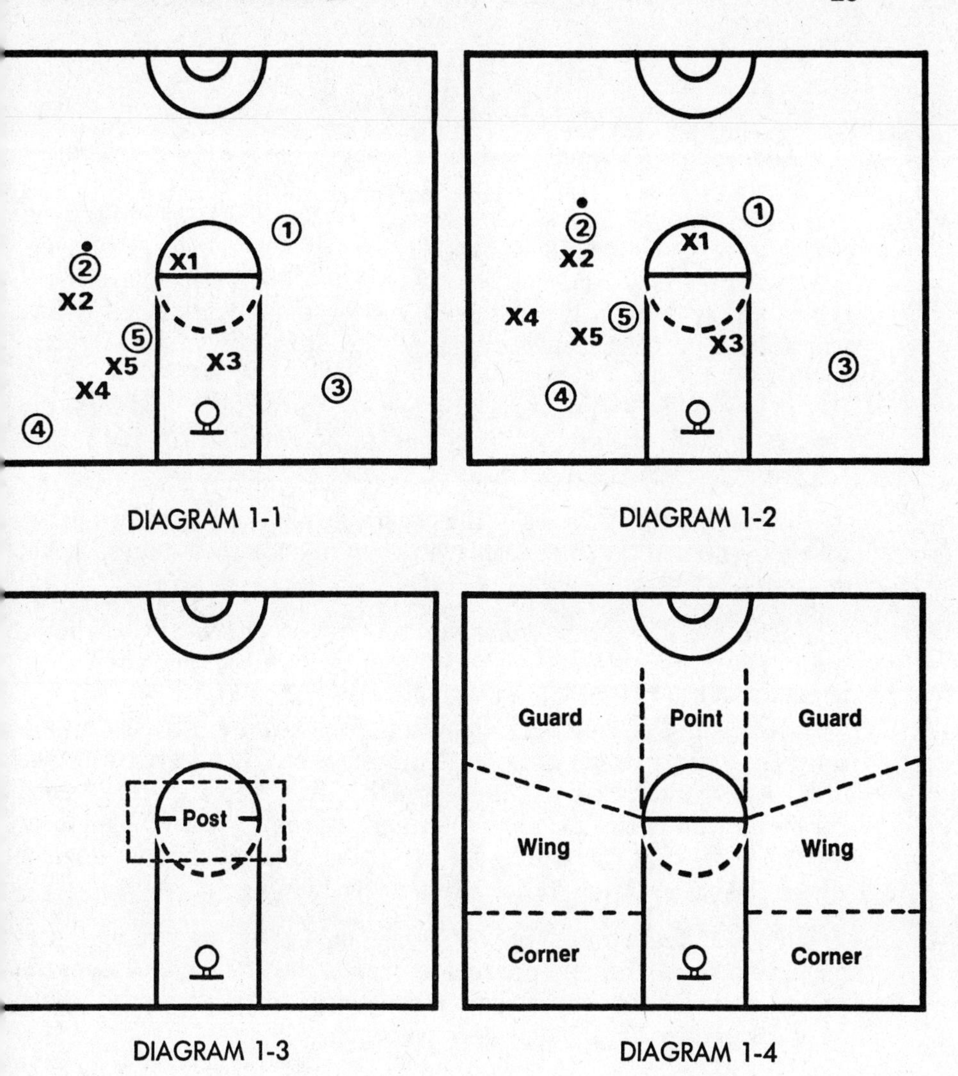

DIAGRAM 1-1

DIAGRAM 1-2

DIAGRAM 1-3

DIAGRAM 1-4

More Nomenclature

Strongside and ballside are synonymous terms. Weakside will be our vernacular for the side of the court away from the ball.

"Switch" will not be used to express how the match-up defenders change assignments. "Shift" will be used instead. Switch is a man-to-man term, requiring two defenders to change men. Shift is the match-up term, obligating two defenders to change assignments.

Formulating the Two Basic Rules

Rules govern the defensive movement of the match-up defenders. Defenders must match the initial alignment of the attackers. This will be called the *coverage rule.* If the attackers remain in those positions and content themselves to passing around the perimeter for shots, the coverage rule is the only guideline necessary. But the offensive players will begin cutting through the match-up, forcing the defense to react and adjust. Those cutters mandate another rule. It is simply called the *cutter's rule.*

These guidelines, the coverage rule and the cutter's rule, allow the defense to stay matched-up throughout the offensive attack. Both rules are presented here and fully covered in later sections in the book.

Coverage Rule. Basically the coverage rule consists of two parts: the perimeter and the post. All players, regardless of their duties, should understand the responsibilities of both.

Perimeter. X1 always takes the man with or without the ball in the point alley. If no player is in the point alley, X1 takes the man with or without the ball in the right guard alley (Diagram 1-4).

Regardless of the initial alignment of the defense, X2 must always cover the first perimeter attacker to the left of X1. X3 always covers the first perimeter attacker to the right of X1. And X4 covers the second perimeter man to the left or to the right, whichever place the attacker locates, of X1. In other words, X4, the matcher, must always recognize where this man is located. X5 covers the center.

Post. If there are no high post men or if there are two high post men, X5 takes the center or perimeter man to the right and X4 takes the post or perimeter man to the left. When there is only one post attacker, he is covered by X5, the defensive post man.

Cutter's Rule. Basically the cutter's rule is twofold: covering a cutter from weakside to ballside and covering a cutter from strongside to weakside.

Weakside perimeter defenders may have to take the weakside cutter to the high post, especially when X5 defends a low post attacker on the strongside. Otherwise weakside to strongside cutters can be released to a ballside defender.

A weakside wing defender must pick up a cutter from the strongside to the weakside. The weakside defender should call "release" when he feels he has the cutter properly defended. This release should occur as near the foul lane line on the ballside as possible. This releases the ballside defender faster: He can hurry back outside to locate and to cover his new perimeter assignment.

General Coaching Guidelines and Drills

Regardless of the zone you contemplate using, your match-up guidelines can stay constant from year to year even when you change your basic zone because of new personnel. These general coaching guidelines can solidify your defenders' coverage of perimeter movement whether by dribble, cut, or pass.

A. The defender on the dribbler stays with the dribbler, allowing no dribbling penetration. All other defenders remain matched-up obeying the rules of the above section and the guidelines of this section. The only time the defender on the dribbler shifts to another attacker is when two attackers cross near the ball, or when the dribbler moves into an alley being defended by another defender.

B. On all crosses of offensive personnel, defenders shift men and call "cross."

C. Whenever the ball is in the corner, the defender covering the attacker in the point guard alley covers the passing lane into the high post region. The high post defender, if there is one, drops to cover the low post area. Usually when the ball is passed to the corner, teams prefer to cut. By having a low post big defender zoning this area, it is difficult to pass inside. Also, teams must have an attacker in one of the guard alleys for defensive purposes. Otherwise they would concede the fast break lay-up. Defensive court balance is a basic tenet of offensive basketball.

D. If weakside deep defender is occupied on the strongside, he yells "clear," telling the weakside wing or guard to slide as wing defender would in a regular 1-3-1 zone. This impels the weakside guard or wing to become the weakside deep defender. Diagram 1-5 shows a drill to teach X2 (X3, X4, or X5) to sag and slide as in a 1-3-1 zone. X2 drops and deflects the first ball passed by the coach; yet X2 must recover in time to defense his own assignment.

E. On successful passes to the high post, wing and corner defenders cover their men's cut toward the basket man-to-man while the guards sink and force the post to pass the ball back outside. The perimeter attackers pass the ball around the perimeter until one of them can hit the high post (Diagram 1–6). The corners and wings cut to the basket. Once the ball is forced out of the high post, passes begin again. You should allow only the lay-up in order to expedite teaching.

F. Ball on the strongside with cut going to the weakside:

1. Any up pass from deepest attacker followed by a cut along the baseline is covered man-to-man.
2. Any pass from wing to corner is covered "over" or "scissored." Anytime you hear scissors, you trade duties and responsibilities with the man you scissored. Diagram 1–7 displays a scissors. X3 simply follows 3 man-to-man yelling "scissors." Now X4 and X3

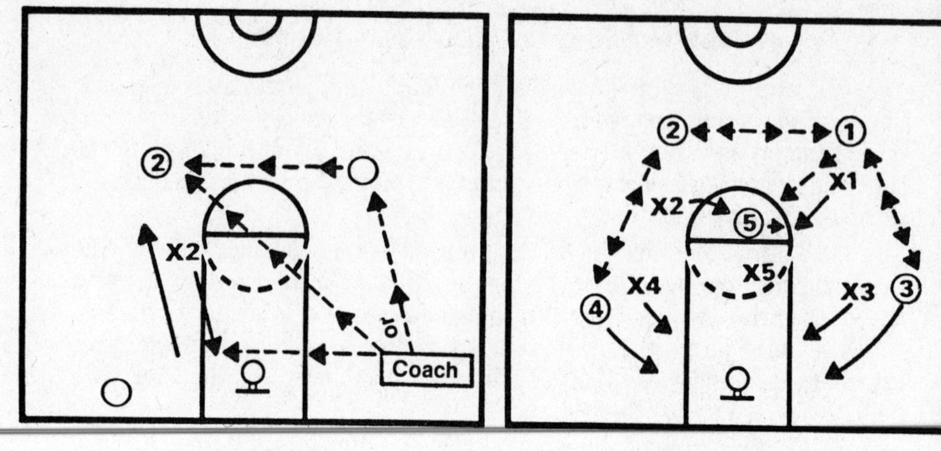

DIAGRAM 1-5

DIAGRAM 1-6

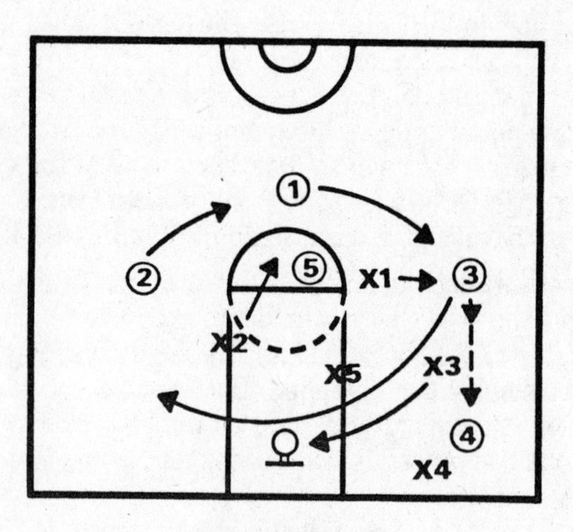

DIAGRAM 1-7

trade duties and assignments. X4 now covers the first player right of X1, and X3 covers second player left and/or right of X1.

3. Any pass from guard to wing is covered "over" or Penn Stated (Slide). Don't Penn State on passes to the corner. Don't Penn State or cover "over" unless your man cuts. The best time to slide is when cutters are coming from weakside to strongside corner or when a guard on the strongside passes and cuts to the corner. Otherwise it is best to cover "over."

G. Ball on the strongside with cuts coming to strongside from weakside:

1. On passes from point alley to guard, from point alley to wings or corners, or from a guard alley to the other guard alley, all followed by a cut, the guard defender covers "over" but defends the high post region until the center who has sluffed and made himself big can return.
2. If the high post is covered, the weakside deep defender can cover a cutter along the baseline man-to-man.
3. If the low post is covered, weakside defender (high or deep) covers a flash pivot from his area man-to-man.

As you read the following pages, you will notice these guidelines and rules are adhered to religiously. They are a brief summary of all the offensive cuts and maneuvers your match-up will face. They form the bases, the fundamental precepts, for your match-up zone.

2 UNDERSTANDING MATCH-UP HYBRIDS

Early in the history of basketball, coaches began to recognize the importance of combining zone and man-to-man principles in the same defense. Although many early coaches played man-to-man, they sluffed on the weakside, a zone principle. Coach Henry Iba of Oklahoma State was a consistent winner, with two national NCAA championships, using such a defense. Three decades later, Coach Bobby Knight of Indiana won an NCAA championship using the same defensive principles.

Between these two masters of defense, the zones began to form and to develop creatively. Many of these newly invented zones also involved man-to-man principles. These earlier zones with man principles, however, did not contain pure match-up techniques. They bordered on the match-up; they were match-up hybrids. Many of these hybrids are still used successfully today. Although this chapter cannot cover all the man-zones or any one completely, it will skim the few selected so you can see the match-up developing. You can use any of the hybrids as a team defense should they fit your personality and team needs.

Yo-Yoing

Yo-yoing permits the defensive team to adjust its front line from an odd to an even zone. The yo-yo begins as a 1-2-2 zone and changes to a 2-1-2 zone as the ball moves from the point to a guard to a wing or to a cornerman. This enables the yo-yo to "match-up" the perimeter attackers.

Diagram 2-1 depicts the yo-yo's starting alignment. X1 must be a tall, agile defender. He covers the point guard initially, but as the ball moves, X1 becomes the defensive center.

The yo-yo has amazing versatility. Should the offense use a high post, for example, X1 could drop off 1 and front the high post. That defensive maneuver would be extremely effective if the point guard, 1, was not an effective outside shooter. Should the offense use three guards, X2, X3, and X1 would cover them. A two guard offense would see X2 and X3 covering the guards. Two inside attackers would face X4 and X5. But three inside offensive performers would be defended by X1, X4, and X5.

Many teams attack the 1-2-2 zone with a two guard front. In that case, X2 and X3 "match-up" the two guards while X1 drops to cover the center.

Diagram 2-2 shows the defensive movement as the ball moves to the wing. X2 guards the ball, and X1 takes the high post. As the ball moves to the corner, X4 would cover the cornerman, and X1 would drop to defend the low post.

X1, therefore, becomes the only moveable defender. He roves until he matches the attack. Should cutters begin cutting through this zone, the yo-yo plays as a standard 2-1-2 or 1-2-2 zone, depending on the position of the ball. This cutter coverage robs the yo-yo from being a true match-up.

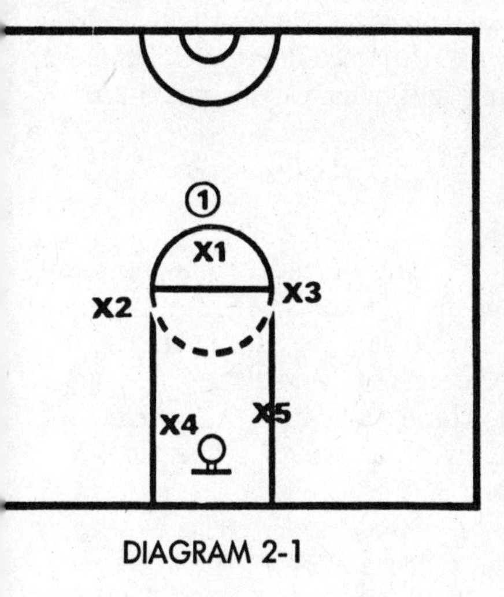

DIAGRAM 2-1

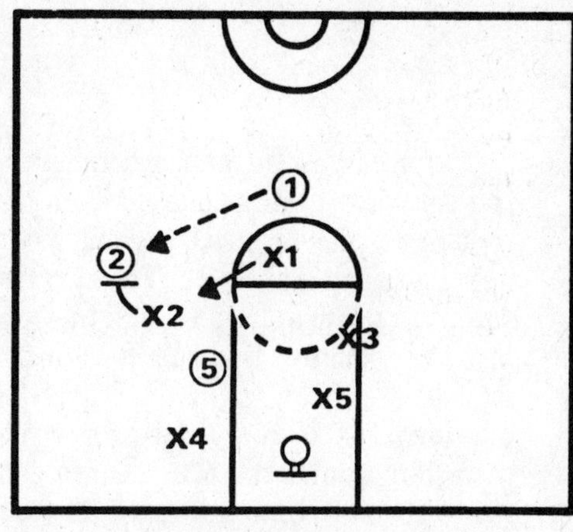

DIAGRAM 2-2

From 1-3-1 into 2-3 with First Penetrating Pass

Most teams attack a 1-3-1 zone with a 2-1-2 formation: two guards, a post, and two cornermen (Diagram 2-3). When one of those guards passes to a cornerman, it is considered a penetrating pass. Under the rule of this defense, the defense would switch from a point (odd) zone to a two guard front (even). Should the guards pass back and forth, the zone stays as a 1-3-1. Of course, the defense could adjust their rule: they could rule that any pass by the first guard automatically calls for a switch to the 2-1-2.

In Diagram 2-3, 1 dribbles into front court. When 1 passes to 3, X4 would cover 3 and stay as the left cornerman of the 2-1-2 zone. X2 would have 1 and would become the left guard of the 2-1-2. X1 covers 2 and remains as the right guard in the 2-1-2. X3 covers 4 and becomes the right cornerman in the 2-1-2 zone. X5 covers the center area in both the 1-3-1 and the 2-1-2 zones.

If 1 passed to 2 and the defense was changing its zone with the first pass, X3 would cover 2 and stay as the right guard on the 2-1-2 zone. X4 would have 4, and would play the right corner of the 2-1-2. X1 defends 1 and plays the left guard of the 2-1-2 zone. X2 defenses 3 and plays the left corner of the 2-1-2. X5 again covers the center in both the 1-3-1 and the 2-1-2.

All the initial slides are those of the 1-3-1 zone. After the defense sets, they play a 2-1-2 zone. This borders on a match-up and would be a pure match-up if the offense did not move. But once the offense cuts, the defense stays in the 2-1-2 zone, robbing it of being a true match-up.

Triangle Zone Match-Up

Match-ups began as combinations, some defenders playing man-to-man while others zoned. When the defensive team had only two men capable of playing pressure man-to-man defense, they frequently would use the triangle and two. The two good defenders would guard the opposition's top two attackers, and the other three would zone. This developed into the triangle (Diagram 2-4) or the inverted triangle (Diagram 2-5).

Teams began to match from these triangles. If the opposition played one low post man and two forwards, the two guards would be played man-to-man and the other three zoned (Diagram 2-5). When the opponents employed two low post players (usually a point offense), their two wings were usually good offensive performers. Such attacks could be stymied with the regular triangle (Diagram 2-4): X1 takes the point; X4 and X5 cover the low posts; X2 and X3 guard the wings man-to-man.

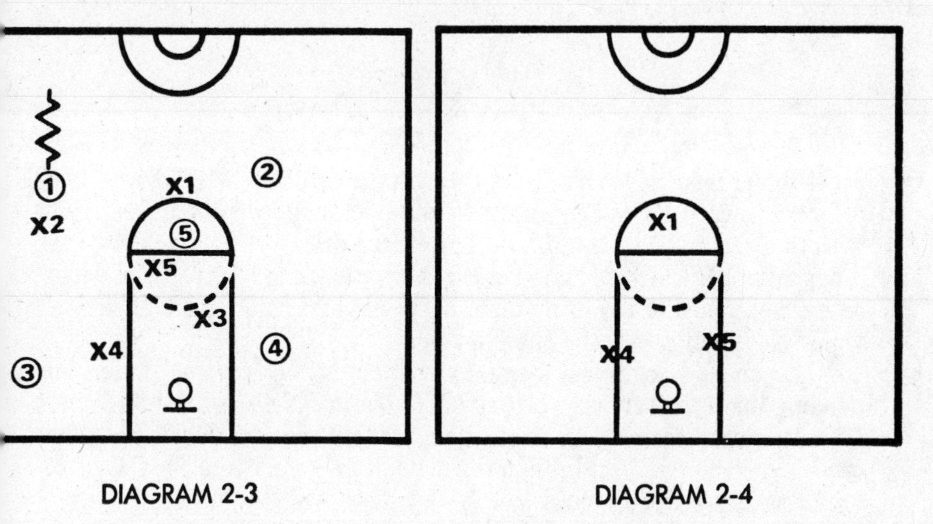

DIAGRAM 2-3

DIAGRAM 2-4

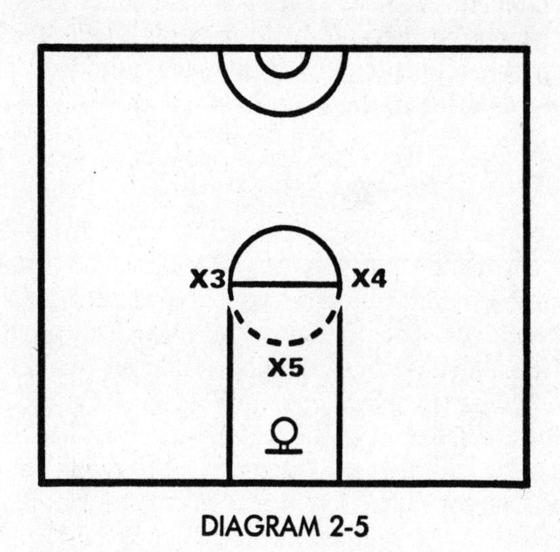

DIAGRAM 2-5

The two man-to-man defenders could press, deny, float, face-guard, three-quarter, sag or use any man technique they preferred. The zone defenders matched up and played their area. The defense can start as a 2-1-2 zone, and at a particular time spring into the triangle and 2.

The triangle match-up, however, is not a game-to-game, season-to-season defense. It is easily taught and could be used as a change-up, but it could never become the team's primary defense. But it has paved the way for deeper match-up concepts.

"T" Match-Up

Diagram 2-6 shows the "T." X1 covers the ball handler, picking up the dribbler near midcourt. X1 stays with the dribbler, whichever side he dribbles toward. Most teams attack the odd zone (the one guard front) with two guards. So when X1 would take the dribbler, X2 would take the other guard. But if X1's man, the dribbler, passes as he crosses midcourt to another guard or to a wing man, X2 would cover the pass receiver. X1 would then play the other outside guard.

X3 and X4 cover the forwards or the wings or the cornermen, depending upon the offense's original alignment. X5 played the post man.

It is easy to see how original alignments were matched. But when cutters began breaking through the zone, it no longer remained a match-up; instead it reverted back to a 2-1-2 zone.

Impatient teams succumbed to the "T" match-up. Because all arrays can be initially matched, even the overloads gain no advantage; the first offensive thrust cannot be successful. But a patient team faces the 2-1-2 zone after a few passes and cuts. Under that condition, the "T" match-up works no more hardship than the even front zones.

"Y" Zone Match-Up

When your opponent's star does not play a guard or the high or low post, the "Y" match-up might be effective (Diagram 2-7). X4 covers the baseline like he would play the baseline of a 1-3-1. X5 covers the post like the post man in the 1-3-1. Because the opposition prefers the two guard attack, X2 and X3 cover the guard alleys. Whichever guard, X2 or X3, is on the weakside as the ball goes to the corner would slide to the basket on the weakside as he would in the 1-3-1 zone. X1, not shown, guards the opposition's star man-for-man. Again, he may face-guard, deny, sag, three-quarter or use any technique his coach prescribes.

Most teams attack a 1-3-1 zone with a two guard front. Because the slides of this defense are the same as the 1-3-1, most teams run two guards against them. When this happens, they are met by defenders X2 and X3.

Should your opponents operate with a one guard front, X2 could pick up the point. X3 would then take the weaker offensive wing while X1 matched the star wing. A rule could require X4 to cover one low post while X5 covered the other. And you have your match-up.

Once cuts begin, however, the zone begins to slide as a 1-3-1 and not a true match-up. Because of its two guard front and its 1-3-1 slides, it can confuse the opposition.

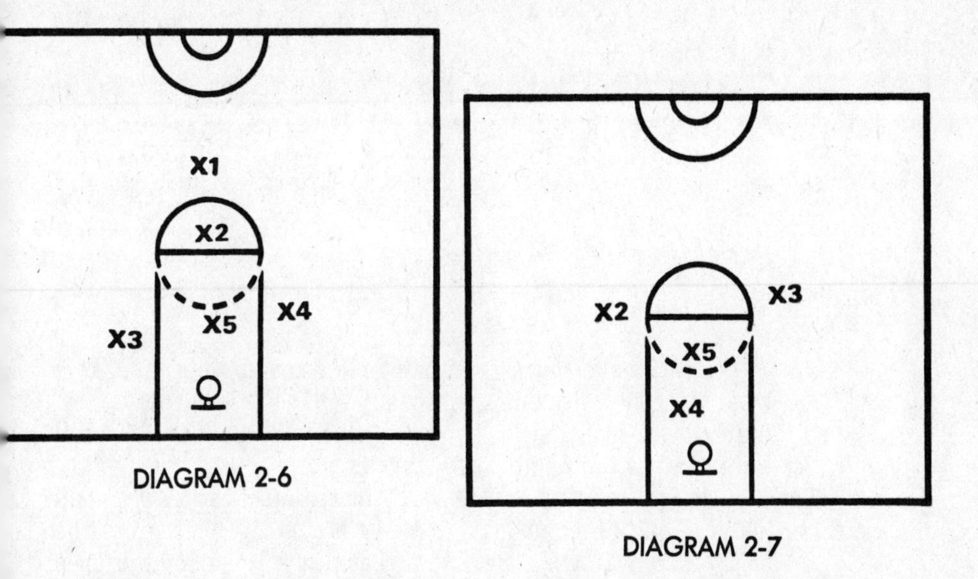

DIAGRAM 2-6

DIAGRAM 2-7

You can invert the Y zone (Diagram 2-8) to make it strong against a star guard. This is best when the complement to that strong guard is a strong inside attack. The opponents, however, must have a weak wing attack.

By inverting the Y, you have strength inside and you play the strong guard man-to-man. You can again "match" the opposition's align-

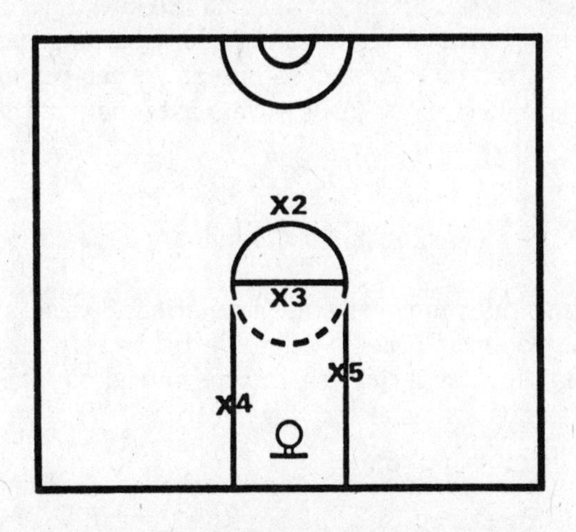

DIAGRAM 2-8

ment; but once movement begins, the shifts are basically those of the standard 2-1-2 zone.

Teams that run the Y and the inverted Y can confuse and match the opposition as well as keep pressure on their one great opponent. They basically slide in a standard 1-3-1 (Y) and a standard 2-1-2 (inverted Y). This sliding movement prevents the Ys from being true match-ups.

Rotating Four and One Stays Home

This defense plays more as a switching man-to-man than zone. It is best employed by teams with an exceptionally tall, agile inside defender. The rotating four channel their men toward this tall defender. This tall defender never leaves the middle. He stays home.

The outside four match up much as our match-up coverage rule—all defenders keying off the point guard. (See Chapter 1.) This gives the defense the appearance of a zone. Most teams use their zone offense against it.

This defense approaches the true match-up. As long as the attackers move around the perimeter by a pass or a dribble, the defenders play a switching man-to-man. They switch when any two attackers with or without the ball cross paths. The big man and the weakside offer exaggerated sags. But when cutters break through, the big center is the player who takes all cutters. Once the cutter moves to the outside, the perimeter defenders rearrange their coverage.

Rotating four while one stays home is effective when you have that one great center who can thoroughly defend the key area. You can even afford to play four small quick outside defenders. Its great problem is that it cannot be a season-to-season defense; for when you lose your big, agile man, you lose your match-up defense. That is not true of the basic or pure match-up.

Zoning by the Rules

Formulating rules to cover most zone attacks borders on the pure match-up. It came about because offensive teams began to place their star attackers in the area of the weaker zone defenders. This meant that the natural holes and seams of the zones were not their only weakness. Now an area of the court covered by a weak defender would have several excellent offensive performers cutting into that area. Easy baskets resulted. An adjustment had to be made. Rules began to form which developed into the pure match-up.

Harry (Mike) Harkins of Eastern Montana College formulated a set of rules in the early 1960's which almost conform to present day match-ups. He began from the 1-3-1 alignment and matched the opponent's initial formation. Everyone keyed off of the point guard. The point guard took the point alley or the right guard alley. The two wing defenders took the first attacker left and right respectively from X1, the point guard. The post defender matched the opponent's post. The baseline defender covered the remaining man.

When cutting began, Coach Harkins ruled, "Whenever a man passes and cuts through, we attempt to stop him for two or three steps, drop off, and take the first man opposite the direction of the pass." This gave the match-up an original line-up "coverage" rule, and it gave the match-up coverage on the passer-cutter (part of the cutter rule). All that remained was coverage on the cutters away from the pass cutting toward or away from the ball. And all the little techniques that make the match-up work so well would develop from usage year after year after year.

Diagram 2-9 shows a cutter, 1, away from the pass cutting toward the strongside. Coach Harkins would send X1 with 1, playing man-to-man. X1 would then become the baseline chaser of the 1-3-1 zone. What has happened is that the defense changed originally from the 1-3-1 to the 2-3 to follow the coverage rule. Then when the cutter broke through, the

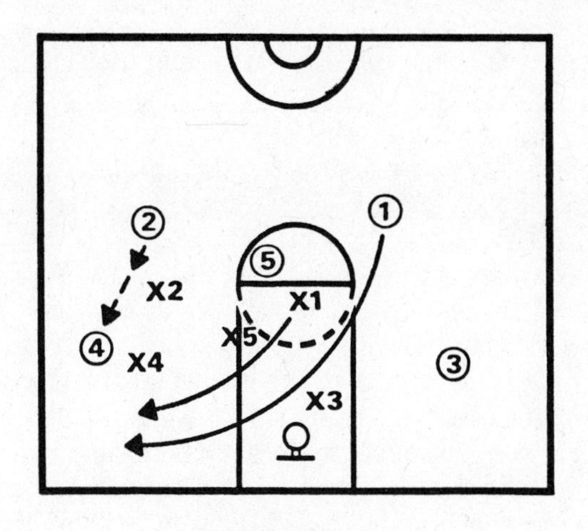

DIAGRAM 2-9

defense changed with the offense back into a 1-3-1. This is a recognized adjustment of the pure match-up. (See Diagram 10-2, Chapter 10.)

Other coaches developed other adjustment rules for zoning. Before long, the "match-up" would become a scientific, solid team defense, a defense capable of being used as a primary defense, a defense which played zone using man-to-man principles. Now the basketball world had a parallel to Coach Iba's man defense with zone principles.

Monster Man-Zones

Half a decade later, Mike Harkins appeared again. He had developed his "match-up" to a greater degree. He had theorized the use of a monster man (a matcher). This one defender needed good basketball savvy, for he was the only defender who must adjust according to the offensive alignment. By then, Coach Harkins was using this defense as his primary defense.

It was still not exactly a pure match-up. His monster man started as a guard if the offense was a two guard front. He started as a baseline man or a post defender if the alignment was a one guard front. On the first cut through by a guard from the two guard front, the monster man followed (Diagram 2-9), becoming the baseline man. If the monster man lined up originally on the baseline, he was to find the open attacker. When cutting movement began, Coach Harkins' players responded by shifting assignments. But his post man still stayed inside and his monster man would have to run the baseline (a regular slide of the 1-3-1 zone).

About this same time, Coach Bill Green and John Males were watching a Purdue-Notre Dame football game, and they noticed the adjustments of the defense to the offense. Only one defender—the monster man—was adjusting to the original offensive alignment. Thus Coach Green developed his rover man in his match-up zone. Later Coach "Digger" Phelps called upon Coach Green to teach his Notre Dame players the pure match-up zone.

The far Northwest and the Midwest did not have a monopoly on the development of the match-up. Coach Charles Ward was defeating stronger opposition in the South with his famous match-up. Coach Ward's rules, however, did not use a monster man. But his was a pure team match-up nevertheless.

Legendary coaching records were springing up throughout the high school ranks in America. Many of these coaches were employing their own made-up rules for a match-up zone. The most notable in our area was Jimmie Bryan, who used the 1-3-1 zone and developed it into a 1-3-1 match-up that led him to be honored as the National High School Coaches Association Coach of the Year (1967–68) and as its president in 1974–75. In twenty-seven years of coaching, he won 22 district championships and four state championships and finished second four times. Few match-ups confused opponents as successfully as Coach Bryan's.

The West and the East also had their contributors, but time and space cannot permit mention of them all. Each coach must make his own rules, although they might only minutely differ, that suit his personality, his basketball beliefs. To mention all contributors would be to mention most high school and college coaches.

The Amoeba Defense

Some coaches chose not to use match-up zones; so they originated their own zone team defenses. By creating new alignments and new slides, offensive teams must practice specifically for that one defensive team. Naturally, their offense would not be as effective against a team zone with unique slides as they would against the regular slides.

And team zones did not stop being invented in the 40's or 50's. Fran Webster developed the Amoeba as late as the mid-1960's.

The Amoeba differs from the conventional zones by the way the players move from one area of responsibility to another. It begins with a 1-1-2-1 alignment. The two guards are in tandem, and they play their areas much as the guards in the "T" Match-Up. The two wing defenders can trap at a wing, can lane a wing, can cover regularly, but must drop to low post when the ball goes to a corner. The baseline defender covers the area of the basket unless the ball is in the corner. Then he slides to the corner, much as a 1-3-1 baseline defender. It is impossible to give this defense the coverage it deserves in such a small space. This section is presented to illustrate that hybrids spring up yearly not only from the match-up but from conventional zones. When Coach Clair Bee designed the 1-3-1 zone, for example, it was a revolutionary hybrid of the then standard zone defenses.

Penn State's Sliding Zone

A major hybrid revolution took place in the 1930's at Penn State when John Lawther developed this change-up from the 2-1-2 zone. John Egli, an assistant at Penn State and player for Coach Elmer Gross, a disciple and player for Coach Lawther, wrote a book on the unique slides of this zone.

Although these slides were developed in the 1930's and 1940's, this defense is still used extensively. It's effectiveness over the standard zones stems from its uniqueness. Our match-up borrows one of its techniques.

Diagram 2-10 illustrates this technique. It must be mastered for your match-up to function by our match-up rules. You can make it a

DIAGRAM 2-10

fundamental drill (see others in Chapter 3) and practice it daily. It is one of the many solid defensive ideas of the Penn State Sliding Zone.

When 2 passes to 4 or when 2 cuts and 4 has the ball, the match-up would want X2 and X4 to shift assignments. X2 follows 2 a step or two below the free throw line to where he can see 4. X2 then slides out to cover 4, "releasing" X4. X4 immediately slides back toward the goal, making himself appear big, keeping 4 from seeing a passing lane to 2. When 2 comes into X4's view, X4 covers 2, and the shift has been successfully performed. X4 must, however, give X2 temporary help on 4, especially if 4 is an outside shooter, before kicking back to the low post to pick up 2.

You can also, with proper drilling, allow X4 to shift to any attacker coming along the baseline. Because this movement is such an integral part of the match-up team defense, it works best when defenders are drilled on it daily. Other fundamentals that must be constantly reviewed are presented in Chapter 3.

3 BASIC MATCH-UP FUNDAMENTALS AND DRILLS

Coaches teach their team defenses by drills. And those drills must present the required fundamentals for developing the defense soundly. This chapter divulges those drills and defensive fundamentals that are peculiar to match-up zones. Drills designed for teaching the different standard zones and the basic man-to-man, although definitely needed to develop the match-up, have been omitted, left for books devoted solely to those subjects.

One-on-One

How we play basic one-on-one defense on the perimeter of the scoring area was covered completely in *The Winning Power of Pressure Defense in Basketball* (Parker Publishing Company, Inc., West Nyack, New York). Whether we play man or zone, we cover the ball handler the same. We will offer here a brief review of those fundamentals.

The dribbler, not the dribble, must be defended. Containment, preventing penetration, is the order. It is too difficult to steal the dribble. To try is to allow the dribbler penetration. Penetration, not the outside dribble, kills the match-up.

Before the ball handler dribbles, his defender must prevent the jump shot. He must not leave his feet on a fake-shot-drive move. But he must stop the lethal jumper. To do this adequately, the defender on the ball starts in a front foot to pivot foot stance. He plays tight enough to prevent the jump shot, knowing he has help from his matched-up teammates. If the defender wishes to turn the offensive man away from his pivot foot, he merely places his front foot outside the attacker's pivot foot (Diagram 3-1). If the defender wants to channel the attacker toward his pivot foot, the defender overplays the prospective dribbler a half a man (Diagram 3-2).

Both of these coverages prevent the jump shot. So the attacker must fake to get his shot, or he will take his all-important first step in the direction we want. If he pulls the ball down to his side to start a drive or to fake one, we retreat step. If he pulls the ball back up into a triple threat position, we use the attack step, pulling our front foot up near his pivot foot, preventing the jump shot with our close play. Should the attacker crossover to go toward his pivot foot, the defender does a swing step. Under this coverage, the attacker cannot shoot, and he cannot gain an advantage with any of his fakes or his all-important first step.

The attacker must begin his dribble before he picks up his pivot foot or he walks. Once we have the dribbler moving, the defender slide-steps with him, placing his head directly between the dribbler's body and the dribble. This slight overplay prevents the dribbler from turning the corner and penetrating. The defender needs to maintain this coverage only a step or two. After that, his teammates can help him close the gap. (See later section in this chapter.)

But it is best when the defender can contain his man for many dribbles. This allows a wider spread by each defender, and it makes the perimeter defense more solid, making the match-up almost impregnable. The more each defender is drilled, the wider the area each can cover, and the better the perimeter defense becomes.

Different fifteen foot alleys should be marked off on the court and used for one-on-one drills (Diagram 3-3). Help will always be available outside the alley. But a defender who can control more than his alley will be worth his weight in gold. And a team which develops four such perimeter defenders could not be penetrated.

Do's and Don'ts of Individual Defense: Defense on your man after he has the ball but before he dribbles.

1. Begin with front foot pivot foot stance. This forces the attacker to use only one of his three alternatives.
2. Dictate which alternative you will permit your opponent; then dominate that dictate.
3. Don't react—act.
4. Constant movement of the feet is essential. Don't raise them high; instead grab at the floor with your toes.
5. Retreat with the leg on the side to which he has faked (retreat step).

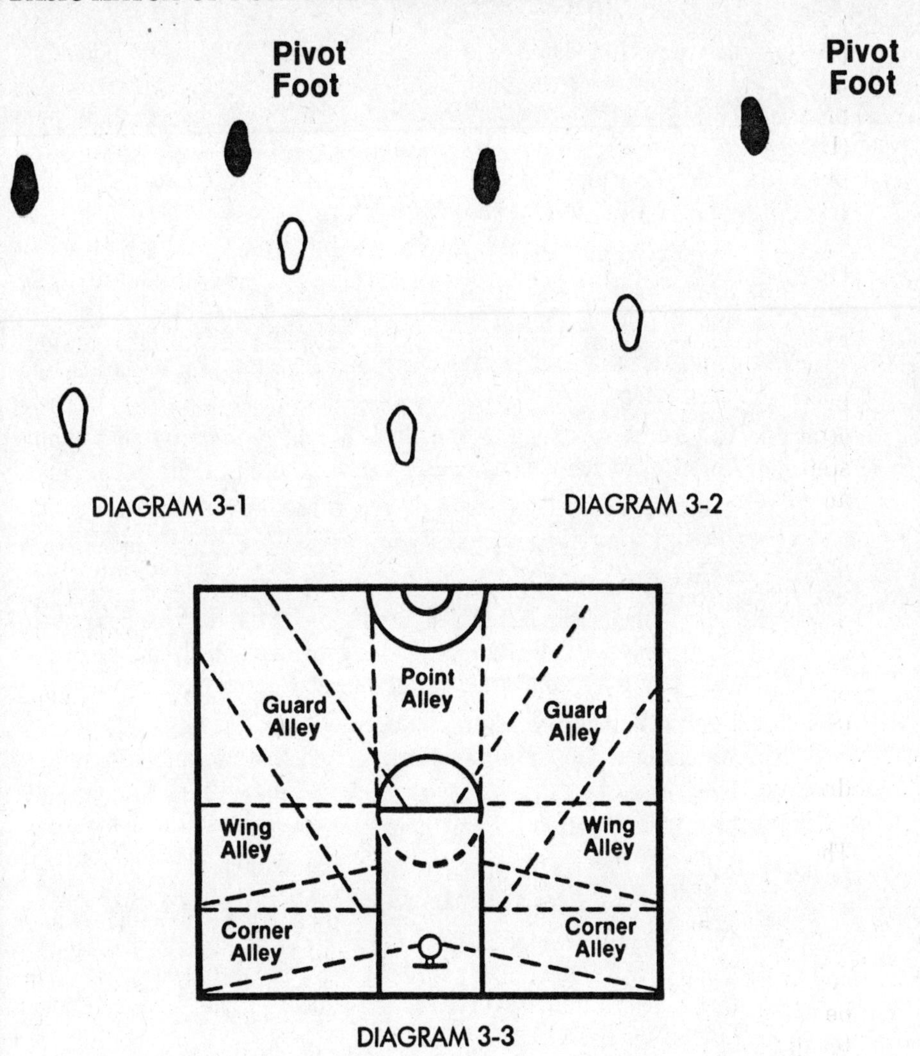

DIAGRAM 3-1

DIAGRAM 3-2

DIAGRAM 3-3

6. Have the hand up that corresponds with the forward foot.
7. Don't commit yourself first. If you fake in, pull back immediately. But get your opponent to do what you want him to do with your defensive fakes.
8. Stay between your man and the basket any time he has the ball.
9. Watch his belt until he begins his dribble. That part of his body moves less when he is faking.
10. Pressure the ball to make him dribble or throw an errant pass. But do not pressure him to the point where he can drive by you.
11. Watch position of the ball: When held low, retreat step looking

for the drive; when held by chest or head, advance step looking for the shot or the pass.

Defense on your man after he has started his dribble:

1. Make your man take a shot he does not want to take. Make him go in a direction he does not wish to go.
2. Keep nose on basketball as it is dribbled.
3. Keep your eyes focused at a point between the dribbling ball and the body. That will prevent reacting to dribbling fakes.
4. Never cross your legs unless you are trying desperately to catch a lost man.
5. Cut your opponent in the direction advocated by your team defense, including any called stunts.
6. Don't reach in. Defense is played with the mind and the feet.
7. If you lose a dribbler because of an excellent fake, sprint to a wise cut-off spot.
8. When his dribble has ended, move in tight and move your arms vigorously without fouling. Keep your arms in the plane of the ball; you may be able to deflect a pass.
9. Be ready to move in on the jump shot of a dribbling opponent by watching for his second hand to touch the ball.
10. Keep your hips low and your hands moving. Your head should be below the dribbler's armpit.
11. Be mentally alert when guarding a dribbler. Anticipate his every move. Always try to stay a half step ahead of him physically and mentally.
12. Keep the trail hand down to steal all crossovers, and try to draw the charge on all reverses when time and the score demands gambling.
13. Otherwise play the man and not the dribble unless forced to gamble. Penetration must first be stopped. It is easier to steal the pass than the dribble.

Three-on-Three Clearouts

Offensive teams must never be allowed to clear a side of the court. In fact, two successive lanes next to and on both sides of the ball should never be left vacated. If a player with the ball is located in the guard's alley, for example, then the defender on the ball must have a helper no further away than in the corner alley (ballside) and the other guard alley (weakside). Any wider of a spread by the defense could allow dribble penetration.

You may wish to channel an offensive team attack in one direction. When you decide to turn a team in one direction, your defenders can play their assignments tighter, preventing the jumpers. The defenders, under this plan, play the jump shooters tighter and concentrate on covering drives in only one direction. They overplay while using front foot to pivot foot defense. They know they have massive teammate help in the other direction. Thus, these defenders can cover their areas better, more efficiently. When you plan to channel, you should channel during this three-on-three (four) clearout drill.

Some individual defenders are not as adept as others. In fact, each team has several defenders who are weak. They remain weak although they improve with proper drilling. If some of these weak defenders are excellent offensive players, you can still play them without hurting your match-up zone. You simply have that weak defender always cut his man in only one direction. This allows the weak defender to concentrate on only one direction and the outside jumper. His teammates must also know that direction. This allows the weak defender and his teammates to control his area. During this three-on-three (four) drill, you should designate the weak defender's channelling direction.

Three-on-Three (Four) Clearout Drill (Diagram 3-4):
Procedure:

1. Line up three offensive players and three defensive players. Let X4 represent the matcher or a weakside helper.

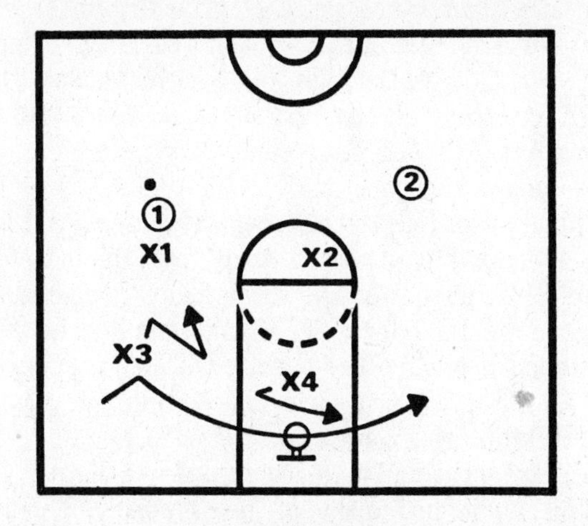

DIAGRAM 3-4

2. Attackers pass the ball around until one of them decides to go one-on-one. He hand signals a man near him to clearout.
3. The defender on that clearout cutter follows him at least to the free throw line on the ballside where he is released to X4 who represents a weakside defender or the matcher. The defender on the cutter then returns to his area or man to cover.
4. The man with the ball then goes one-on-one if he can.

Objectives:

1. To teach defenders proper sag (three step drill, later in this chapter) as ball is being passed.
2. To teach defenders to go with the cutters to the ballside free throw lane line before releasing their cutters to a weakside man (basic rule, Chapter 1).
3. To teach closing the gap (a later section in this chapter).
4. To teach defenders how to cover one-on-one on perimeter.
5. To teach defenders away from the ball the interceptors stance, using proper peripheral views (a later section in this chapter).
6. To teach defenders not to allow a side of the court to be cleared.
7. To teach the matcher(s) proper coverage (a later section in this chapter).

Close the Gap Drill

When playing a match-up defense, each attacker on the perimeter will have a defender covering him. Because of this coverage, there should be no holes for a dribbler to drive through. But each attacker with the ball can drive to his right or to his left. And occasionally this driver can beat his defender. To prevent dribbling penetration, the nearest defender on the side of the drive closes the gap.

Before the drill is presented, the interceptors stance must be understood. This stance, used only by attackers away from the ball, forces the offense to pass a step further out on the floor, keeps perfect defense on the cutter, and enables the defender to offer maximum help on the driver. The interceptors stance is always used when we face a reverse action team. Such teams are always laned. Sometimes while we play containment, we use the interceptors stance as a change of pace.

Defenders away from the ball align themselves so that they are able to deflect any pass on the defensive side of their receiver. This is usually one step off the line between the ball and their man. It is frequently two steps toward the ball, while we play our match-up. These defenders play in a closed stance with pressure on their forward foot. This close stance permits a quick open front pivot and interception if the ball is passed on the defensive man's side of the intended receiver (Diagram 3-5). To pass to 2, 1 must pass away from the defender, spreading the offensive attack further out on the court. Should 2 begin cutting toward the basket, his defender can easily slide with him until he releases the cutter. He already has the advantage on the cutter: his pressure is on his outside foot, making his slide quicker and easier to perform. X2 also positions his body so he has maximum peripheral view of the court (see next section). Should 1 begin dribbling toward X2, X2 does a reverse pivot and jab steps toward the dribbler to slow him down (Diagram 3-6). Now X2 almost faces the dribbler, trying to help X1 stop 1's dribbling penetration.

2 can react in three ways. He can stand still, waiting for a pass from 1. If 1 does pass to 2, then X2 approach steps toward 2 to defense him, cutting 2 back toward the pocket (where X1 is). 2 can cut behind 1. If 2 does cut behind 1, X2 and X1 automatically shift. 2 can cut backdoor. If 2 does cut backdoor, X2 hedges toward 1, then retreats with 2 until he releases 2 to the matcher. X2 then returns to help cover the first attacker to the right of X1. While we run this drill, 2 steps off the court after being picked up by the matcher and X2 covers a new 2, the first player in that line. The situation would be reversed if 2 handled the ball and 1 was cutting.

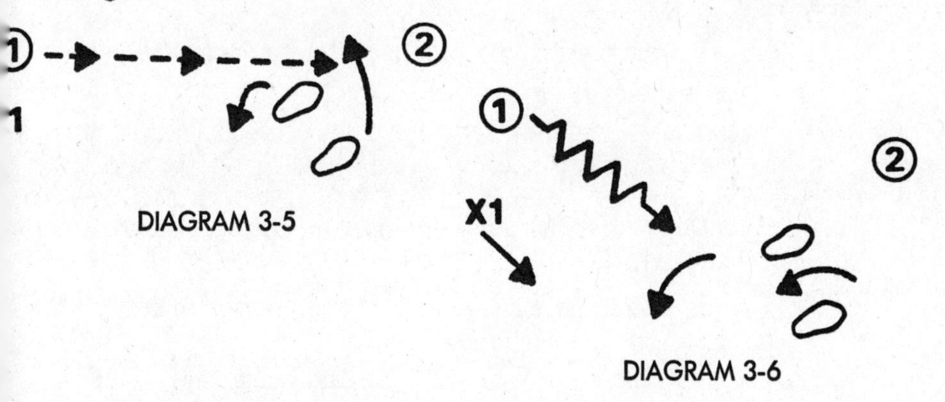

DIAGRAM 3-5

DIAGRAM 3-6

Close the Gap Drill (Diagram 3-7):

Procedure:

1. Line players up as shown. Rotate from offense to defense to end of the line. Use different alleys on the court from day to day (Diagram 3-3).
2. Let 1 and 2 pass the ball until X1 and X2 get their front foot to pivot foot and interception stances perfected.

DIAGRAM 3-7

3. Let 1 drive while 2 exercises his three options. Then let 2 drive and 1 exercise his three options. Make sure the defense of X1 and X2 is more than adequate.
4. Use X4, your intended matcher, to receive the cutter when that option is permitted.

Objectives:

1. To teach front foot to pivot foot and interceptors stance.
2. To teach closing the gap against all options.
3. To teach playing on the plane which gives the defender maximum peripheral view of the court.

Do's and Don'ts of Individual Defense: Away from the Ball Before Your Man Gets the Ball.

1. Use peripheral vision and constant foot movement to keep both your man and the ball in view.
2. Do not relax when your man does not have the ball. Play ballside, one step off the line between your man and the ball and two steps toward the ball (the three step drill).
3. Talk constantly to help your teammates out.
4. Be willing to help a teammate who has been beaten by a dribbler. Close the gap.
5. After a shift stay with the man you have just picked up until you shift again.

6. Keep at least your hand, head, arm, and one foot in front of and on ballside of any inside attacker. Keep your ear on his chest. Make yourself appear as big as possible.
7. When using the interceptors stance be prepared for a badly thrown pass.
8. Take the path away from a cutter before he gets to the most advantageous receiving point.
9. Make a cutter cut behind you. The backdoor is not a dangerous cut against the match-up—the give and go and middle cuts are, and they should never be successful.
10. When on the weakside, protect the middle of the court and be prepared to accept and release cutters.
11. Defense does not end until you or your teammates have the ball.
12. Learn the weakside rebounding techniques (Chapter 4).
13. When guarding an inside man or a cornerman on the weakside, keep your back parallel to the baseline.
14. Never let the knee of your lead foot advance beyond the toe of that foot.
15. Retreat quickly on defense. When you don't have a man in your area, double-team or sag to the middle.
16. Never trail your man on cuts toward the basket.
17. Move in the direction of the pass before your man does.
18. Any time you have better than 50% chance to intercept a pass, go after it. You have help behind you.
19. When your man cuts away from the ball, release him and hurry back out to find your new assignment.
20. Don't turn your head to watch a pass by the man you are guarding. Move in the direction of the pass.

Weakside Coverage

Because of the nature of the match-up defense, weakside defenders have many responsibilities. They must cover cutters toward the ball. They receive cutters away from the ball. And, in general, they offer maximum help to the ballside.

To accomplish these objectives, weakside defenders must master the three-step drill, they must play on the plane which gives them maximum peripheral view of the court, and they must deny the cutter.

The Three-Step Drill (Diagram 3-8):

Procedure:

1. Use five attackers and five defenders. Because we teach containment first, we sink two steps toward the basket and one step toward the ball on every pass. This gives us ideal help positioning.
2. Let the attackers come down floor and align in a pre-determined formation. Now let the defense match-up with the perimeter. It is best to use your next opponent's offensive formation.
3. Let the offensive players pass the ball around the perimeter and the defensive players make their three step adjustments. No cutters. After you are satisfied, let the offensive players begin again in a new formation.

Objectives:

1. To teach the coverage rule (matching the perimeter).
2. To teach the three-step concept.
3. To teach positioning of the body for maximum peripheral view (see next drill).

Coaches, spectators, and players laud the deceptive passer who seemingly has eyes in the back of his head. But if they watch the same player on defense, they will find him stealing more passes, recovering more loose balls, helping his teammates more. This is excellent usage of offensive and defensive peripheral vision. Such vision comes from proper body positioning: playing on the plane of greatest peripheral view. These defenders see all cutters, especially their own assignment; and they never lose sight of the ball, knowing when it is passed, when it is loose, and when it is being dribbled toward them.

The Peripheral View Drill (Diagram 3-9):

Procedure:

1. Use five offensive players and five defenders. Each off-of-the-ball defender plays with pressure on his front foot and each has the foot forward that corresponds to the side of the ball. Diagram 3-9 shows their approximate back positioning.
2. As ball is passed, if it is thrown on the inside of the receiver, the defenders can intercept the ball. If ball is thrown away from the defenders, the three-step drill is used. At the end of each pass check the positioning of each defender.

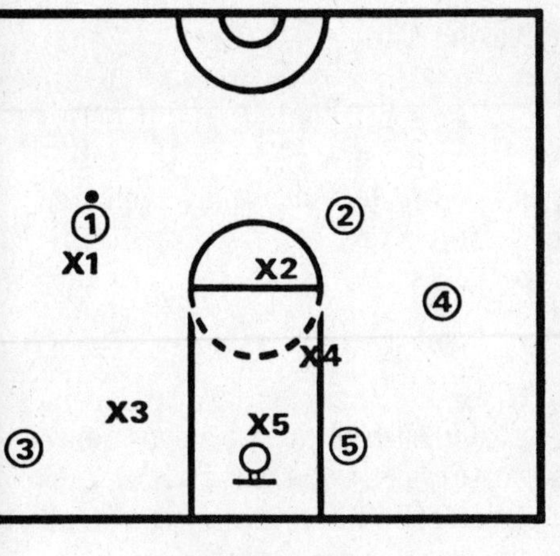

DIAGRAM 3-8

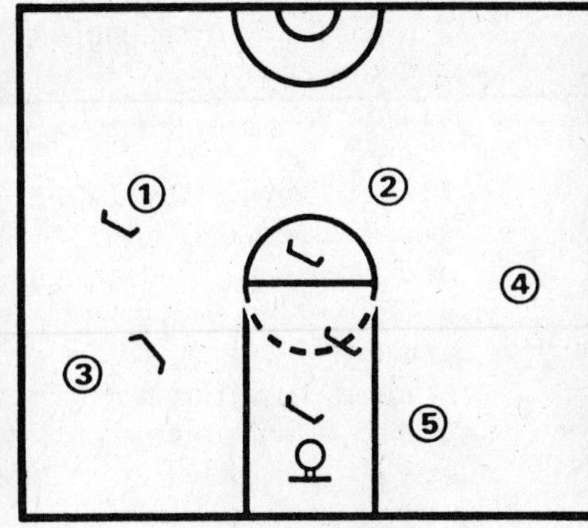

DIAGRAM 3-9

Objectives:

1. To teach the coverage rule.
2. To teach the three-step concept.
3. To teach maximum peripheral view positioning.
4. To teach the interceptors and front foot to pivot foot stances.

Deny the Cutter Drill (Diagrams 3-8 and 3-9):

Procedure:

1. Use the same alignment as the other two drills.
2. Let a player from the weakside cut to the ball. His defender denies him the cut, forcing him to go in the opposite direction or outside.
3. If the defenders have learned the cutter's rule, you may permit the proper shifts.

Objectives:

1. To teach the coverage rule.
2. To teach the three-step concept.
3. To teach the best positioning for maximum peripheral vision.
4. To teach the cutter's rule and denying the cutter the cut or the ball.

Accepting and Releasing Cutters

Defenders on cutters take them to the foul lane ballside, if necessary, before they release them. These defenders stay between the cutter and the ball, denying the cutter the pass. These defenders may even step in front of the cutters, hoping to draw the charge, at least slowing the cutter down, ruining the timing of his cut. And if it is a team continuity type offense, stepping in front of any cutter will ruin the precious timing of the entire offense.

Cutters moving from strongside to weakside should never receive a pass. Their defenders need only to defense them a step or two before "releasing" them. Defenders on these cutters must mentally realize that their new outside assignments might get a shot off before they can reach him. They must be prepared to hurry back outside.

Cutters moving from weakside to strongside are infinitely more dangerous. If they get the ball, they can quickly score from the inside. Any shifts must allow no seams. And many times this defender will play his cutter man-to-man, especially to the high post area. Body checking this cutter will ruin his timing.

Receiving a cutter quickly from the strongside helps the strongside outside defense. It frees the defender on the cutter to hurry back outside. A weakside acceptor can see the entire court. He should have no trouble anticipating this reception if he has played on the plane of greatest peripheral view. He picks up this cutter at the strongside foul lane line, makes himself big, and stops in the lane near his defensive basket, adjusting his position between the ball and his new assignment (the three step drill). This defender must also momentarily zone the passing lane between the ball and his old assignment. He does this mentally while playing his new assignment physically.

Receiving a cutter from the weakside requires split second timing. It must constantly be drilled upon. Any inside seam that opens might lead to a successful penetrating pass and easy basket. This defender's proper sag (three-step drill) and our rule of picking up the cutter at the foul lane strongside enable the team defense to eliminate the inside seams. The sag will clog up the middle, compressing the passer's angle inside. Tight coverage on the ball reduces the passer's vision. And shifting at the strongside foul lane line decreases the area of inside coverages.

Devise drills that correspond to your next opponent's offense as often as you can. That would permit your team to drill against the next offense they'll face. And its breakdown factors will permit excessive drilling on accepting and releasing cutters from all angles and the other fundamental techniques of the match-up zones.

Let's consider an offense you will face from your next opponent. From Diagram 3-10, you can see that 2 is the first cutter, trying to find the seam of your zone. Let's break that one cut down and make a drill out of it.

By the coverage rule of the match-up, if X1 takes 1, then X2 would have 2, X3 would cover 3, and X4 would defend 4. X5 has the pivot.

Diagram 3-11 depicts the breakdown drill. Of course X5 would make himself big when the pass enters the corner. X5 could offer a lot of help to X2 and X3. But not putting X5 in the drill puts an overload on X2 and X3, making those two defenders more aware of their coverage responsibilities:

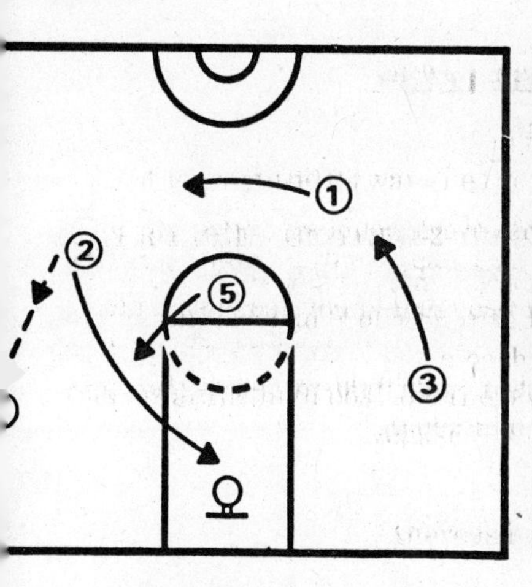

DIAGRAM 3-10

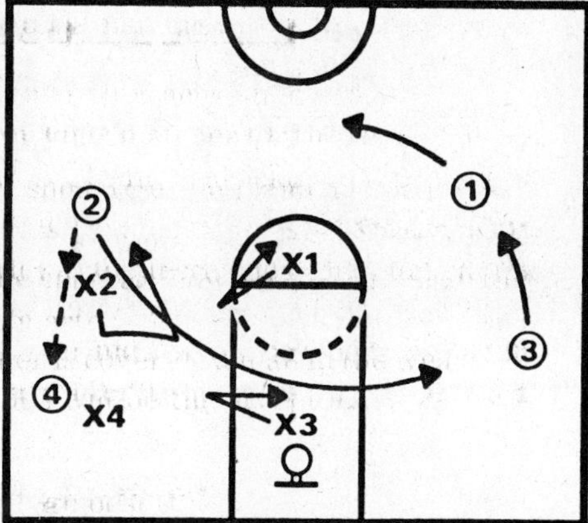

DIAGRAM 3-11

Procedure:

1. Line up four perimeter attackers and drill on coverage on the outside.
2. X2 has moved a step toward the pass and two steps toward the basket—the three-step drill.
3. X3, the weakside deep defender, is located near the basket. X3 plays on the plane of greatest peripheral view, meaning he sees all of the court.
4. X2 is in an interceptor's stance, sliding back to the area of the free throw lane line on the ballside. X3 picks the cutter, 2, up there. X3 knows he must also mentally play in the lane between 4 and 3. X3 also knows that the quicker he picks up 2 the quicker X2 can slide back out on 1 who has rotated to 2's old spot. The offense must rotate a player to that spot, or 4 will not have anyone to receive a pass if 4 gets into trouble.
5. When X3 feels he has 2 covered, he says "release." This cues X2

to hurry mentally back into position on 1. If 1 can get the shot off before X2 physically arrives, we want him to shoot. If 1 cannot, we want 1 to pass to 4 and cut through with each offender rotating one more position. This continues until X2 and X3 learn to release and accept cutters. The drill may be run from any alley (Diagram 3-3) on the court.

Objectives:

1. To teach proper coverage rules.
2. To teach the three step drill.
3. To teach accepting and releasing cutters.
4. To teach adjusting with each pass.
5. To teach playing on the plane of greatest peripheral view.

Devise the drill that suits your match-up concepts. After all, to be ultra successful you must use your own techniques, ideas, drills. You may borrow, but you must rearrange to suit your personality and team needs. By drilling and drilling and drilling your players become excellent reactors to any offensive move. Drilling makes team defense instinctive, adding a step or two to its quickness and cleverness.

The Matcher's Coverage

Regardless of the initial zone alignment, the matcher has the responsibility of making sure the offensive formation has been matched. He is the defensive quarterback, the equivalent of the monster defensive back in football.

This man—or men, if a team is fortunate to have more than one—must have an astute knowledge of basketball. He must be willing to spend some time with his coach, learning what the coach wants and directing the team in those techniques. All teams have at least one player who can become a matcher. Many teams have more.

Matchers must play on the back line. This enables them to see the entire attack and the entire defense with one quick glance. If the matcher is a center or forward and you have another center, you will want to begin in a 1-3-1 alignment. If the matcher is a center type and you have another center who can also become a matcher, you will want to consider the 1-2-2 alignment. But if you have two forwards who can become matchers and you have a man who can play defensive center, your best formation will be the 2-1-2. Each of these formations have four chapters devoted exclusively to them. Basically, you must decide which is best for your team for that year.

No discussion of the matcher's duties and rules will be presented in this section. Because they are numerous, they will be discussed in detail when we consider each zone. The next two sections explain the matcher's relationship to inside coverage and to perimeter coverage. He must be proficient at both. The best way to drill the matcher is with five-on-five drills used above.

Center and Matcher Coverage

Matchers help the centers defend the inside. The rule is simple: Center covers the high post and the matcher takes the second attacker either left or right of X1 (wherever the second man is located). If there is no center or if there are two centers (high post only), the defensive center takes the offensive center to his right. The matcher takes the center or perimeter player to the left.

All inside attackers are fronted or three-quartered. Fronting usually occurs at low post on ballside. The defender tries to feel his man's movement by body contact. This enables him to keep a front position. When the attacker locates outside the low post (but not at high post), his defender three-quarters: places three-fourths of his body between the ball and the attacker. This defender can see both his man and the ball. In both cases, as well as at the high post, the defender need not play his man tight as in man-to-man. Instead, he should make himself as big as possible, offering maximum help inside on cutters. In essence, the center should, along with the matcher or weakside defender, patrol the middle area.

To understand these coverages fully, we must consider the three basic offenses used against match-ups: five perimeters, four perimeters, and three perimeters (Chapter 1).

Five Perimeter. This means there are no high post attackers, only low post or perimeter players. It is very easy for the center to cover the inside man to his right and the matcher to get the man to his left. *X4 will represent the matcher and X5 the center in all the diagrams in this section.*

Diagram 3-12 shows the typical five perimeter formation and the defensive coverage. Most offenses attack to their right, defensive left. The most obvious move is for 5 or 3 to break toward the wing, 2, who receives the first penetrating pass from 1. If 5 breaks, X5 denies him the ball. But if 3 breaks to the high post area, X5 would shift men with X3 because X5 will cover the high post man whoever he is (Diagram 3-13). It is an easy shift. Because of the three-step drill, X1 has the passing lane to the high post covered. X5 has sagged and places his body on such a plane

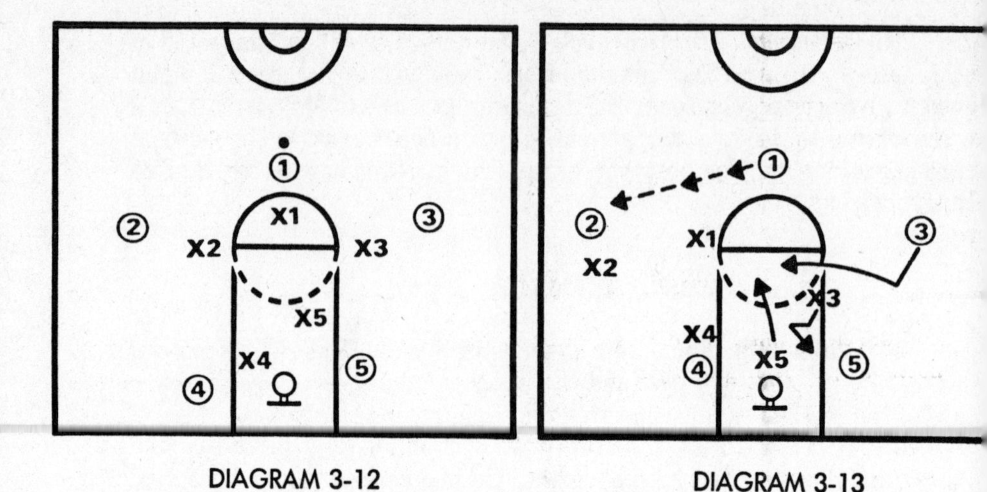

DIAGRAM 3-12 DIAGRAM 3-13

that he can peripherally see the entire weakside. X3 also has sagged and can easily shift with X5 upon X5's beckon.

Another typical move from this formation is represented by Diagram 3-14. The weakside wing would cut baseline to strongside. As 3 cuts through, X3 fronts him until X5 fronts him. X3 then would take 5, the first man right of X1. X5 would subsequently change with X4 as 3 cuts by 4. This gives X4 the second man left or right of X1, and X2 has the first man left of X1. So the coverage rule is obeyed as the matcher and the center react to the cutter's rule.

5 could cut along the baseline, forcing a simple shift by X4 and X5 as 5 cuts by 4.

The ball could go down the right defensive side. And if the defense is operating with two matchers, X4 and X5, the coverage would be the same. But if X4 is the only matcher, then each of the above situations would be covered as follows: When 2 cuts to high post area, X2 would cover him as a flash pivot, denying 2 the ball. X5 would not shift because X5 has a man in low post strongside to defend. If 2 cuts through to the corner, X4 and X2 would shift men, with X4 covering 2 all the way to the corner.

All the shifts above permit X2 to remain the first perimeter defender left of X1, X3 the first perimeter defender to the right of X1, and X4, if there is only one matcher, covering the second man left or right, whichever is applicable, of X1. X5 covers the high post or low post according to his rules.

Four Perimeter. This means that the offense operates with a post man, either a 2-1-2 or 1-3-1 offensive formation. Let's consider both from only the center and matcher's viewpoint.

Let's let 3 begin with the ball (Diagram 3-15). Let's let 4 flash pivot while 5 rolls to low post. If X4 sees this occurring, he can release X5 who goes a step with 5 before returning to high post. Remember X1 and X2 will have sagged into the high post passing lanes. If X4 does not see this cut in time, then he controls the flash pivot and X5 covers the low post. But with proper drilling, these two defenders can execute an effective release.

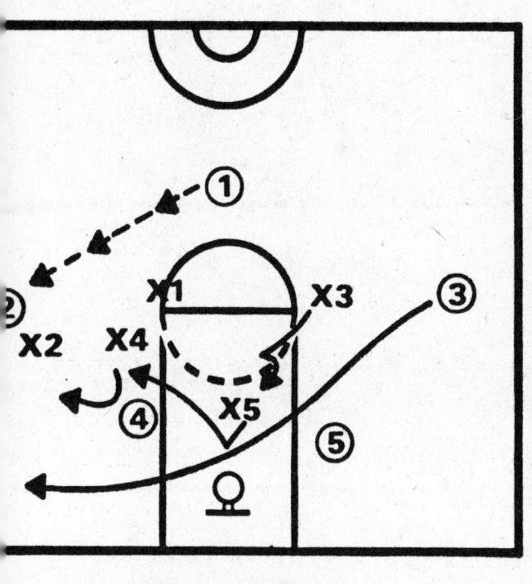

DIAGRAM 3-14

DIAGRAM 3-15

If 5 stayed high and 4 cut to low post, naturally X5 would stay high and X4 would cover 4 as a flash pivot cutter. (This is exactly as the coverage rule dictates.)

The only other possibility from the 2-1-2 formation is for 5 to cut to low post weakside and 4 still to flash to high post. X4 would take 5 at the low post and X5 could easily cover 4's flash pivot (Diagram 3-16).

Offensive coaches do not want too many players congregating near the basket. Consequently, when the offense operates from the 1-3-1 alignment, most of the cuts involve the high-low interchange (Diagram 3-17). Usually, the high post lines up on the ballside, stays for a count of two, then rolls low. The low post breaks high, timing his move for 5's exit. Because of the three-step drill, it is very easy for X5 to carry 5 to about middle post area before X4 picks him up. X5 would go back to cover the high post. X1 would be in the passing lane between 3 and the high post area, helping defense that area before X5 arrives.

The screen down or the screen up can be easily defensed with a man-to-man switch. Should the high post break to weakside low post while the weakside low breaks to strongside low, a simple shift would be in order.

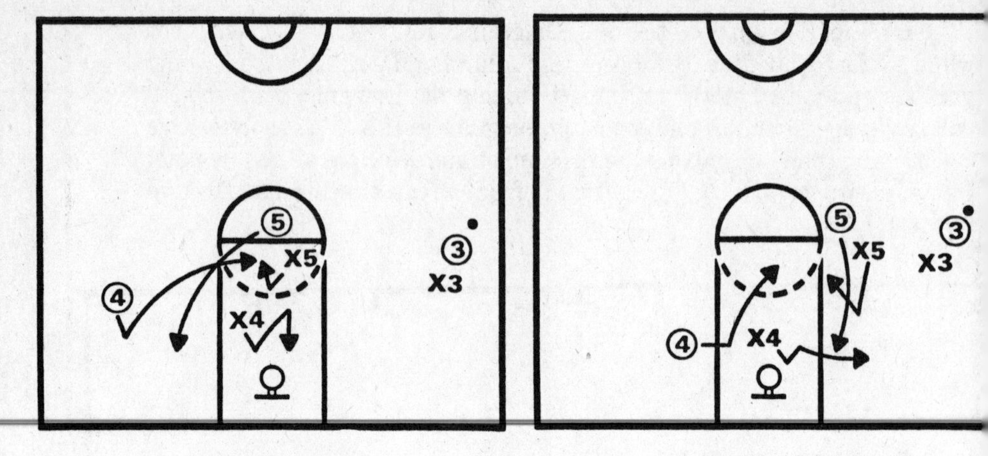

DIAGRAM 3-16

DIAGRAM 3-17

All these defensive movements should be drilled upon and drilled upon until they become second nature for the defenders. Automatic reactions, which are gained only by repetitive drilling, speed the shifts and make the defense more solid, more instinctive.

Three Perimeter. The only way the offense can have only three perimeter players is to have a double-high post, most likely the 1-4 formation. By the rules of double-post defense, the left high post is defensed by the matcher and the right high post is covered by the center. Let's observe a few of their basic maneuvers.

Diagram 3-18 depicts one favorite maneuver. 5 cuts to low post as 2 receives the pass from 1. Naturally X1 sinks one step off of his man toward the ball and two steps toward the basket, the three step rule, into the passing lane between 2 and the high post area. X4, upon hearing from X5, sags toward the goal, ready to pick up 5. X5 covers the only high post left, 4. You could, however, have X5 cover 5's cut man-to-man. This also follows the rule: When X5 has a low post strongside attacker, weakside cuts to high post are covered man-to-man. It is easy to see that 5 is a low post strongside attacker. You can imagine 4 as a flash pivot cutter to high post.

Should 4 originally slide down to low post and 5 break across to the high post, both would be covered man-to-man. This leaves X4 on a perimeter man and X5 on the high post.

The only other ordinary post action in the double-post is a double-cross. 4 breaks to low post weakside, and 5 cuts to low post strongside (Diagram 3-19). X4 would pick up 5 as he crosses the basket area, and X5 would sag his two steps toward the basket, letting 4 cut on to the weakside.

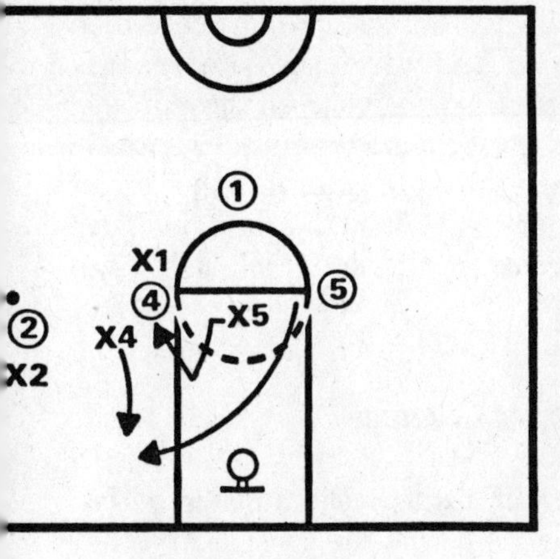

DIAGRAM 3-18

DIAGRAM 3-19

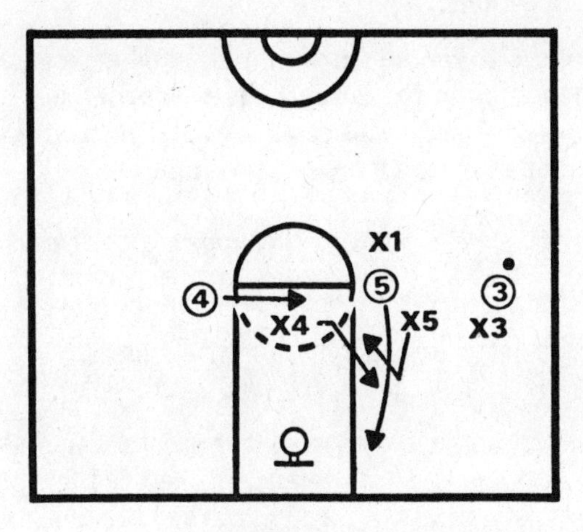

DIAGRAM 3-20

Should the ball be in 3's hands, the coverage is virtually the same. If 5 drops low and 4 flashes high, the post defenders shift (Diagram 3-20). This leaves X5 on the high post and X4 playing the low post, a perimeter player. X1 helps in the high post passing lane.

If 4 decides to cut to the low post strongside, X4 merely plays the cut man-to-man. X5 stays man-to-man on the high post. If the two attackers double-cross, as in Diagram 3-19, it is easy for the two defenders to shift. X5 merely slides a step or two low while X4 slides to the area of the basket.

When these defensive maneuvers have been drilled until they become instinctive, the interior defense begins to form. When these men can act in unison, it becomes easy to teach the rest of the defense. It is hard work, but then any worthwhile defense usually is. All these moves have one common thread: they follow the post coverage rule of Chapter 1. That is, the post man covers the post, and the matcher covers the second man left or right of X1. The lone exception: When the post defender defends the low post strongside, the weakside defenders might have to cover flash pivots to the high post.

Perimeter and Matcher Coverage

Matchers have perimeter responsibilities as well as inside duties. Matchers often have to cover the ball while it is in the corner. And they frequently guard the weakside deep attacker. They must cooperate with their teammates who also have these duties. The following three divisions explain these cooperations.

Fourth Man Around the Perimeter. Now the matcher is a perimeter defender. When the ball is in the corner, the weakside backline defender sometimes becomes confused on his coverage. This man will be X2, X3, or X4. All must be drilled on their proper coverage.

Four Men Around the Perimeter Drill (Diagrams 3-21 and 3-22):

Procedure:

1. Line up four attackers against four defenders.
2. Let the ball be passed into the corner.
3. Have the four outside offensive players cut through the lane in an assortment of ways. Have defenders execute their proper shifts. After each player has cut through the key area, he moves back to the perimeter.
4. Check to see if X3, X2, or X4, whichever is weakside deep defender, has counted and is defending the fourth perimeter man from the corner.

Objectives:

1. To teach defense of the cutter.
2. To teach cutter rule (shifting).
3. To teach sagging (the three-step drill).
4. To teach playing on the plane of greatest peripheral view.
5. To teach proper coverage of perimeter men with ball in the corner.

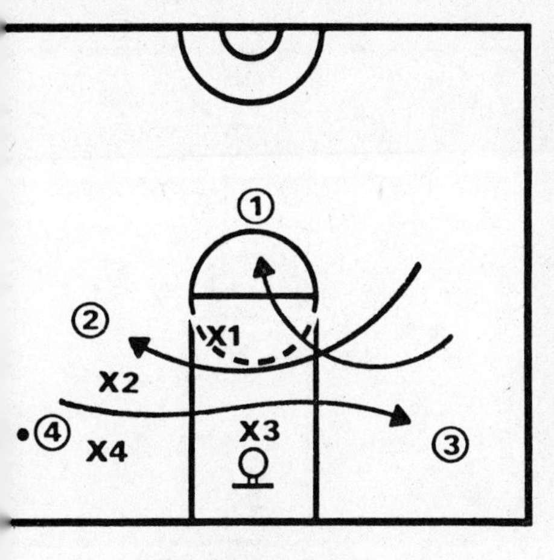

DIAGRAM 3-21

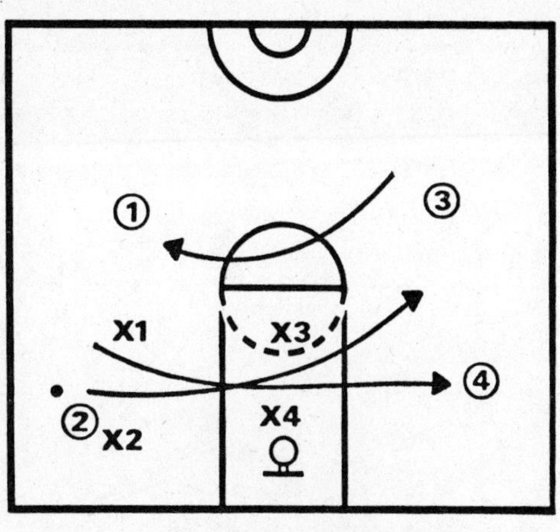

DIAGRAM 3-22

Three Men on the Backline. Three men on the backline will be covered by X2, X3, X4, and X5 (Diagram 3-23). If X4 covers the cornerman with the ball, then X3 or X2 will have to help X5 patrol the middle. Therefore, X3 or X2 should receive the same drilling as X4, the matcher, did with the center. (See section on matcher and center coverage.) X1 and X2 or X3 are left out of the drill so X4, X5, and X3 and X2 will have to respond more alertly. Of course, when you face a team that runs three men on the backline exclusively, X1 and X2 or X3 can offer exaggerated help from the outside. X1 would have lob coverage in Diagram 3-23.

Four Men on the Backline. When the ball is in the corner, the defense may have to match four men on the backline. Diagram 3-24 shows one such example. When X5 fronts 5 and X3 denies 3 the cut, X1 may have to cover 1 as the fourth man on the backline. We prefer shifts by X3 and X1. But occassionally, with the ball in the corner, X1 will have to drop fast and X3 and X1 will not be able to shift men.

We drill on this coverage with X3 (X2 if ball is on the other side) covering 3 on his high post cut. Then when the ball is reversed to 2, 3 steps out as the other guard. This merely means that X1 and the man guarding 3, X3, (X2 guarding 2 if on the other side) exchange responsibilities. X1 now takes the first man right of X3 (3's defender). The other defenders still follow their coverage rules. This can happen only when the matcher, X4, covers the cornerman with the ball and X3 and X1 cannot shift. This exception to our perimeter coverage occurs very rarely. But drilling on it prevents coverage adjustment problems when it does happen.

It also works well as an adjustment to the coverage rule. (See Chapter 18.) The wings and the point exchange duties for a possession or two. It can create the illusion of a different defense (man-to-man, for example).

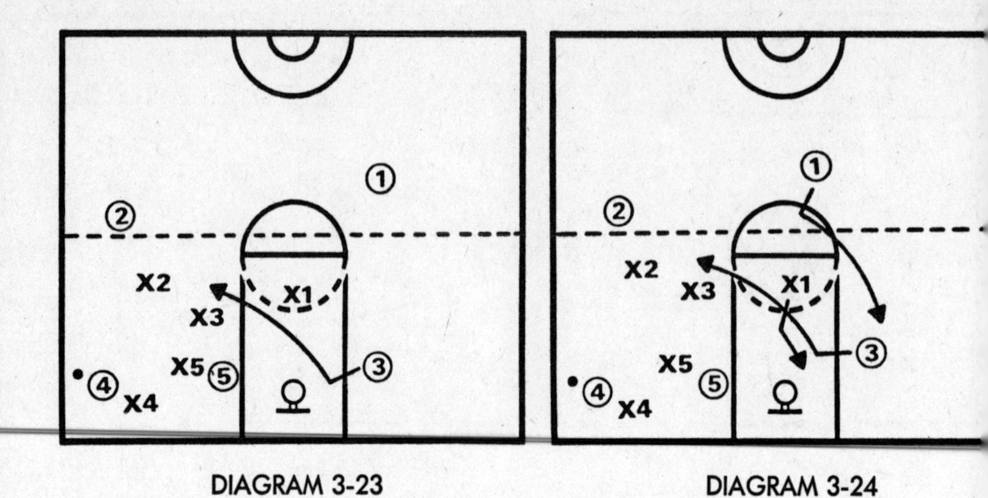

DIAGRAM 3-23

DIAGRAM 3-24

4 UNDERSTANDING DIFFERENT TEAM MATCH-UP CONCEPTS

It is hard for a coach to establish a rule, devise a drill, or play a defense he does not believe in. Players would know it, and the coach would fail. So down through the years, different coaches have conceived different team match-up concepts. This chapter presents some of them.

Matching from the Baseline

Probably the earliest method of matching the perimeter was to assign a defender the first man from the baseline. A second defender would get the second attacker from the baseline. Both of these would be on the ballside. There would be two defenders on the weakside with the same assignments: The bigger defender would take the first player from the baseline and the smaller the second from the baseline. The defensive center would cover the offensive post.

This method prevailed for a short period before the 1-3-1 overload took advantage of this 2-1-2 match-up theory.

Coach Charles Ward wrote a book describing his match-up in 1964. In Coach Ward's match-up, he used the baseline ballside defender as a parameter. He began from the same 2-1-2 alignment, just different assignments. The baseline man on the ballside guarded the first man from the baseline nearest the sideline. He was called corner position, strongside. The front position, strongside defended the second man from the baseline nearest the sideline. These two men played their attackers aggressively, using man-to-man tactics. The front position weakside defenses the "third man from the baseline around the perimeter on the side of the court in which the ball is located." And the corner position, weakside "zones his area by sluffing off to get good rebound position." The middle position, as the center is described by Coach Ward, "defenses the potential scoring threat nearest the basket in his area with aggressive man-to-man play." Coach Ward's match-up is still very effective and very much in use in the area where I coach.

Other coaches who have advocated matching up have channelled the ball into the corner. Once the ball reaches the corner, the defense matches up the perimeter with much the same assignments as advanced by Coach Ward. This method, however, leaves the offense attacking a standard zone until they pass the ball to a corner position. Some teams, when playing against this defense, never take the ball to the corner, preventing the match-up from ever becoming operative.

If you prefer one of these methods of matching, you can set up your match-up assignments. Your rules should prevent a hole in the perimeter. Then you can use our cutter's rule and have a perfect match-up. Or you may use our coverage rule, described in Chapter 1 and in the last paragraph in the next section.

Matching from Ball as It Comes Downcourt

Teams that match as the ball crosses the midcourt line must execute excellent defensive transition. They must be waiting as the ball crosses midcourt. They can match-up in two ways, match from the ball, or match from a particular defensive man.

Matching from the ball can result in some initial confusion, especially when the ball is passed near the midcourt line. Let's say that the opponents have two guards and three big men. They run from a two guard front. Now if the two offensive guards line up on the same side of the court (Diagram 4-1), the defensive guard could end up covering a big man near the basket, especially if the first passer at midcourt is a forward type who passes to the second guard who brings the ball into front court by dribbling toward the second defensive guard. 4 would clear to a corner before 2 dribbles. 1 would cut outside to the point guard position.

But the best way to match the perimeter is to match off of a particular defensive player. X1, your offensive point guard, and usually your quickest defensive player, is your best choice. X2, your other guard, should take the first player to the left of X1. X3, ideally the smallest

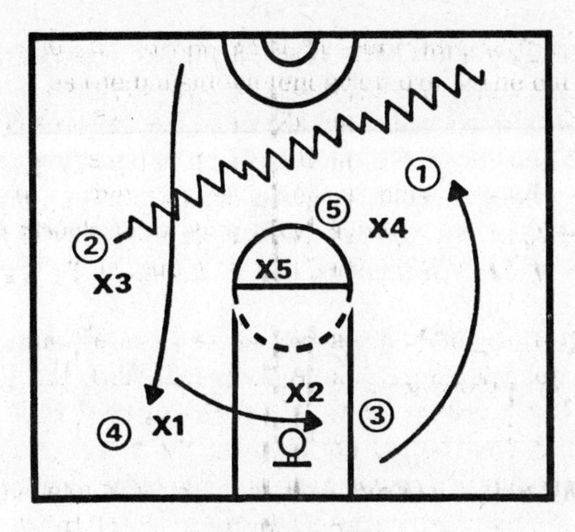

DIAGRAM 4-1

forward, will always take the first attacker to the right of X1. X4, the matcher, ideally the tallest forward, takes the second player either left or right of X1, if there is a fourth perimeter player. If not, X4 takes the left post, and X5 always takes the post or the right post if there are two. All defenders can see X1, and all know where to find their men. This type of initial matching should not be confusing. And this type of matching keeps X1, your smallest player, away from your defensive basket.

Matching from Odd Zones

When you use an odd zone, you should anticipate an even offensive front. This gives the offensive team a perfect three attackers to hit the offensive boards—and a perfect two defenders to stop your fast break.

However, if the opposition likes to run from a point guard offense, matching from an odd zone would pay the best dividends. The offense would be matched one-on-one, or they would be forced to go to their second best offense, which would also be matched.

An odd zone can force the offense outside as they cross midcourt. From there the odd zone has the option of forcing inside or outside or both.

Your own personnel, however, should be the major factor in your decision for an even or odd match-up. And, if not placed correctly, your personnel can cost you games, can ruin the effectiveness of your match-up.

Start with your matcher. He is your most important person. If you have a forward style matcher and a center to go with him, the 1-3-1 match-up will probably work best. If you have two center types who will make excellent matchers, the 1-2-2 will be your defense.

What makes a good matcher? He must be agile with better than average size and quickness. He must have an outstanding knowledge of basketball, or be willing to work to obtain the knowledge contained in this book. He must have above average basketball intelligence. And he must earn the respect of his teammates. He is going to be their defensive leader.

If your matcher cannot adequately cover an inside attacker and you want to play an odd match-up, you must operate from the 1-3-1, putting the matcher on the baseline. If he is a second guard type player, you might prefer to put your bigger forwards at the wings of the 1-3-1.

But if the matcher is a center type and you have another center, you have a perfect 1-3-1 match-up. And if the other center can also be trained to be a matcher, you want to work from the 1-2-2.

Your other personnel, of course, will need to fit your defense. But your matcher will make your defense. You might even hide a misfit defender for the entire season, but you won't hide a poor matcher for even one night.

Matching from the Even Zone

Even zones have tendencies to force the attackers into a point guard offense. This is ideal if you intend to fast break. They only have one defender back to stop your fast break. Also, odd front attacking teams usually play with two men inside. These two hit the offensive boards hard. Point offenses usually leave their other two players in limbo, sometimes defensing the fast break and sometimes hitting the offensive boards.

Offensive teams with two excellent guards should be matched by the 2-1-2. These teams either remain matched, or they play one of their guards out of position. By using the even match-up, you will have dictated to such attackers.

Even zones can force the attackers inside or outside at midcourt. They are better used to channelling the attack to the inside. After the offense passes midcourt, the defense can still dictate inside or outside to the offense.

Again, your personnel should dictate your match-up formation. If you have two matchers who are forward types, but neither of them can cover the inside and if you have a center to go with them, the 2-1-2 match-up will win you the ultimate championship. You could, of course, run the 2-1-2 with only one forward type matcher and an excellent defensive center. But you must scout well to help out the other forward. It might be best, under the last condition, to play the 1-3-1.

From your schedule, your personnel, and your opponent's theories on offense, you should decide which formation is best for your initial alignment. This book will cover all three.

From the first two sections in this chapter, you can begin to formulate how you want to match up. After deciding on your techniques of matching and your formation, you are ready to study the remaining parts of the book that are applicable.

Scouting and How It Will Help Your Match-Up

This section is not designed to tell you how to scout. Many books have sections on that subject. This section discloses the more important points of scouting that will aid your match-up. How you gather that information is up to you.

First you must check the opponent's offensive formations against zone defenses. You should check the zone they face and record the offensive formation they use against that zone. This may sound simple, but it is extremely important as your defense must first match that formation. You should make a note of where each offensive player plays. This might help you decide where to put your best defender. While observing the attacking methods, you should get their formation against man defenses. Often teams will run their man offense against your match-up just to get more offensive movement. If you know their man formation and they decide to run it against you, you will have no trouble matching it.

After recording the offensive formations you will see, you will want their various cutting maneuvers. Most teams use continuities against zones; so their options are usually predictable. If the defense can predict the offensive movement, they can practice against that movement. Their releases would be pre-drilled. The offense can be immobilized, almost shut out. Also, stunts that would disrupt the offensive team plans could be pre-planned.

Now that you have the formation and the movement, you should gain all the knowledge you can about each individual's strengths and weaknesses. Any peculiarities should be noted. Shots should be charted, and the defense will know each player's favorite shooting area. You can never gain too much information about each individual opponent. Should, for example, the opponents free-lance, this knowledge would be extremely valuable.

Next you must learn the opposition's system of play. Do they move quickly through the zone? Do they move the ball rapidly? Will they attack the zone in a slow methodical manner? Or will they shoot after a pass or two. After determining the plan of action, the defense can force the offense into another style of play, thereby helping to defeat their attack.

Lastly, you should chart their out-of-bounds play, their jump ball situations, their press offenses, and all their special game plans. If you should discover, for example, that they turn the ball over a lot, you might consider pressing, laning, trapping. But if they handle the ball well but can't shoot, you would want an exaggerated containment.

Anything you discover will help. But don't try to get too much. Too often, you end with a mess and get nothing. Make sure you get the basics: the formations, the movements off those formations, the team's style of play, and all the individual strengths and weaknesses you can. You should never trust one report; get two or more.

Again, you should make your own forms, devise your own methods for scouting. Make those methods suit your personality. You can live and coach with nothing less.

Remember: To defeat a zone, coaches must have a carefully planned attack. When the defense knows this planned attack, it becomes difficult, almost impossible, to penetrate and to defeat the defense.

Match-Up Rebounding

Rebounding is a weakness of all zone defenses. Because the rebound often goes to the highest jumper, positioning plays a minor role. But in the match-up zone, because every defender guards a man, positioning can be emphasized. Blocking out can be taught. Because all match-up defenders are responsible for a man as they play their zone, match-up rebounders can block out on every play.

Weakside. Rebounding has complete manuals devoted to it. Match-up rebounding from all alignments will receive attention in this section; techniques will be left to those manuals which cover rebounding completely.

Weakside defenders, because of their sluff, can be caught too far under the basket when the shot is taken. Yet most missed shots ricochet to the weakside. So this primary rebounding area must be covered aggressively. The weakside defender should approach slide toward the weakside attacker. He should go toward the shoulder of the weakside attacker which corresponds to the proper rebound angle of the shot. This will take the weakside offensive rebounder away from the area of the carom. Statistics indicate that the majority of shots taken from the baseline rebound on the baseline. Balls shot from forty-five degree angles rebound at a forty-five degree angle on the opposite side of the court. So a weakside baseline defender should slide at the shoulder on the baseline side of his assignment if the ball is shot from the opposite corner. He should slide at the shoulder corresponding to the midcourt side if the ball is shot from out on the floor. Most offensive rebounders will start away from this defensive overplay. When the attacker takes his first step toward the rebound, the defender should front pivot, making contact and maintaining it. He should keep his weight on his back foot while he approach slides; this enables a proper front pivot. He should keep his weight evenly distributed after he contacts his assignment; this allows movement in any direction the attacker chooses. This positioning should be maintained until that weakside defender or one of his teammates gain control of the carom.

The two most difficult teaching points: getting the weakside defender to go out after the offensive rebounder, and getting the weakside defender to watch the offensive rebounder until he front pivots. Too many tip-ins occur on the weakside because the weakside defender waits and watches for the ricochet.

Strongside. Strongside rebounders are near their men. They do not have to go find them. One of the attackers will be the shooter. Other defenders on the strongside will never be more than one step away.

Strongside perimeter rebounders slide to a point directly between their assigned attacker and the basket. The defender watches his man and not the ball as he defensively slides. When the attacker takes his first step, the defender slides one step in that direction, still facing the potential offensive rebounder. The defensive rebounder, during all this movement, keeps his weight evenly distributed over both feet. This enables him to move quickly in any direction. The defensive perimeter player needs to watch his man longer because the attacker has a large area in which to fake and go to the boards. He need not watch the ball because it takes three seconds for a medium arch fifteen foot jump shot to reach the board and ricochet. When the attacker takes the second step, the defensive rebounder front pivots, making contact and holding it with a slide as the offensive player moves one direction or another. The defender's upper arms should be parallel to the floor, and his lower arms and hands should be up. This arm positioning enables the defender to hold his attacker even if the offensive rebounder should slide around the defender's buttocks. The defender keeps the offensive rebounder on his back until the ball has been secured by himself or a teammate.

A difficult point to teach: getting the defender not to go to the basket but to go to the line between the strongside perimeter attacker and the basket. A second difficult point: teaching the defender to keep his eyes on the attacker and not on the ball. Of course, should the potential offensive rebounder make no effort to go for the carom, after a reasonable time the defender should go to the basket.

Inside Rebounding. When fronting at the low post, it is impossible to block the attacker out. So this defender gets a position beside and even with the low post attacker while the ball is in the air. He gets the side that corresponds with the shot. In other words, a shot taken from the corner position usually ricochets to the corner, and a shot taken from out on the floor usually caroms to the center of the court. So a defender who has fronted the low post strongside gets the baseline side of his assignment on shots from the corner, and he gets the midcourt side on shots taken from out on the court.

Because all inside defenders play very near their assignments and because the ball arrives off the board quickly, they must see the ball quicker. Because their assignments have less area to fake and maneuver, the inside defenders don't need to watch the offensive rebounders. So inside defenders, who do not front, reverse pivot, making contact with their assignments, and go get the ball. Usually, these defenders are the matcher and the center. These are usually your two best rebounders. They should control the boards with this positioning, especially when the weakside and strongside perimeter attackers have been effectively blocked-out.

PART TWO

THE 1-3-1 MATCH-UP

5 UNDERSTANDING THE BASIC 1-3-1 ZONE

Before you can match-up, the offensive team must show an attacking formation. Their formation often depends upon the defense they face. So you show a zone. The offense lines up to attack it. Then you match that alignment. How long you run your zone depends upon your views, your personality, your personnel. Some match-up coaches run their zone only one possession. Others run it a set number of possessions at the start of each quarter. Still others run their zone a set number of possessions and then stay with it until the opponents score. Then the defense matches. But regardless of your preference, you should show your zone every time down the floor although you may know the alignment your opponent will be in and where each defender's man is. Then your defenders can stay zone, match-up, or go man. Plus your opponents may think you are in a standard zone.

Whichever plan you prefer—and they all have merit—you must know your zone. You must know its strengths, its weaknesses. You must adequately anticipate what the opponents will do against you. In short, you must understand your basic zone defense. This chapter deals with the 1-3-1 zone as it leads to the 1-3-1 match-up.

Areas of Strength

The 1-3-1 zone is strong against the inside game. It is strong against teams that shoot from the wings. This zone offers maximum protection inside even with laning. The 1-3-1 also offers the best defense for trapping, either extended or contained.

Your best defensive rebounders are kept near the basket. Two tall forwards, played at the wings, can contest vertical penetration. A quick baseline defender can intercept many vertical and inside passes.

Offensive point guards have trouble getting shots against this zone. Frequently, teams that ordinarily attack with a point offense will change to a two guard front. This weakens their attack at least psychologically. Plus they now have a few people out of their area of maximum efficiency.

Teams whose attack centers around driving and/or screening dread facing the 1-3-1. This zone can virtually stop any screening maneuvers. Drivers constantly face a closed gap.

Big pivot men who are dangerous scorers near the basket cannot operate as effectively against the 1-3-1. Because of the defensive power down the middle, it is difficult for a team to pass the ball inside: The big pivot can be fronted as well as played behind. And even if a team successfully completes a pass inside, the defense can collapse (triple-team if need be), forcing the big pivot player to pass back outside.

When a team's attack focuses around the post, the 1-3-1 is the defensive answer. When that attack features strong shooters in the foul line area, the 1-3-1 provides the remedy.

The 1-3-1 zone defense neutralizes the popular triangular overloads. Because of the positioning of the perimeter defenders, three defensive players can always match three offensive overloaders.

Areas of Weakness

Good corner shooters and good guards can destroy the 1-3-1 zone. An excellent weakside rebounding club can get many extra shots against this zone. Many offensive coaches send three rebounders to the weakside, overloading the lone defensive weakside rebounder.

It is very difficult to find three defenders (both wings and the baseline) quick enough to defense these vital areas. Their movements must be quick, and they must react as the ball is passed. If they don't move while the ball is in the air, defense of the wing jump shots and the baseline jump shots will not be satisfactory.

The 1-3-1 is also the weakest zone for the fast-break minded ball club. The other zones provide a better springboard from which a team can launch the outlet pass and fill the lanes. Of course, 1-3-1 zone advocates can release their point defender for a long pass.

Selecting and Positioning of Personnel

Selection and placement of your personnel will either make your match-up or break it. Your baseline man must be your matcher, your most important defender. But that's getting ahead. Let's take each position man for man, step by step.

Your point defender, X1, will probably also be your point guard, your offensive quarterback (Diagram 5-1). He will be your ball handling guard, your fast break leader. He receives the outlet pass on both sides of the floor, or releases if that's your theory of fast breaking. He is usually a pepper pot, a talker, with lots of energy to burn. On most teams, he is the

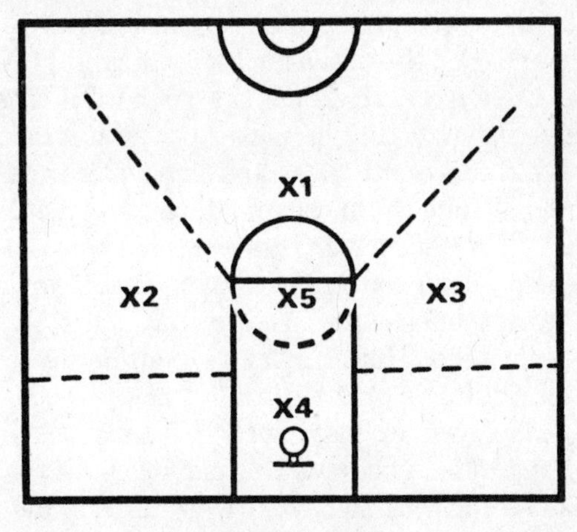

DIAGRAM 5-1

smallest player, but that does not have to be a characteristic. For defensive purposes he must possess above average lateral movement, the quicker the better. His forward and backward steps are secondary to his lateral slides. Drills can increase the quickness, but most teams possess at least one potential point defender. This defender should pressure the opponent's ball handler, frequently turning him to one side of the court or the other. He will often play the opponent's ball handler man-to-man, pressuring him yet keeping him from penetrating with a drive. If you can't pressure and stop penetration, it is better not to pressure, unless you plan to trap or stunt teamwise. When X1's man gives up the ball, he usually passes to a wing. With the ball on a wing, this defender must not let the offensive wingman drive into the middle. He must protect the high post area by stationing himself in the passing lane to the high post. Should the ball go inside, he must sink, double-teaming the ball if necessary, to force the ball back outside.

The left wing defender, X2 in all our diagrams, is usually the other guard, usually the bigger guard. He must be taught to box out to rebound, because he will be the weakside rebounder when the ball goes down the right side of the court. He should be the better defender of X2 and X3, but you can hide your second worst defender in this position. If he is quick and can cover a lot of ground laterally, your laning match-up will be more effective. Frequently, this man will have to cover out front, the other attacking guard, because most teams face a 1-3-1 zone with a two guard front. He talks to X1, letting X1 know where he is and which man he has. With the ball in the corner, he must help the corner defender stop the drive to the middle. He must know where the ball is at all times, and he must account for the first attacker directly to the left of X1. He will have to release players to the opposite wing or the matcher when the ball is on his side of the floor. He will have to receive cutters from the right side of the floor when he locates on the weakside.

X3, the defender on the first attacker to the right of X1, is a position for your weakest defender. He is usually your third largest player, the smallest offensive forward, and he must be a good weakside rebounder. He must be taught to box-out. He can be slow unless you are planning to lane or stunt or trap. If he has excellent lateral movement, your match-up will be that much more effective. This is a good place to put your great scorer who does not play good defense. Of course, if you have a big, tall, slow man who cannot defense the inside as adequately as a smaller man, you could play him here. His primary responsibilities are the same as X2's, just on the right side of the court.

X4 is the reason you are playing the 1-3-1 match-up. You evaluated your personnel and found you have this player with excellent basketball savvy (or he can be taught this savvy) who can help defense the inside. He first lines up on the baseline of the 1-3-1 zone. He checks to find his man. It will be the second attacker on the right or left perimeter from X1 unless there is a double high post. Then he takes the left high post man. If there are five perimeter players (counting low post), X4 takes the second left attacker from X1. Ideally, this player is your second tallest player, but he does not have to be. If he is smaller than most forwards, he will need to be an excellent jumper. He should possess better than average quickness for his size. He needs to be your second best rebounder, but boxing his man out is more important. He will need to learn to play in front of the offensive attacker on the inside backline. He must have the ability to stop the baseline drive by a corner player. He will probably play inside on offense; so he must recover quickly in your defensive transition, yet hit your offensive boards hard. He must be a good athlete. He sees the whole court. He is your defensive quarterback. He keeps in constant contact with X5. He always knows where the opponent's big men are. He must be able to help X5 defense the inside, yet he must be agile enough to cover a forward on the outside. He must be able to accept cutters from the strongside, both while he is on the strongside and while he is on the weakside. He must recognize when the defense is in trouble and relay the "home" signal to his teammates. If you plan stunts, traps, and switching defenses, he must keep his teammates abreast of what is happening.

X5, probably your offensive center, is your defensive center. Ideally, this is your largest player. He must understand the defense second only to X4, but he does not have to possess the basketball intellect of X4. X5's primary responsibility is the opposition's center, but don't tell him that. Often, your 1-3-1 zone will face no high post player, but your zone will frequently see two low post men or three men on the baseline. If there are two low post attackers, X5 takes the right man. Or if there are two high post attackers, X5 takes the right high post. If there is only one high post, X5 must learn to shift with X4 so he can stay with the high post. Drills were offered in Chapter 3 so these two men could coordinate their efforts. This man must be your best rebounder; he'll always be in a position to defensively rebound. He must be able to stop all breakaway drives into the middle. If an attacker drives by his defender on the baseline, he must stop the advancement of the dribble. He must be able to play in front of, on the side of, and behind the post man. He must constantly be in verbal contact with X4. If his man goes to the corner, he must shift with X4. In this condition, he must be able to cover a smaller, perhaps more mobile, man inside. He must be able to slide in his zone slides as the ball moves. He must be taught a technique for making himself appear big.

If you have this type personnel or you can adequately compensate, this is the match-up you will want to run. If you think your personnel is better suited for another zone, go to the other two match-ups described in this book. There is a match-up for every type of personnel.

The 1-3-1 Zone Works Best Against Which Personnel

Teams that have only one ball handling guard will not defeat your 1-3-1 match-up. Even if they have two small offensive guards, your 1-3-1 match-up will give them trouble.

Many coaches try to hold the ball until they can get it inside for the high percentage shot. These teams will not be very successful against the 1-3-1 match-up.

Teams with five smallest type outside players will have trouble against this match-up. Because of their obvious lack of offensive rebounding, the match-up can pressure, even lane, them outside and not lose anything inside or on the defensive boards.

Teams with an effective passer at the post would hurt the 1-3-1. If this passer-pivot could drive, that would hurt this zone tremendously.

The 1-3-1 Zone Forces the Opponents into What Offense

Most teams meet the 1-3-1 with a two guard front. They set two shooters in the corners or will rotate them there. They either put their post man high as a feeder-shooter or low as a baseline screener-rebounder. These 2-1-2 attacks seem to be the most popular.

Several teams have run 3-2 attacks in recent years. They feel that by matching up on the outside, movement of the ball is more rapid. They allow the two inside players much freedom of movement, and they try constantly to pass inside, often forcing their passes.

A few teams think the best formation to attack any match-up is the 1-4 (double high post). It does clear the area near the basket on the initial match-up. But when cuts begin, and the offense must cut to get near the basket itself, the match-up adjusts by proper shifting, again defensing the inside more than adequately.

All these offenses will be defensed in the last chapter in this part (Chapter 8). Most of the options and cuts will receive extensive treatment in the next two chapters (Chapters 6 and 7).

6 DEVELOPING THE COVERAGE RULE FOR THE 1-3-1 MATCH-UP

This chapter will develop the coverage rule of the 1-3-1 match-up zone. (See Chapter 1.) Because completeness is one of the determined efforts of this book, all popular attacks against the 1-3-1 match-up will be presented, defensed. Defense of the basic sets, overloads, and ball movement will receive extensive treatment here. Movement by the offensive players, however, will be held to a minimum because that involves the cutter's rule, the subject of Chapter 7.

Coverage Rule Using One Matcher

You chose this zone because you feel you have at least one matcher and another player who can become an adequate inside defender. If you have those two spots filled, your 1-3-1 match-up will please you. And should your point defender and your two defensive wings also happen to possess quickness, your 1-3-1 match-up will be unbeatable.

X1 is the guard your other defenders will use as their key (Diagram 5-1).

X2 takes the first attacker to the left of X1. If your opposition attacks with a two guard front, you should instruct X1 to take the guard to his right. That communication need exist only between you and X1. It does not change X2's duties. During any game condition, it is difficult to relay messages to more than one defender. In the match-up, other defenders adjust to X1, making communication to only one player necessary.

X3 covers the first attacker to the right of X1.

X4 matches the second offensive player around the perimeter to the left or right of X1. Some teams overload left one trip down the floor and overload right the next. That is one reason why you must train X4 and he must possess basketball intellect.

X4, your matcher, must check the offensive alignment while you are using your regular 1-3-1 zone. You may run your standard 1-3-1 zone one possession or as many as you like. If X4 is an astute observer, one possession will be enough. We have had great success running the 1-3-1 for three possessions, then matching up on the possession following an opponent's field goal. A good scouting report often helps X4 locate his ever changing assignment. The matcher must always determine the offensive set, and he must pick up the loose cutters.

X5 covers the offensive high post. If there is no offensive high post, X5 takes the low post man if there is only one. If there are two high post, or side post, or low post, X5 covers the attacker on his right and X4 checks the one on his left.

Sometimes confusion results or the defense meets an offense they have not seen. When this happens, X4 calls "home," and the defense stays as a basic 1-3-1 zone. After the coaches figure out what is happening, the match-up can adjust.

But before we show the matching coverage from the most ordinary offenses to the trumped-up complex ones, let's drill the defenders on their proper coverages.

A Drill to Teach the Coverage Rule

Procedure:

1. Allow five offensive players to bring the ball downcourt while the defense sets in a standard 1-3-1 zone.
2. Start by requiring that the offense line up in a typical or basic set used against the 1-3-1. Check to see if the match-ups are correct according to who has whom and according to positioning (three-step drill and the plane of greatest peripheral view).
3. You may then allow passing with no offensive player movement.

4. You can advance to allowing drives, forcing defenders to close the gap, but still no man movement.
5. Allow cutters after you teach the cutter's rule (next chapter).
6. Repeat the first four steps by having the attackers start in an overload alignment.
7. Repeat the first four steps by having the attackers start in any free-lance array they wish.
8. Repeat the first four steps by having the attackers use the formations of your next opponent.

Objectives:

1. To teach closing the gap.
2. To teach the coverage rule.
3. To teach the three-step drill.
4. To teach defenders to respond to the next offense you will face
5. To teach playing on the plane of greatest peripheral view.

Matching the Basic Sets Used Against the 1-3-1

2-1-2 offenses line up in two basic arrays against the 1-3-1 zone. They leave their post man high (Diagram 6-1) and use him as a shooter-passer; or they station him low and use him as a screener against the baseline defender (Diagram 6-2).

Offenses using the alignment of Diagram 6-1 attempt to move the ball rapidly, trying to get the ball to their shooters who are stationed in the corners. Or they pass the ball to the post man, 5, who turns for his shot or passes to 3 or 4. When 5 gets the ball against the standard 1-3-1 zone, 5, 3, and 4 have a three-on-two advantage against X5 and X4.

X1, complying with the coverage rule, matches the guard to his right when there is a two guard front. X2 would take 2, the first attacker to the left of X1. X3 covers 4, the first player to the right of X1. X5 takes the center 5. X4 deduces all this and covers the second attacker on the perimeter either left or right of X1. X4 figures his man is 3, the second player to the left of X1. Diagram 6-1 shows the three-step drill (one step toward the ball and two steps toward the basket) from each defender. All the other diagrams throughout this book will depict the containment sluff unless otherwise stated.

Diagram 6-2 displays no high post. So instead of having a four perimeter situation (as in Diagram 6-1), this formation activates the five

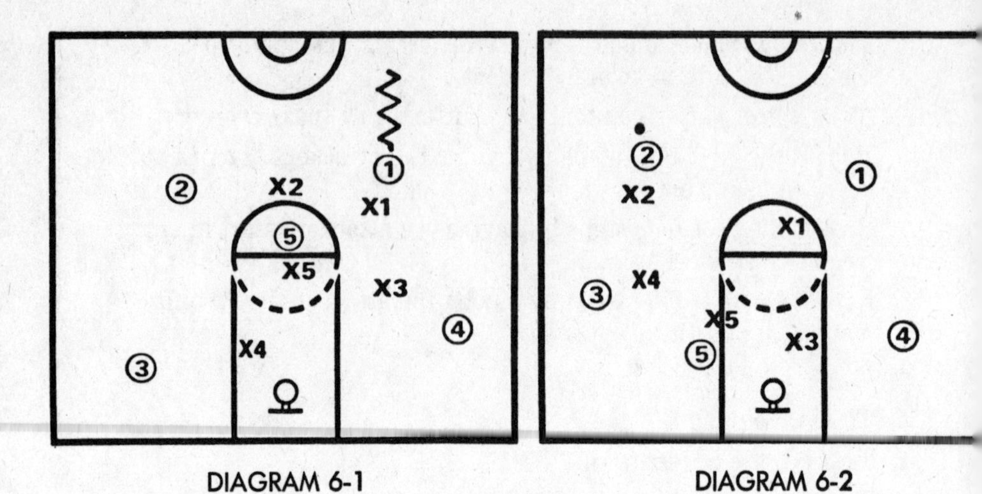

DIAGRAM 6-1

DIAGRAM 6-2

perimeter rules. X1 takes the guard to the right of a two guard front. X2 covers the first attacker left of X1, in this case the ball handler. X3 takes 4, the first attacker to the right of X1. X4 and X5 see this. X5 knows X4 will take the second attacker to the left or right of X1 around the perimeter. 5 is on the ballside. So X4 counts around the perimeter finding 3 the second attacker to the left of X1. X5 would naturally check to his right first; but when he finds no one there, he immediately looks for the next closest offensive performer around the perimeter. 5 fits that description. 5 is the most likely candidate to move to the high post. (See the next chapter for the switching techniques as 3 cuts off of 5 or 4 flashes to the high post, etc.) If 5 had lined up on the weakside low post, X5 would still have covered him.

Some teams attack with the 3-2 alignment shown in Diagram 6-3. X1 always takes the player in the point alley if there is one. This does not mean it will be the opponent's point guard. It means the attacker who locates in the point guard's alley. X1, therefore, covers 1. X2 takes 2, the first attacker left of X1. X3 blankets 3, the first player right of X1. X4 counts a five perimeter offense. He looks for the second player to the left of X1. X5 receives communication from X4 and locates his man 5. But X5 knows he takes the right player if there is a double-low or double-side post.

Offensive numbers have been mixed up in Diagram 6-4, which shows the standard 1-4 alignment. The mixing was done to keep X1 off of 1, the offensive point guard. This should help you see the matching techniques more clearly.

X1 takes the attacker in the point guard's alley (Diagram 3-1)—3 in this case. For variety, Diagram 6-4 shows 2 bringing the ball into the

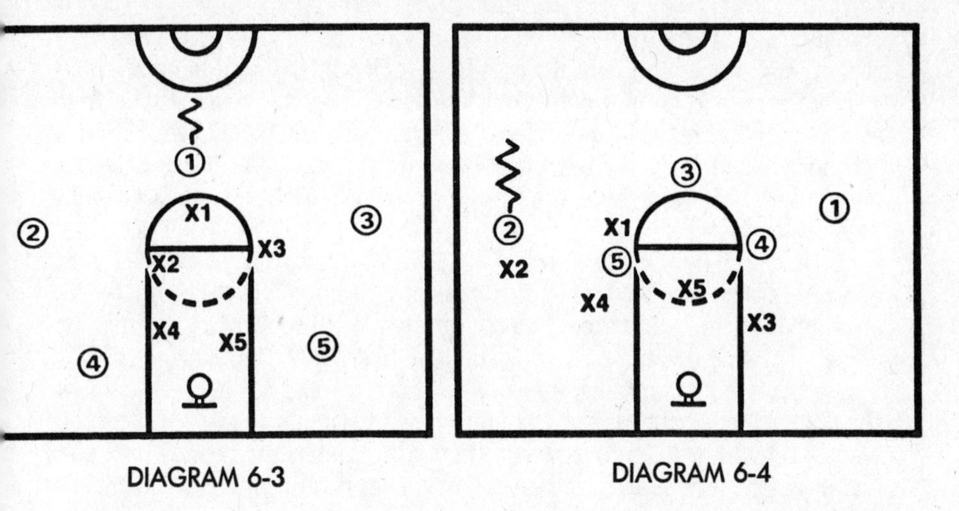

DIAGRAM 6-3

DIAGRAM 6-4

scoring area. X2 picks up 2 because he is the first attacker left of X1. With the ball at the wing, X1 sags to cover the high post area. He can do this with his three-step drill. X3 takes 1, the first player right of X1. Notice X3 has sagged two steps off his man and four to the basket. (His man is two passes away from the ball.) X4 takes the left high post, and X5 takes the right high post.

There are many offenses used against the 1-3-1 zones, but these are the basic ones. The many other offenses have elements of these, and the special trumped-up formations will be dealt with later.

Matching the Overloads Used Against the 1-3-1

This section is designed to match the teams who come down floor and line up in the basic overloads. These are some of the trumped-up formations you will see when you employ your 1-3-1 match-up. Some teams will line up in a regular formation and cut into these overloads. Those teams will meet our cutter's rule, a subject for the next chapter. We will again match up with no movement.

X1 covers 1, the offensive point guard (Diagram 6-5). X2 takes 2, the first perimeter player to the left of X1. X3 checks 3, the first perimeter player to the right of X1. X4, the matcher, finds the second player left of X1; so X4 discovers 4. The perimeter, as we define it, goes along the sideline then in by the baseline. This particular overload fits into the five perimeter category. X5 would cover 5, the only inside attacker.

If 2 had lined up as the second low post man, X2 could cover him, obeying the coverage rule. Or the defensive coach, armed with a scouting report, could pre-plan for this lopsided overload. He could have X1 take 3. Such an assignment would give 1 to X2. X3 would cover 4, the first attacker to the right of X1. Under these conditions, X4 would cover 2, the second perimeter player left of X1. Or you could invoke the double-low post rule, letting X4 take the low post left, 2. Either way, X5 would defend 5.

Diagram 6-6 displays an alignment that started as a 1-3-1 and evolved into an overload when the weakside wing man cut through to the strongside corner. X1 takes the point guard, 1. X2 covers the first player left of X1, which would be 2. X3 takes the first player to the right of X1. There is none if the offense lines up in this overload as they come down the floor. Most teams, as stated before, use this overload after cutting the weakside wing through toward the ball. Under any condition, the match-up should never let either defensive wing man cut cross the lane to cover an attacker. This would clear out a side for an easy drive. So if a post man exists, let the wing man cover him. X3, therefore, must cover the high post man 5. This is a coverage which would conform to the coverage of a cutting wingman. (See next chapter.) X4 guards the second player left of X1 (or right). In this case, he would guard 3. And X5 would release the high post man to X3, and he would take 4, the low post attacker. These exact same coverages would result if 3 had cut through to the strongside corner on the pass from 1 to 2.

If the offense always pre-sets in this formation, the defensive coach could adjust by starting X1 on 2. This would put X2 on 3 and X3 on 1. X5 could keep 5, and X4, by the rules, would have 4.

Diagram 6-5 shows a triangular overload. Diagram 6-6 depicts a box overload. And Diagram 6-7, explained next, displays the diamond overload. These three examples seem to be the most popular overloads against the 1-3-1 zone—in fact, against all zones.

Most teams that attack the 1-3-1 with a two guard front move into this overload by the guard to guard pass. When 1 passes to 2 in Diagram 6-7, 4 cuts from his weakside wing position to the low post. But we are not defensing cuts here, although they would be defensed in the same way. (See diagrams in the next chapter.) We will defense this array as though the team initially sets in this overload.

A scouting report would permit several pre-planned adjustments. We will begin by defensing this overload without a scouting report. Then we will discuss a few adjustments.

X1 would begin with 1, unless we make an adjustment because of a scouting report. X2 would have 2, the first man left of X1. X3 would not come across the lane as long as there was a man on or near the lane. So X3 would take 5, the first attacker right of X1. X4 would take 3, the second

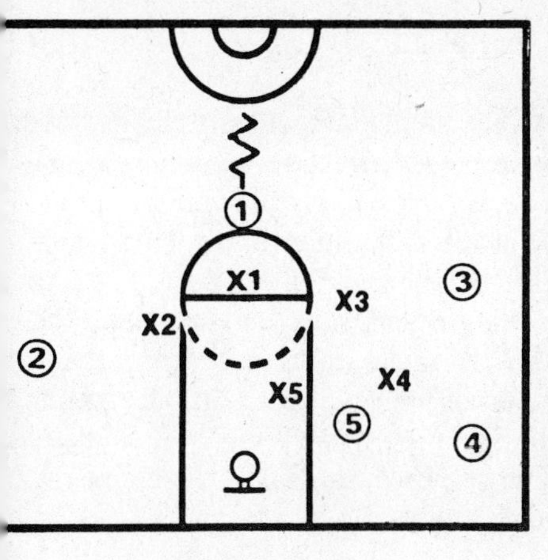

DIAGRAM 6-5

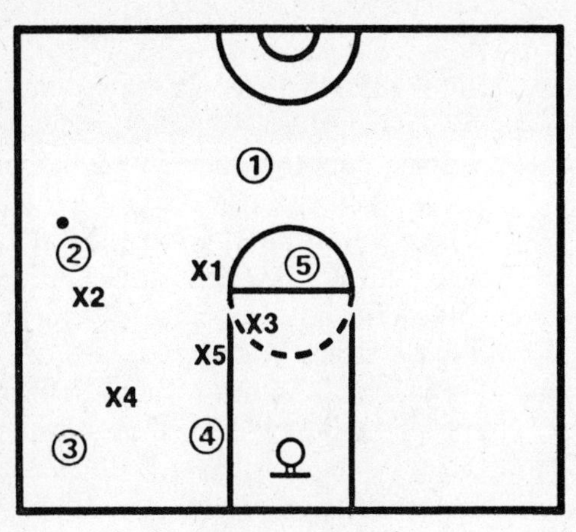

DIAGRAM 6-6

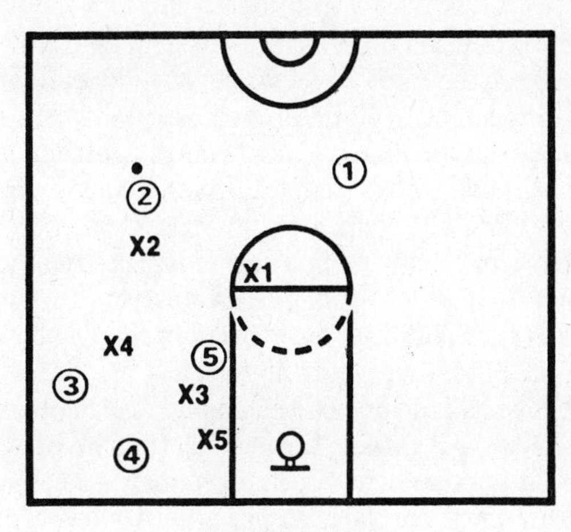

DIAGRAM 6-7

attacker to the left or right of X1. X5 would switch off of 5, using the exception to the basic rules and cover 4. (See the next chapter for an explanation of the switch between X3 and X5.)

A scouting report could permit X1 to cover 2. That would put X2 on 3 and X3 on 1. X5 could keep the high post man 5. And X4 would follow his second man left or right rule and cover 4.

Another possible adjustment: X1 covers 1, giving 2 to X2. X4 takes 3, and X5 keeps 5. X3 would then cover 4, the strongside low post. This adjustment requires a deviation from your basic coverage rule. This you would not want to do from game to game. But you could change your rules from season to season allowing your post to stay high and your wing to take the low post attacker.

From these examples, representing the major three overloads, you can see how the basic match-up coverage rule can be applied and adjusted. You can also see how a scouting report will enable you to make a simple adjustment, letting X1 cover a different man and letting your match-up automatically adjust according to the basic rules. You can make these adjustments without a prior scouting report simply by watching the offense attack your standard zone. And to make matters even safer defensively, all X4 has to do to pull you out of your match-up into a regular 1-3-1 zone is say "home." A good scouting report can allow you to make the more complicated adjustments. The good scouting report permits you to pre-plan and pre-practice these adjustments.

Defensing Ball Movement

The match-up is a team defense. As such, each defender must always execute the proper team and individual fundamentals.

Drilling on defensing only ball movement kills two birds with one stone. First, many teams attack the 1-3-1 zone by getting into an overload and passing the ball, holding cutting maneuvers to a minimum. So drilling against ball movement helps your team defense when you will be attacked by an overload and ball movement. Teams which employ cutters do so almost reluctantly. They will cut one or two players through the middle, analyze each, then cut another or two through. So it's almost like defensing ball movement. Secondly, by drilling against only ball movement, you can require that the ball stop on your command. You can check to see if all your defenders have sagged their three steps (this helps in defensing the inside, closing the gap, and in receiving and releasing cutters), have played where they have the largest peripheral view of the court (this helps in seeing cutters and ball movement), and have defensed the weakside properly (this helps when this defender must receive a cutter). Let's check these coverages using a drill against an offense that's basic against a 1-3-1 and using an overload that's basic against the 1-3-1.

Basic 2-1-2 Offense Versus 1-3-1 (Diagrams 6-8 and 6-9).

Procedure:

1. First let the five offensive players break downcourt and set up. See if the defense knows the proper match-up coverage rules. Let X1 take 1 one trip, and then let X1 take 2 another trip. In the diagrams, X1 takes 1. (The lines in the diagrams show the approximate shoulder-to-shoulder line of each defender.)

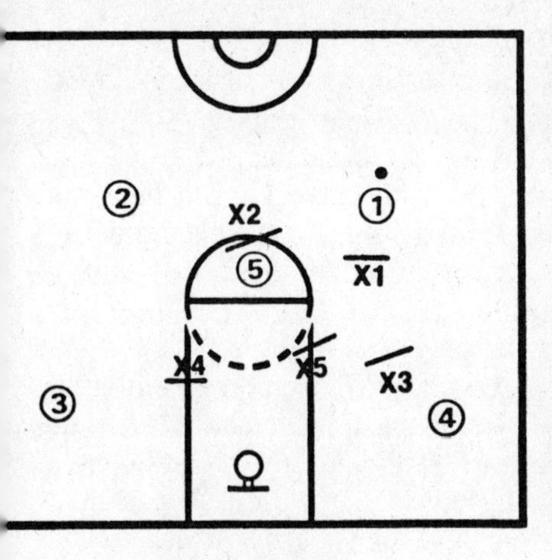

DIAGRAM 6-8

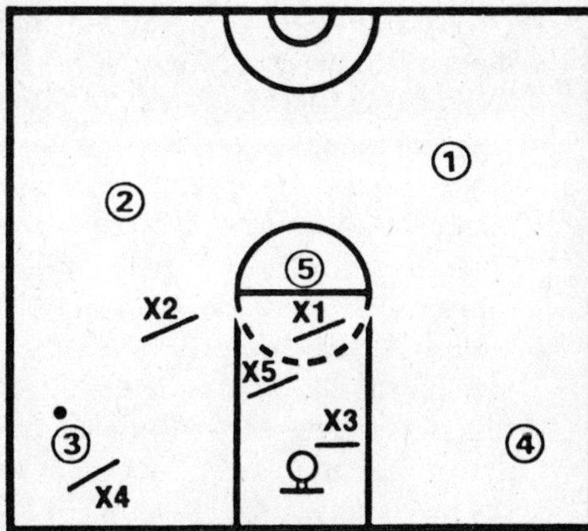

DIAGRAM 6-9

2. X2 must sag into the passing lane into 5. He should be in his interception stance if we are laning. (See Chapter 3.) He can cut off the drive by 1 into the middle. His body must be such that he can peripherally see 1, 2, and 3.
3. X3 positions himself so he can see almost all of the court, using his interception stance if we are laning. If we are containing, X3 should see all five attackers, and he should be two steps toward the basket and one step from his man (three-step drill).
4. X4 would cover 3 according to the match-up rules. He must play on the plane of greatest peripheral view: He must see all of the court. He can probably locate four steps toward the basket and two steps from his man. From this positioning, he can protect the middle and he can accept strongside cutters.
5. X5 can play to the side of 5, preventing 5 from getting the ball. Or X5 can play behind 5, trusting X2 to discourage the inside pass. You, as the defensive coach, can decide. But, in either case, X5 should make himself big, arms up or to the side, making 1 think the inside passing lane to any cutter is closed.

Objectives:

1. To teach the match-up coverage rule.
2. To teach proper weakside sag.
3. To teach the interception stance.
4. To teach proper positioning of the body so it will always be on the plane of greatest peripheral view.
5. To teach the three-step drill.

If 1 passes to 2, the coverage would be the same, just opposite defenders reversing their roles. Diagram 6-9 shows the pass continuing from 1 to 2 to 3. Let's stop it at 3 and check the coverage.

X4 would cover 3 so he cannot drive the baseline. X2 drops two steps toward the basket and one step from his man. He can be in an interception stance if we are in a laning match-up. But he should easily see 1, 2, and 3 from his body positioning. He must also close the gap on a drive by 3 to the inside. X1 can sag drastically off of 1. He should be where he can see everyone except possibly 4. X5 can sag two steps toward the basket and one step from his man. X5 should make himself big, preventing 3 from finding a passing lane inside. X5 must stop 3 if he drives baseline. And if X2 cannot prevent the middle drive, X5 must help there. If any cutter should break through the middle, X5 can help momentarily by being big in the passing lane. X3 should be at least even with the basket, his back almost parallel with the baseline. He should see everyone. He must be ready to accept a strongside to weakside cutter, probably 2 or 1. And he must be willing to deny 4 a cut to the low post until he releases him to X5. 5 then would be his man. (See next chapter.) If 4 breaks to high post and 5 rolls low, he would play 4 man-to-man. No man with the ball and no cutter should be open.

Box Overload Against the 1-3-1, a Drill

Diagram 6-6 shows the box overload with the ball at a wing. A discussion of the coverage was offered with the diagram. Let's let 2 pass to 3 in the corner and see how the defense adjusts.

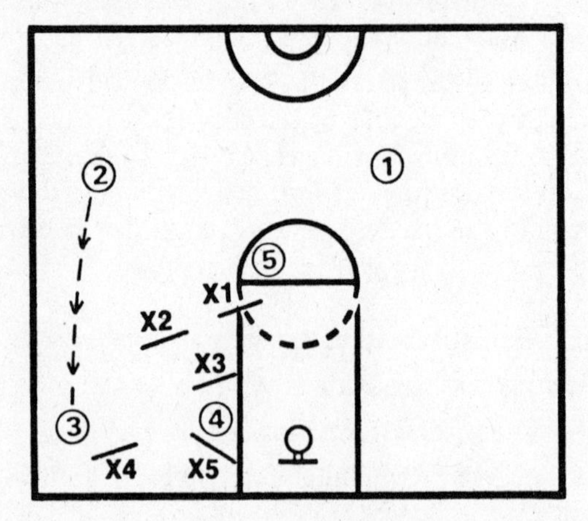

DIAGRAM 6-10

Procedure:

1. Let the attackers bring the ball up the floor and get into their overload formation. See if the defenders can match the line-up using the coverage rule.
2. X4 takes the cornerman 3. X4 prevents the baseline drive. When the ball is in the corner, the weakside can afford an exaggerated sag.
3. X2, using his three-step drill, helps on the inside drive by 3. X2 can play his interception stance if he wishes or if we are in a laning match-up. X2 should see 1, 2, and 3.
4. X1, sagging four steps toward the basket, can see the entire court. If his man, 1, breaks backdoor to the weakside, he can easily trade with X3, keeping the coverage rule intact.
5. X3 plays big, arms out and waving, making 3 think the inside and cutting lanes are covered. X3 must also help X4 if 3 gets by X2 on a drive to the middle. X3 can also discourage a pass inside to 4, especially to 4's right. X3 can see all attackers.
6. X5 can see the entire court. With the ball in the corner, the defensive center must front the low post or play in the three-quarter denial position. X5 must keep 4 from getting the pass. X5 must help X4 on a baseline drive. X3 would have to sink onto 4 if X5 had to cover a breakaway baseline drive. (See last section in this chapter.)

Objectives:

1. To teach the match-up coverage rule.
2. To teach the proper weakside sags when everything is on the strongside (overload).
3. To teach interception, fronting, denial and three-quarter stances.
4. To teach proper positioning of the body so it will be on the plane of greatest peripheral view.
5. To teach the sagging three-step drill.

Defensing Offenses That Penetrate the Holes and Seams

Offensive coaches use this principle to attack all zones. Holes are the areas between the perimeter defenders. And they are plentiful against the standard 1-3-1 zone (Diagram 6-11). Seams are the openings on the inside of the zone. There are no seams inside the 1-3-1 zone unless you count the areas on the foul lane line near holes #3 and #4. Some coaches may think the high post area is a seam, but there is adequate defense to prevent passes there. In fact, a strength of the 1-3-1 zone is its interior defense.

Attackers plan to penetrate the holes with a dribble, passing to a nearby teammate when two defenders converge on the driver. Attackers always look inside, whether they are dribbling or passing around the perimeter, hoping to pass into the seams of the zone. At least the defense must assume that the attackers will constantly be checking inside. The seams can have an attacker cutting into it, or the potential receiver can be stationed there.

There are no holes to defend in a true match-up. That is one of its greatest advantages over the standard zone. A perimeter attacker is always matched-up with a defender. Sometimes, as the zone slides, seams appear inside for cutters to take advantage of.

To eliminate drivers into pockets, there are no holes; defenders can be drilled on closing the gaps. (See Chapter 3.) The more drilling, the better the defense. Should one defender be matched against a quicker offensive player, that defender should be instructed to halt a drive in only one direction, preferably to the baseline side. The slower defender can overplay that potential driver. That defender need concentrate on drivers in only one direction. Although he may be slower, the defender should more than adequately cover a drive in only one direction. The teammates of this slow defender must be told how the slow defender intends to play the drive. A team concept or rule could improve this coverage, and it would avoid confusion. The slower teammate's defenders sink toward the open pocket, concentrating on closing the gap.

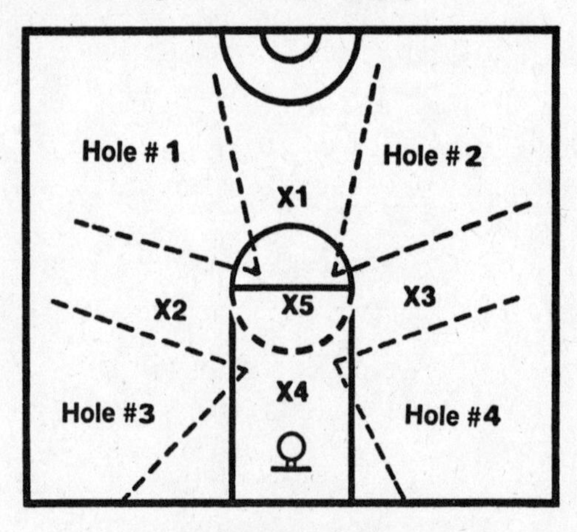

DIAGRAM 6-11

A lot of points must be considered before activating this strategy. Does this quicker driver shoot better going left or going right? How does he pass when he drives into a pocket? Does he like to go all the way, or can he pull up short, shooting or passing? A wise and accurate scouting report can stop an attacker who should, because of his physical superiority, dominate the defender in his area.

Match-up defenders will body check all weakside cutters who flash toward the ball. Because defenders have excellent pre-positioning, the three-step drill, they should never allow a cutter between themselves and the ball, making it impossible for the cutter to get to the seam.

Denying and three-quartering inside stationary seam seekers should keep them from the ball. Inside defenders do not have to intercept passes directed toward the seams. They need merely deflect them, directing the errant pass to the inside key area. All the other match-up defenders are there, and they can recover these deflections. A few such recoveries quickly discourage further inside passing.

Releasing and accepting cutters, especially from the strongside to the weakside, sometimes creates an open seam. Constant drilling on the correct techniques eliminates many of those openings. (See fundamental drills, Chapter 3.) Drilling will make this exchange smooth and second nature, making it quicker and easier during game situations.

"Bust Out" and "Bust Over"

Two important terms individual defenders use to inform their teammates of their intended coverages are *"bust out"* and *"bust over."* "Bust over" means that the defender intends to release his man, a cutter to the weakside, and he intends to cover the next man around the perimeter from the ball (Diagram 6-12). 2 passes to 4 and cuts to weakside. Before X2 releases 2 to the weakside, he can use the Penn State Sliding Maneuver and "release" X4, or he can call out, "Bust over." This tells X4 to keep 4. It tells X5 to keep 5, and it forces the weakside defender, X3, to "release" X2. Because X2 or the coaching staff has called, "Bust over," X2 slides to cover the first man away from the ball—1 in this diagram. This also informs his teammates to slide over a man. X1, therefore, takes 3, and X3 has 2. This conforms to the coverage rule: X2 has first attacker left of X1, and X3 covers first player right of X1. This strategy is used over the Penn State rotation when scouting reports show 4 as an outstanding offensive player.

"Bust over" and Penn State strategies can be used simultaneously in the same game. This allows continuous coverage on the great offensive players and yet keeps the defense obeying the coverage and cutter rules.

Couple these strategies with the traps of Chapter 18 and you can see how confused the attackers may become.

"Bust out" is used primarily by weakside defenders who may have sagged near the basket only to be caught by a skip pass (Diagram 6-13). Diagram 6-13 depicts 2 passing to 4 and cutting to the weakside. X2 and X4 execute the Penn State maneuver. 4 skip passes to 2. X5 must go out quickly to cover 2. As X5 goes, he shouts, "Bust out." This keeps X3 and X4 aware to the potential help they must provide should 2 drive around X5. Busting out allows a team a strategy of an exaggerated inside sag. This strategy can work simultaneously with the three-step drill during any game.

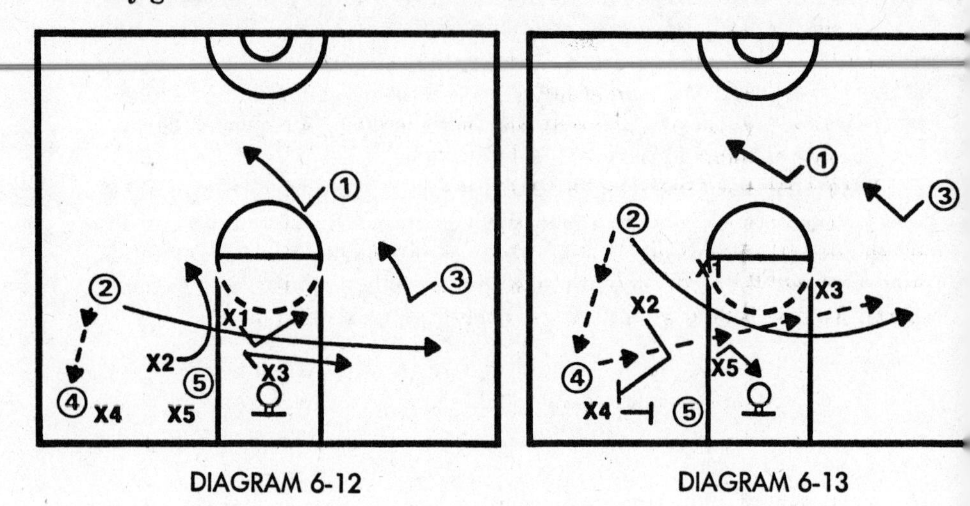

DIAGRAM 6-12

DIAGRAM 6-13

Stopping the Breakaway Dribbler

Diagrams 6-14 and 6-15 display a breakaway dribbler and a breakdown by a baseline or corner defender. When this happens, the weakside center must stop the driver should the helper (X2 in Diagram 6-14 and the baseline in Diagram 6-15) not close the gap. When a dribbling breakdown occurs, each defender rotates ("bust over") one man. X4 yells, "Bust over," and all the other defenders react. X3 must drop fast to prevent the lay-up. X4 can trap before rotating. (See Chapter 18.)

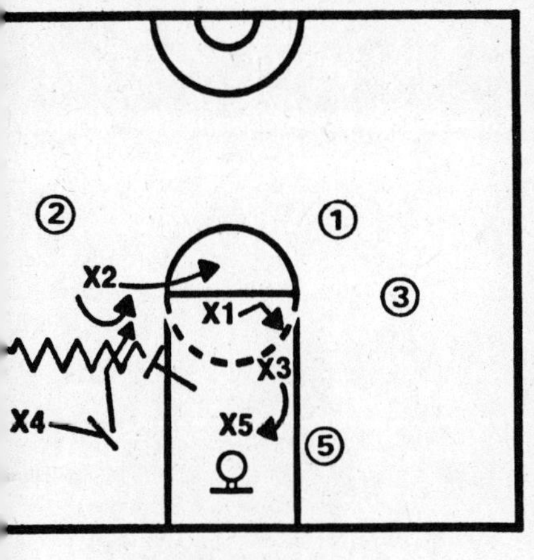

DIAGRAM 6-14

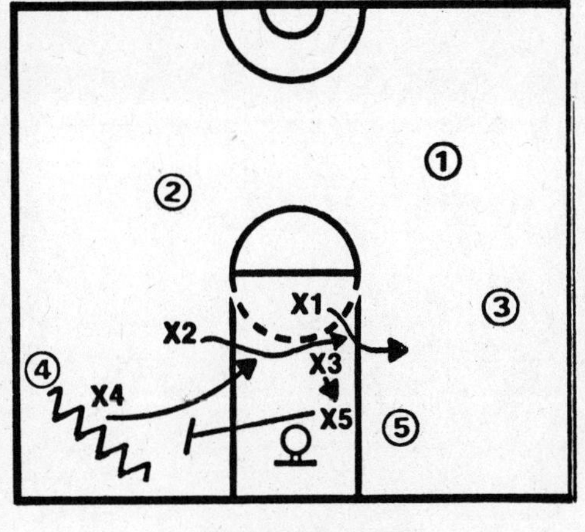

DIAGRAM 6-15

7 DEVELOPING THE CUTTER'S RULE FOR THE 1-3-1 MATCH-UP

If offensive teams contented themselves to stay in their formations or overloads and pass the ball around until they found a hole or a seam, you would have all the defense you would need to counteract the offense. But attackers begin cutting, usually as their continuities call for them to cut. A cutter rule must be developed to defend against this cutting, yielding no inside openings to the cutter, yet keeping the perimeter matched-up according to the coverage rule. This chapter develops such a cutter's rule.

The Cutter's Rule for the 1-3-1 Match-Up

Weakside wing defenders must pick up cutters coming from the strongside heading toward the weakside. Sometimes the matcher also takes this responsibility. He must read when he becomes involved. Usually he becomes involved when his man is in the weakside corner area. Strongside defenders maintain the coverage rule by switching to cutters coming from the weakside to the strongside.

Weakside perimeter defenders may have to cover the weakside cutter flashing to the high post. Although it is best for the defensive center, X5, to always cover the high post attacker, there is one condition where such a shift is impractical. If the ball is on the wing or in the corner and X5 already has the low post man covered, the weakside wing must cover the flash pivot cutter to the high post. This is consistent throughout our match-up. It leaves the wing man only one attacker away from X1, his coverage rule. It also prevents the momentary opening to the low post that would occur if the wingman and X5 tried to shift. The weakside wing man should body check this cutter, preventing him from receiving the pass into the high post. If the ball is at a wing, the weakside defender against the flash pivot should three-quarter the high post. If the ball is in the corner, the weakside defender against the flash pivot would sag two steps toward the basket and one step off of his man (three-step drill), making himself appear big, using proper body positioning to see all the players he can, and helping on the strongside to weakside cutters.

Those two axioms comprise the cutter's rule. But teaching points must be learned so there will be no openings when the releasing (shifting) occurs. Releases should occur as near the foul lane line on the ball side as possible. This frees the ballside defender guarding the cutter to get back to his new assignment before his new man can get a shot. And it means there is greater denial coverage on a cutter coming from the weakside. But no defender should release his cutter until he hears "release."

A defender on a cutter should always be between the cutter and the ball. He should open to the ball around the foul lane line, making himself appear big as he would in any zone. He is zoning it, waiting to hear "release," readying himself to pick up his new assignment.

A defender who is to accept the cutter should, by playing on the plane of greatest peripheral view, see the cutter coming. He must momentarily cover his man and the cutter. He does this by physically stepping toward the cutter, appearing big, but staying in the passing lane between the passer and his original man.

Drill to Teach Cutter's Rule

Procedure:

1. Line up five attackers and five defenders as shown in Diagram 7-1.
2. You can switch from five perimeter to four perimeter to three perimeter as you feel you need the drill. Here we will describe a five perimeter drill. Chapter 11 will disclose a four perimeter drill, and Chapter 15 will present a three perimeter drill.
3. Coach numbers offensive positions and calls out the numbers when he wants a cutter. That cutter can be ordered to cut to the

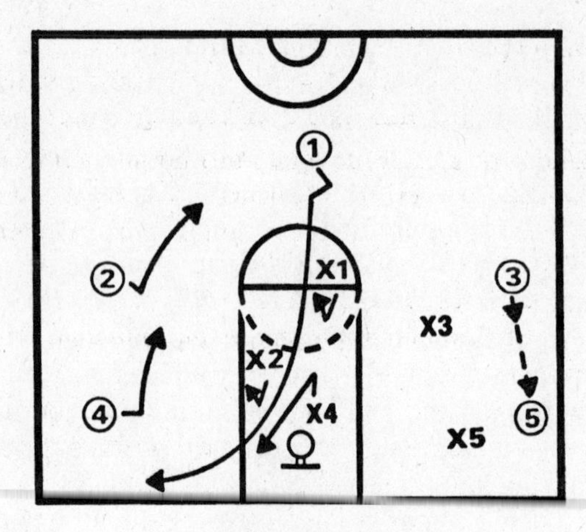

DIAGRAM 7-1

baseline or wherever you want him. Or the cutter can decide for himself.

4. The other offensive players fill in the holes, keeping the continuity alive.
5. Diagram 7-1 shows, for example, our weakside coverage of cutters. If you go back and look at each diagram in the book, you will notice that this coverage is consistent. Whichever part of your cutter defense is weak, work on that in this drill. Or allow your players to cut freely, especially after you have taught them your complete defense. In this diagram, as you will recall, X1 comes one step below the free throw line where X4 calls "release." X4 keeps 1. X2 meanwhile has rotated down on 4. X1 would pick up 2.
6. 2 and 4, for example, could exchange places. 2 could flash to the strongside while 4 rolls to fill 2's vacant spot. If 2 does not get the ball, 2 would fill 4's vacant spot. Where Diagram 7-1 exposes coverage from a point guard cutter, the explanation in section 6 here deals with the weakside wing coverage. You could let 3 cut and 1, 2, and 4 fill one position over. This would teach strongside wing coverage.
7. Proper fundamentals of releasing and accepting cutters must be observed and corrected.

Objectives:

1. To teach coverage of the cutters.
2. To teach accepting and releasing cutters.

3. To teach the cutter's rule.
4. To teach the three-step drill.
5. To teach closing the gaps (by letting players drive while cutters cut).
6. To teach body checking.
7. To teach interception stance. (X3 could be in an interception stance in Diagram 7-1.)
8. To teach playing on the plane of greatest peripheral view.

The Passer as a Cutter from Point, Guard, Wing and Corner

When the cutter is the man who just passed the ball, he is only one pass away. He is a strongside cutter going to the weakside, or he is a strongside cutter going to the strongside. He must never be permitted to cut between his defender and the ball. This can be avoided by the cutter's defender jumping toward the pass receiver as the ball is in flight. This defender must move with his three-step concept. He should watch the passer while executing his three-step drill. This prevents the quick backdoor cut.

From the Point. 1 must pass to a wing or a guard. Any further pass should result in a defensive steal; or if it is completed, a teammate would be a more logical cutter. As 1 passes to 2, X1 executes his three-step technique, watching 1 until he completes the three-steps (Diagram 7-2). His completion of the three-step drill should correspond to 2's reception of the ball. All the other defenders react with their three-steps. As 1 cuts, X1 would take him a step below the free throw line. X5 and X3 both see the cutter coming. X5, the weakside deepest defender, steps to take 1, making himself appear big. X5 does not get out of the line between the ball, 2, and his man, 5, until X3 has 5. X5 would yell "release" to 1, keying 1 to locate a new attacker, 3. X3 positions himself on the proper plane where he can see the entire court. X5 covers 1; but if 1 cuts to the corner, X5 stays near the basket, his proper sag. If 1 breaks on up the weakside, intending to go back out front, X5 and X3 shift. In all of this, X3 remained one player removed from X1, his coverage rule.

What if 1 breaks to the strongside? X5 would still shift with X1. X5 would appear big, and he would either deny 1 the ball or three-quarter him. If 1 continued along the baseline, X4 would shift with X5, giving X5 the attacker nearest the inside. X4 would be taking the second perimeter attacker from X1. X1 would have 3 while X3 covers 5.

From the Guard. tpassing from the guard following with a cutting maneuver means a guard-to-guard pass or a guard-to-corner pass. The guard-to-corner pass was discussed as a drill in Chapter 3. Let's consider the guard-to-guard pass here (Diagram 7-3).

When 2 passes, X2 watches 2; X2 performs his fundamentals well, including the three-step drill. X5 appears big, helping on the area of the shift yet guarding his own man. X3 sags his three-steps, guarding 3 and helping on X5. X4 can see it all. X4 calls "release." X2, when "released," has almost perfect coverage on 4. He may have to drop a step or so. X4 would stay with 2 if he continued toward the corner on the strongside. Of course, he would sag his three-steps, not going directly into the corner. If 2 came back out front, X3 and X4 would shift as the two offensive players crossed. If 2 ran along the baseline weakside, X2 and X4 would shift back as those players crossed. All of this, as you have noticed, keeps the defense equal to the coverage rule.

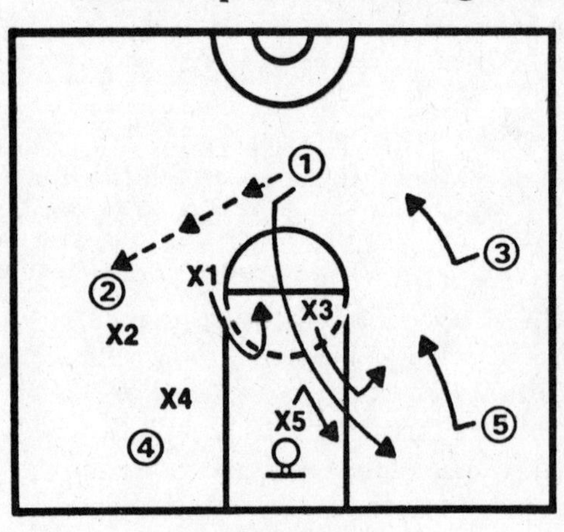

DIAGRAM 7-2

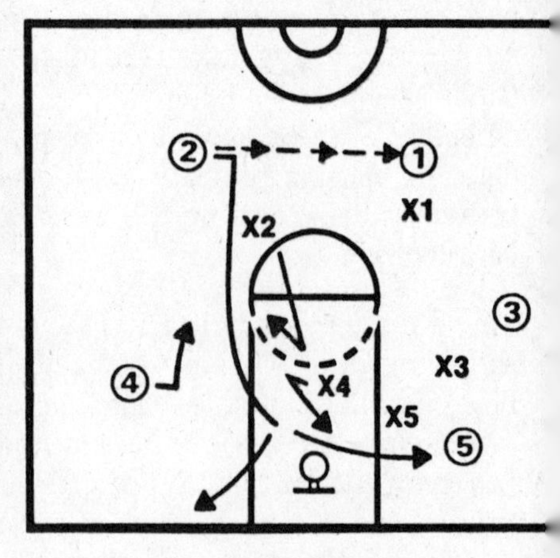

DIAGRAM 7-3

From the Wing. tcoverage on the pass from 2 to 4, the wing to the corner, resembles the drill explained in Chapter 3. So here we will let the pass go from wing to point, and let the wing cut through an open center seam (Diagram 7-4).

All defenders, as shown in Diagram 7-4, have proper weakside and strongside positioning. X2 again executes the proper fundamentals of sliding and watching the passer, a fundamental that you should have drilled and drilled and drilled your players on. Now the cutter is coming toward the ball; so we describe it as a weakside cutter. A cutter moving away from the ball is a strongside cutter. X2 goes with 2 until he reaches the foul lane line on the far side of the court if he has to, or until he hears "release." X4, however, should "release" X2 at the foul lane line on X2's side. X4 plays his release fundamentally (as shown in our drills). X2 takes 4, the first attacker left of X1. X4 covers 2 down the lane and out the side where 5 is located. We prefer for X4 to go over the top of 5 if he is at the low post. Again, if 2 breaks outside, X3 and X4 would shift coverage. If 2 breaks along the baseline on 4's side, X4 and X2 would shift back.

From the Corner. Diagram 7-5 depicts 4 passing to 2 and breaking off the low post. While 4 has the ball, X5, to be consistent with our

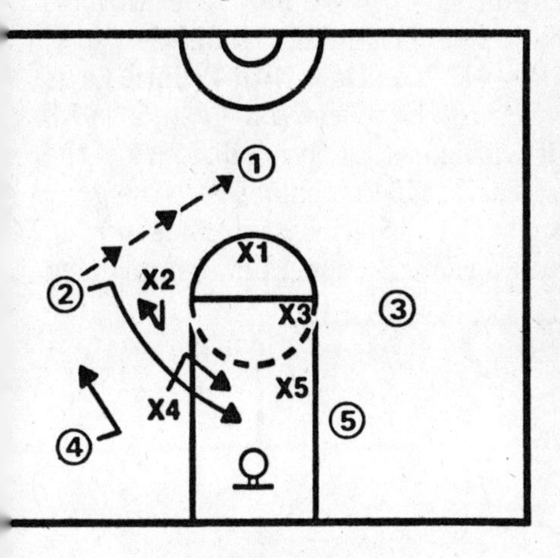

DIAGRAM 7-4

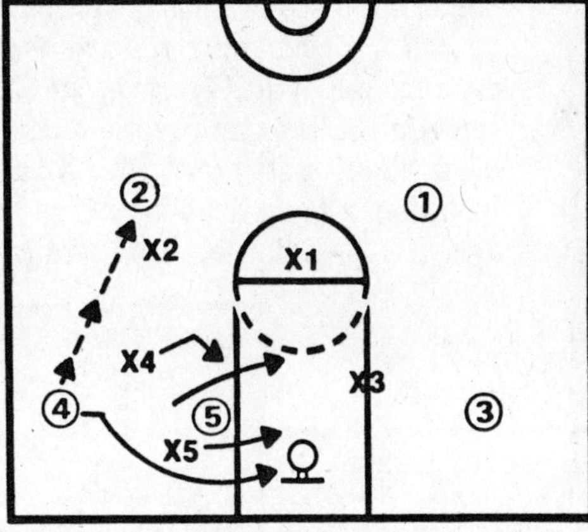

DIAGRAM 7-5

coverage, either fronts 5 or three-quarters him from his baseline side. As the ball moves to 2, X4 adjusts his three-steps, watching 4. X5 can either two-step around 5 to get upper three-quartering positioning or X5 can slide baseline side of 5, knowing he has X4 in the passing lane between 2 and 5. As 4 cuts by 5, X5 "releases" X4. X5 will cover 4 if he breaks on up to high post or if he breaks to weakside low post. If 4 continues on up the weakside sideline, X3 and X5 trade men as 4 goes further outside than 3. X4 stays with 5 until he moves, the subject of a later diagram.

These movements are standard offensive attacks against the 1-3-1 zone. Other similar categories, but against the 2-1-2 and 1-2-2 zones, will be presented in Chapters 11 and 15. But different diagrams there will explain basic attacks against the 2-1-2 and the 1-2-2 respectively. Now let's go to cutters who break without having immediately passed the ball.

Strongside Guard Cutter

Diagram 7-6 depicts a typical strongside guard cutter from a formation that many teams use against a 1-3-1 zone. The original match-ups follow the coverage rule. As 2 moves down below the free throw line a step or so, X5 can make himself big, preventing 4 from passing to 2. X2 can "release" X4 from covering the ball, a defensive maneuver made famous by John Egli's Penn State Sliding Zone. X2 must do this to maintain the coverage rule. X2 goes with 2 until he is assured by X5 and until he is at least even with X4 and 4. X2 slides out on 4, calling "release." The farther 4 is from the basket, the less dangerous he is as a scorer, and the quicker X2 can call a release. This gives X4 plenty of time to get into the basket lane between 4 and 2. X4 slides directly toward the basket with his hands up, discouraging the pass from 4 to 2. When X4 regains view of 2, he can stop his slide toward the basket. X5 stays with 2 until he is comfortable with X4's coverage. X1 has the lane between 4 and 5; so X5 can afford this extra coverage. If 4 is within easy shooting distance of the goal, X4 must stay on 4 until X2 arrives. But if 4 is that close to the goal, he does not have the best passing angle to 2, especially since 2 is moving away. If 2 continues to the strongside corner, X4 covers him, employing

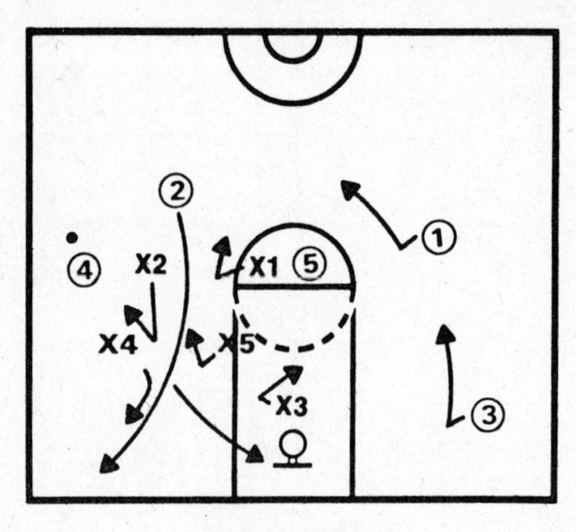

DIAGRAM 7-6

the three-step drill. If 2 cuts to the weakside, X4 stops in the lane. As 2 moves up the weakside, X3 and X4 would shift assignments as their men cross.

As stated before in this book, each defensive match-up coach must devise simple rules he can live with. His personality and ingenuity along with the personnel he has must dictate to the greatest degree how he rules his match-up. In conjunction with that concept, we will from time to time offer a different coverage possibility, hoping it will help the reader to devise rules for himself. It should also help you to see the match-up concepts better. The next paragraph represents a deviation from our basic match-up cutter's and coverage rules.

Let's say that both of your guards are astute, knowledgeable basketball players, capable of defending the inside for a few possessions each game. X2 could go with 2 all the way to the baseline. If he does this, he must let X4 know he has switched roles with him. A key word would do it. X2 now becomes the matcher; X4 becomes the first defender to the left of X1. We have used this type of coverage in years when we had the big knowledgeable guards. The great disadvantage: The offensive team believes you are in a man-to-man instead of a zone. They may run their man offenses. And if you prepared mainly against their zone offenses, you may confuse your own players. The coverage in Diagram 7-6 is a typical zone coverage, leaving no doubt in the attacker's minds. They will want to run their zone offense.

Strongside Wing Cutter

Some teams try to dribble around the horn in an effort to confuse the match-up. In Diagram 7-7, 1 and 2 begin at guards and 3 and 4 at wings. 2 vacated the guard alley, going to a wing. 1 dribbled over to that guard alley. X1 usually takes the right guard, which he did in this case. Because X2 has gone to the wing, X1 stays with the dribbler. X3 covers the first attacker to the right of X1 while X2 covers the first attacker to the left of X1. X4 takes the second man left or right of X1, and X5 takes the center. Of course, the team could have come down the floor and set in this alignment, a typical offensive array against the 1-3-1. But you will face unorthodox moves by teams attacking your defense.

2 now is a strongside wing cutter, the subject of this section. X2 would cover 2 to the free throw lane line, maybe a step beyond. X5 should command, "Release." X2 drops to cover 4, and X4 hurries to match 5. Now we have proper coverage according to the coverage rule. X1 must offer pressure on the dribbler to keep him from finding an open receiver. X2 and X4 are executing typical wing and baseline slides of the basic 1-3-1 zone. X2 must, upon release of 2, get into the passing lane between 2 and 4. X3 covers the high post area, appearing big, preventing 5 from being seen. X5 has the same big coverage and picks up 2 if he stays at the high post. If he cuts on the baseline, hoping to rub the baseline defender off on 5 as the ball is reversed, X4 would pick up 2 as he goes to the weakside corner. X5 would cover 5. In both cases, the match-up conforms to the coverage and cutter rules. No attacker is open in the seams for more than a fraction of a second. And proper drilling cuts down on that fraction.

Strongside Corner Cutter

This 2-3 alignment appears frequently against the 1-3-1 (Diagram 7-8). A cutter from strongside corner never offers any real challenge to

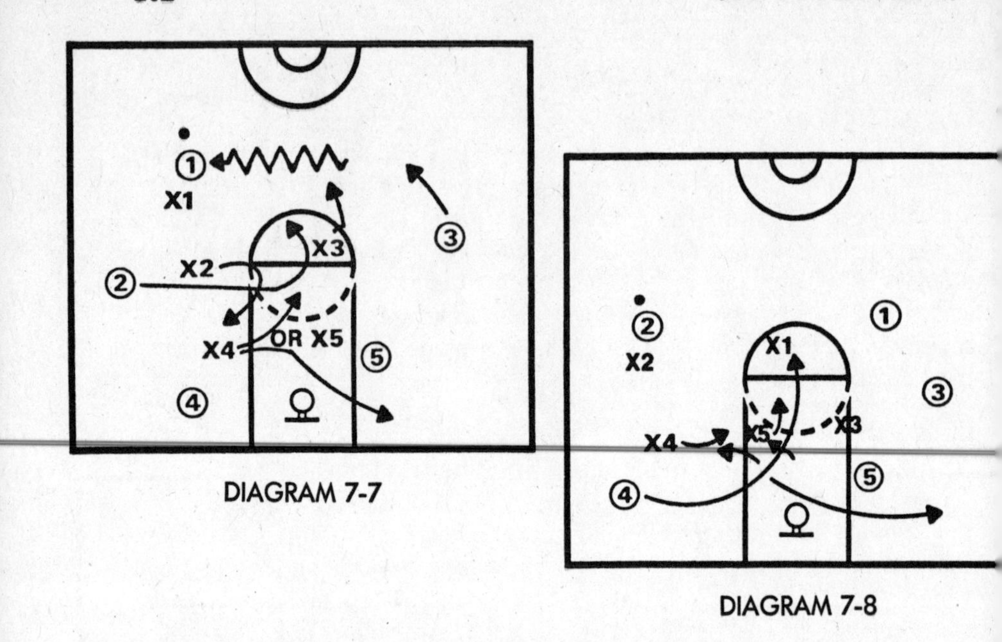

the defense. X4 would cover 4 if he tried to post low. If he tried to cut to a higher post position, X5 would "release" X4. X1 and X3 offer more than enough help inside. If 4 cuts through the lane and around 5, X4 will keep 4 until he crosses the path between 3 and the ball. At that point, X3 and X4 exchange men. If 4 breaks to a high post, X5 will have him and X4 will have 5. But X4 must not go beyond the basket because 2 would have a clearout on X2 (see 3 on 3 clearout drill, Chapter 3).

Weakside Guard Cutter

2 passes to 4, and 1 cuts from the weakside guard (Diagram 7-9) down the lane and out to the strongside or to the weakside. Sometimes 1 will post at the side post or low post strongside.

The coverage rule places X1 on 1, X2 on 2, X3 on 3, and X4 on 4, and X5 on 5. As 1 cuts, X1 will take him to one step below the free throw line. X5 commands a "release." When X1, X2, or X3 releases a cutter, he checks for his new assignment by looking for the next offensive player around the perimeter away from the ball (see section on "Bust Over," Chapter 6). X3 trades onto 5, and X1 covers 3. If 1 continues onto the strongside, X5 would cover the action. If 1 breaks to the weakside, X5 and X3 again trade. 1 might, during the continuing action, go all the way back out to a guard. When 1 and 3 cross, under that condition, X1 and X3 shift.

Weakside Wing Cutter

Weakside cutters should never present match-up problems. And because of the break toward the ball, no worries about clearouts immediately concern the defenders. In Diagram 7-10, 4 has the ball and 3 breaks to either the high post or around the low post into the corner.

Any cut from the weakside should be met with a body check by that weakside cutter's defender. On the weakside, away from the ball, a good defensive ball club will body check all cutters. By virtue of our three-step drill, our defenders are in a perfect position to body check. The idea is to beat the cutter to a spot and draw the charge if he continues cutting. This throws off his timing and discourages him from cutting again.

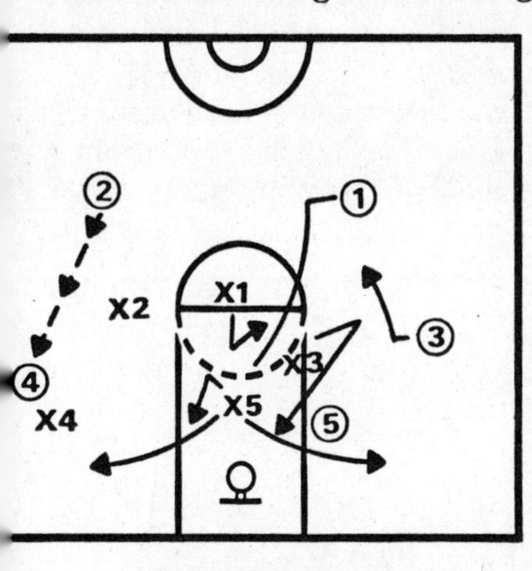

DIAGRAM 7-9

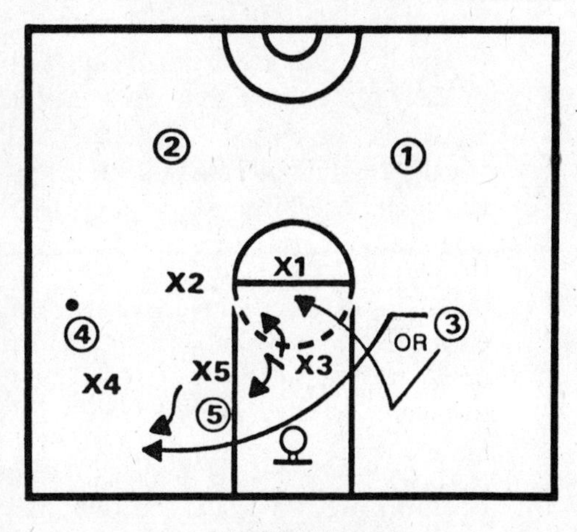

DIAGRAM 7-10

To achieve body checking, the defender needs to have good defensive position and let the cutter bump him. To do this legally, the defender needs to be ever alert to beat the offensive cutter to the advantageous offensive spot. The defender does not have to have the good defensive position that he must have to draw the charge. Usually, body checking is ruled as it should be incidental contact or charging.

Body checking does not have to involve torso contact; arm contact will do. Its purpose is to throw off the timing of the cutter; and, if it is a patterned offense, to throw off the timing of the next several cuts, forcing the offense to re-set. On occasions, a body check will cause the cutter to stop; and perhaps a lead pass has already been directed into the cutter's route, causing a turnover.

In Diagram 7-10, if 3 breaks to the high post, he is covered like a flash pivot attacker. (See Chapter 3.) 3 would be body checked by X3, trying to force him out high and away from the ball. X3 receives more than enough help from X2 and X1, both of whom have activated the three-step drill. Should 3 cut baseline using 5 as a screener on the baseline man of the 1-3-1, X3 and X5 trade men as the two attackers cross. X5 would front 5 and X3 play behind him until the ball goes to the corner. Then X3 could receive help from a sagging X4. X3 must alert X1 as he leaves. X1 under these conditions is the lone weakside defender. He is responsible for the lob and for 1 cutting backdoor. If the ball is reversed back to 1 for a clearout, X3 would move to the area near the basket. X5 would cover both 3 and 5 with help from X4.

Weakside Corner Cutter

3 can cut only to one of two positions and be effective: he can post up at the low post or break completely to the corner (Diagram 7-11). X4 initially plays no further from the ball than the basket area. Otherwise 2 would have a clearout. X3 has excellent position on both 4 and 3. As 3 breaks by 4, X4 "releases" X3; and they shift assignments. X4 would three-quarter 3 if he stopped at the low post, X4 playing baseline side. If 3 continued to the corner, X4 could sag if 3 were not a shooter, could play half-way if 3 were a shooter. X5, who has excellent help from X1, appears big inside. X5 helps X4 on inside passes to 3 if 3 posts up at the low post.

Combination of Two Cutters

Completeness is a basic tenet of this book. And to have a complete defense, every possible cutter must be reviewed. Couple these cutter movements with the fundamental drills of Chapter 3 and you will have a most solid defense. I hope that you thoroughly understand the 1-3-1 match-up by now and that the following examples will serve to reinforce what is already known.

Two cutters, even when cutting at the same time, should be broken into individual cutting drills and defensed as such. Defensing dual cutters inside was covered completely in Chapter 3 while working on the center and matcher's coverage. Here we will defense outside breaks toward and/or away from the ball.

X1 takes 1 back to the free throw line and one step beyond (Diagram 7-12). X5 calls "release," but 5 also begins to flash toward the ball. X3 slides back to pick up 5, but 5 is gone. X5 "releases" X3. X5 body checks 5 as he breaks toward the ball. X3 picks up 1 as he goes toward the basket, and X1 uses his peripheral view to pick up 3. This coverage stays with the coverage and cutter rules; it corresponds with covering the weakside corner and the point guard. Although 5 is lined up at the low post weak-

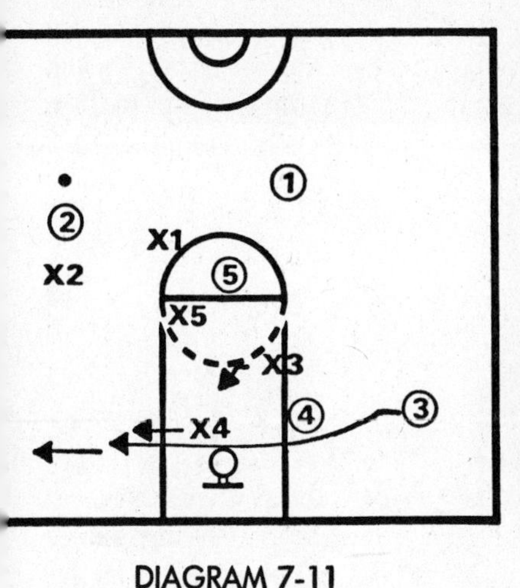

DIAGRAM 7-11

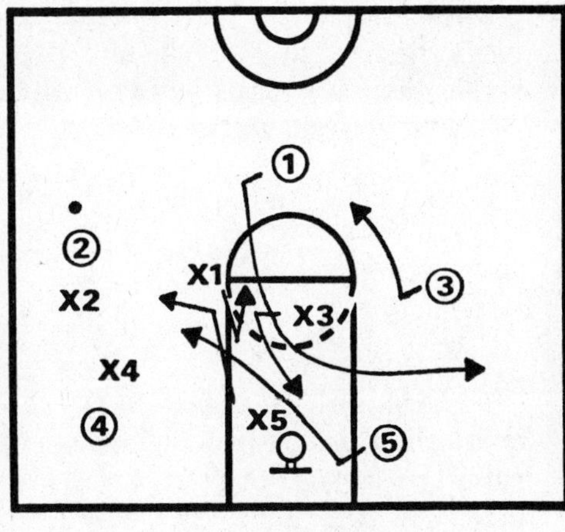

DIAGRAM 7-12

side, he is covered as if he were in the corner. Both positions are counted as perimeter positions. (Only the high post is not counted as perimeter—see Chapter 1.)

Combination of Three Cutters

Three cutters cutting at the same time pose no problems for poised, well-trained match-up defenders. Defensing three cutters represents three separate match-up moves occurring simultaneously.

Diagram 7-13 displays the passer as a guard cutter (2 passing to 4 and cutting), the post man rolling low (5 cutting behind 2 to the low post), and the weakside wing as a cutter (3 flashing to high post). The match-up defenders activate two sections in this chapter and a fundamental drill in Chapter 3.

X2 jumps his three-step drill on the pass from 2 to 4. As 2 cuts, X2 stays between the ball and 2. X5 has made himself appear big. 5 intends to cut into the vacuum created by 2's cut. X1 has perfect positioning to help at the high post. X2 drifts back to "release" X4 when 2 gets even with 4. (See Strongside Guard Cutter, this chapter.) X4 sinks toward the basket and then picks up 2 as 2 breaks to the corner. Of course X4 could sink if 2 is not a shooting threat. As 5 rolls to the low post, X5 prevents him from receiving a pass, appearing as big as possible, three-quartering if 5 tries to post up. (See Chapter 3, Center and Matcher Coverage.) 3 meanwhile has broken into the high post area. (See Weakside Wing Coverage, this chapter.) X3 has helped on the other action as much as possible. X1 now helps X3. X3 should body check 3, forcing 3 high and away if possible. Remember, if X5 has an attacker at the low post strongside, X3 plays the flash pivot to the high post. Throughout this coverage, all the applications are consistent with other coverages and adhere strictly with the coverage and cutter rules.

Matching Cutter Movements into Overloads

Diagram 7-14 depicts a typical 2-3 beginning evolving into a box overload. This offense also involves three cutters. 2 passes to 4 and executes the strongside guard cut. X2 and X4 perform the proper match-up defensive technique, borrowed from Egli's Penn State Sliding Zone. Meanwhile 3 cuts to the low post. X5 "releases" X3. When 5 flashes to the side post, X3 defenses the flash pivot cutter, body checking and sending him high and away.

If the last two cuts occurred in different order: 5 cuts first then 3 breaks low, the coverage would start different but end the same. When 5 cuts, X5 would bodycheck 5's cut. Then when 3 cuts, X5 would shift with X3. (See Diagram 3-16 for this coverage.)

X1 must, in both cases, be notified that he has 1 alone on the weakside of the court. The weakside, as stated before, is not a clearout. It becomes a clearout when 1 gets the ball. But then that would become the strongside, and the weakside defenders would sag toward the ball, eliminating the clearout. The only immediate danger is for 1 to cut backdoor. But X1 is made aware of this, eliminating that danger. X1 would also have weakside lob responsibility.

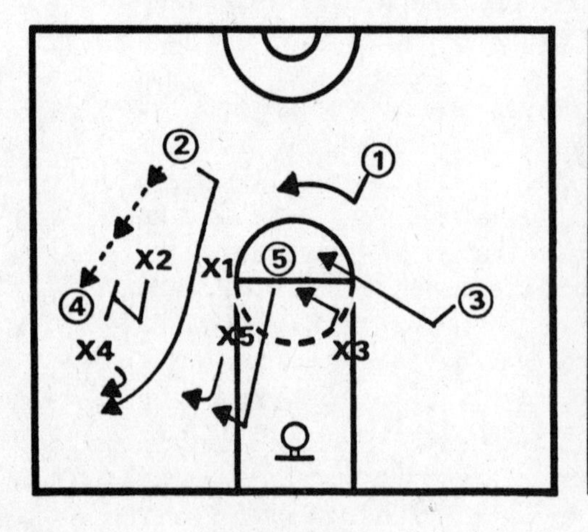

DIAGRAM 7-13

DIAGRAM 7-14

Defensing Dribbling Moves

Some offensive minded coaches believe it difficult to match a 1-4 formation. Our three perimeter techniques enable us to match it perfectly. Those coaches believe that by dribbling to another alley (Diagram 3-3) they force the match-up out of position.

Diagram 7-15 shows a dribbling move from the 1-4 alignment. Our match-up rules and techniques keep us in perfect coverage.

As long as the dribbler does not move through three alleys, his defender stays with him. If the dribbler moves farther than three alleys, we prefer for the defender to release the dribbler to the next defender. Of course if there is no next defender, the man covering the dribbler stays with him. This might necessitate the key word which changes the match-up to man-to-man coverage.

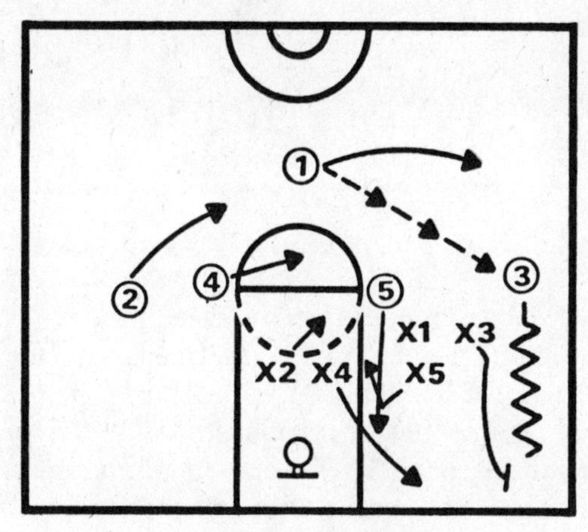

DIAGRAM 7-15

You can make a defensive adjustment by refusing to allow the dribbler to go where he wants. For example, X3 could have overplayed 3, forcing him back to the inside, not giving him the drive to the corner. Teams who like to use the dribble against the match-up have favorite avenues for dribbling. They are pre-planned. A good scouting report will enable you to take those avenues away from the dribbler.

In Diagram 7-15, X3 stays with 3. 3 dribbled only from the wing to the corner alley. 3 must have an outlet pass so 1 must move to the ball. X1 would sink into the high post area. While 3 dribbles to the corner, 4 and 5 roll in an ordinary 1-4 attack technique. X4 and X5 cooperate in the matcher and center coverage methods described in Chapter 3. Diagram 3-18 shows this exact movement. It also explains how and why X4 and X5 trade attackers. This dribbling move enables the offense to evolve from a 1-4 array into a box overload. But proper coverage should yield nothing to the offense.

8 DEFENSING BASIC CONTINUITIES WITH THE 1-3-1 MATCH-UP

Most coaches attack man-to-man defenses with pet patterns, passing games, quick-ending plays, or complete free lance. But most coaches try to defeat the zone with a continuity. And that is superior strategy.

Zones cannot be defeated with haphazard offensive play. Defeating them requires the ultimate in offensive planning. That means there must be a plan for continuous movement without resetting.

Throughout years of observing offenses against zones, some have been seen repeatedly. Those often-used offenses can be considered basic. This chapter presents several of the basic continuities used against the 1-3-1 zone. This chapter also includes a gimmick offense used against us sometime during the last eighteen years. After you see these basic continuities and the gimmick offense defensed, using the techniques of Chapters 6 and 7, you will recognize how solid the match-up defense is.

A 2-1-2 Offense Defensed

Diagram 8-1 represents an ingenious method of attacking a 1-3-1 zone that intends to match up. As long as the defense stays 1-3-1, the offense does not move but stays in the holes of the zone. The guards, from this standing position, can pass between themselves until they hit the post man, 5. 5 and 3 and 4 have a three on two offensive advantage. 3 and 4, the team's best shooters, set up in the corners. 1 and 2 try to catch the baseline defender out of position for the corner shooter. When 1 and 2 pass to the cornerman, 5 rolls to that side low post. Any defensive mistake gives 5 the lay in. When the cornerman shoots, the weakside cornerman has off-side rebounding responsibilities, and the center has on-side rebounding duties. But if the 1-3-1 zone matches, the offense begins its continuous cutting (Diagram 8-1).

The continuous motion of this pattern can be broken into parts, then defensed. The first part begins with 2 passing to 1 and cutting (Diagram 8-2). This is a weakside guard cut. X2 would take 2 to a step below the free throw line where X2 would trade with X3. X2 drops to cover 4. X4 would take X3's man as X3 picks up 2. This puts X1 on 1, X3 on 2, X5 on 5, X2 on 4, and X4 on 3.

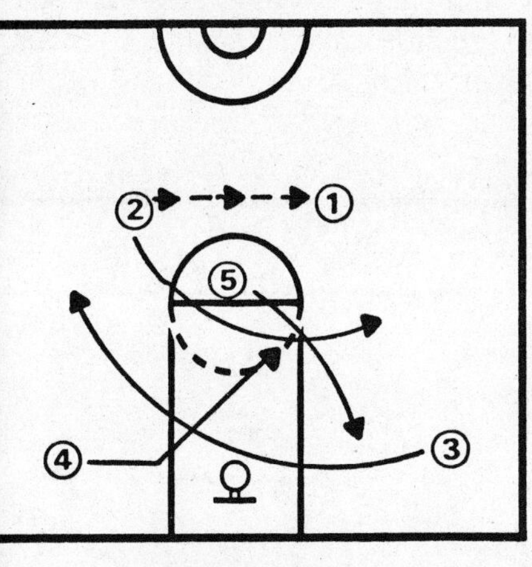

DIAGRAM 8-1

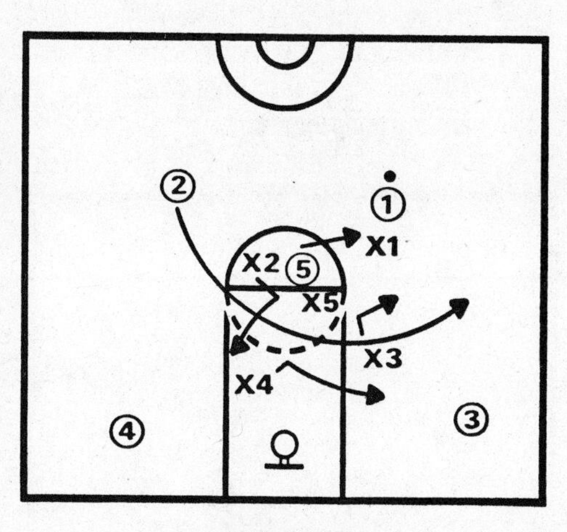

DIAGRAM 8-2

The inside cuts represent the second part. 5 rolls low while 4 flashes high. X5 stays with 5 and X2 covers 4's flash pivot cut. These are just individual moves. Our defense obeys both our coverage and our cutters rules.

Diagram 8-3 depicts the finishing cuts before the offense has completed one full turn. X4 stays with 3 until he cuts to the free throw line extended. X2 stays on 4 until X4 releases him. 5 rolls back to high post and 4 rolls to the corner. And 2 drops to the other corner. X1 stays on 1. X2 now has 3. X3 covers 2. X5 still has 5, and X4 remains on 4. The offense has gone from a 2-1-2 set into a box overload and back into a 2-1-2 set, ready to overload the opposite side with a swing of the ball. Throughout it all, the defense has remained matched up in compliance with the cutter and the coverage rules.

During all this cutting, it is important that each defender execute his fundamentals properly. They must play on the plane of greatest peripheral view, take the necessary three steps, release and accept cutters properly, and body check each cutter. The fundamentals executed skillfully, and not the cutter and coverage rules, make the defense work. Fundamentals win.

A 3-2 Offense Defensed

Most teams do not cut as much as the team offense described above. Most teams use simple basic cuts to try to find inside seams.

5 flashes as 1 passes to 2 in Diagram 8-4. X1 slides into the high post lane. X5 appears big. As 3 cuts through the lane, X4 "releases" X3. X5 drops to help X3 cover 4 because X1 can help on 5. No attacker is open even momentarily because X1 has the high post lane and X5 and X4 cover the side and low post lanes. X1, however, must be notified that 1 might try a backdoor cut.

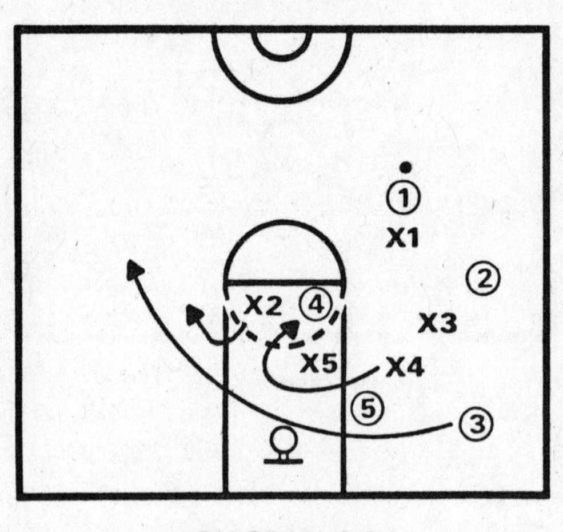

DIAGRAM 8-3

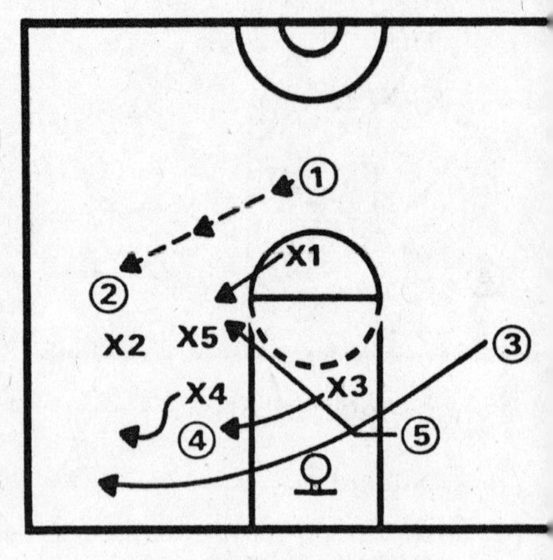

DIAGRAM 8-4

The offense is now in a box overload (Diagram 8-5). When 2 passes to 3, 2 cuts through. X3 "releases" X2 as 2 cuts by 4. X2 "releases" X4, executing the Penn State sliding zone maneuver. 5 then breaks to baseline weakside. This offense now intends for 4 and 5 to act as two screeners against the baseline defender of the 1-3-1 zone as the ball is reversed. But there is no baseline defender: the zone is a match-up although it started as a 1-3-1. 3 either passes directly across the court to 2, or 3 reverses the ball to 1 who passes to 2. The offense has moved from 3-2 to a box overload back to a 3-2.

A 1-4 Offense Defensed

Let's say a team has an excellent shooter at the point and they want to free him for a shot. Diagram 8-6 is a reverse action attempt to get 1 the corner shot against a 1-3-1 zone.

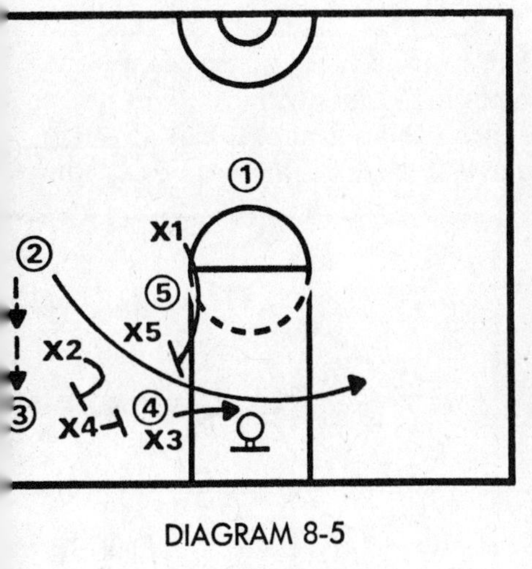

DIAGRAM 8-5

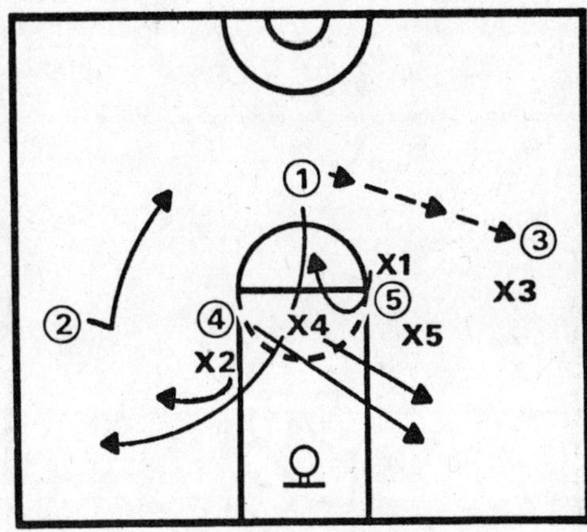

DIAGRAM 8-6

1 passes to 3 and cuts (the passer as a cutter from the point, Chapter 7). It is easy for X1 to go one step below the free throw line, and it is equally easy for X2 to release X1. X2 stays in the lane as 1 cuts to the weakside corner. 2 rotates up to a guard position to get the quick return pass from 3. X4 covers 4's individual cut to low post. Sometimes 5 will roll low and 4 fill in high. X4 ends up on the low post, and X5 ends up on the high post in either case (discussed in Chapter 3 in section on center and matcher coverage).

When the ball is passed from 2 to 1 (Diagram 8-7), 5 and 4 crisscross (another coverage discussed in detail in Chapter 3 in the section on center and matcher coverage). X4 and X5 trade men. If 1 can get the shot, he takes it. If 1 cannot get the shot, he has two centers breaking to the ball for a pass. Adequate execution of the defensive match-up fundamentals will prevent the shot or the pass inside. 1 can dribble outside, pass to 2, while the two centers fill the high post by sliding over one position. The offense is now set and ready to begin again. The offense has rotated from a 1-4 into a triangular overload, reversed into a triangular overload, back into a 1-4.

A 1-3-1 Offense Defensed

Some coaches prefer to match their offensive alignment with the defense, trying to force one-on-one play inside. This means a minimum of perimeter cutting, which should be a blessing to the match-up.

Diagram 8-8 represents this type of offensive thinking. 1 and 2 exchange places after 1 passes to 3. X1 and X2 naturally shift assignments. 5 slides down to low post on ball side and 4 flashes to a seam at the high post. X1 helps close off the high post. X5 slides with 5 until he hears X4 say "release." X5 zones the area, making himself appear big. X2 offers lob pass help. X5 regains defense on 4. 3 reverses the pass to 2, who

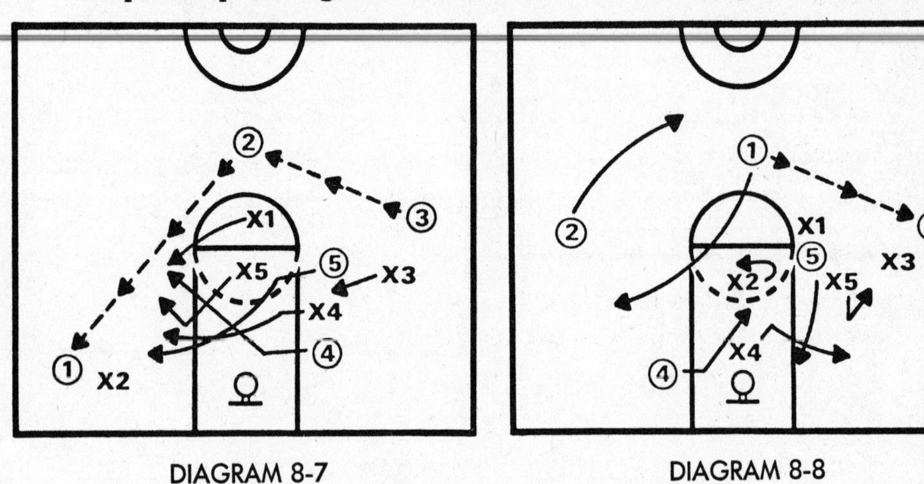

DIAGRAM 8-7

DIAGRAM 8-8

passes to 1. These perimeter attackers punch the ball into any hole (perimeter) they find. Meanwhile, 4 follows the pass from 3 to 2 to 1, hoping he can receive an inside pass at the high post. X5 should prevent it. But if 4 receives a pass, he pivots, faces 5 on the baseline, hoping to get the one-on-one high-low pass on X4. If none of this works, the offense is set to run on the opposite side of the court. It is a simple, but highly effective inside one-on-one offense. The defense must be alert and aware to stop it. This offense stays in a constant 1-3-1 triangular overload. The high post is always on the ballside, always breaking to low post as the wingman receives the pass.

A Special Gimmick Offense Defensed

Teams that prepare special gimmick offenses for your match-up cannot be as well prepared, as well drilled, as they would be using their basic offenses. They concede that your defense scares them. Like it or not, they convey that atmosphere to their players. With such thinking, victory is already half yours.

Diagram 8-9 displays an offense that hopes to take advantage of both systems: special gimmick and/or part of the opposition's basic patterns. X1 contains 1. When there are double stacks, your outside defenders should be X2 and X3. They will take the outside cutters. They line up on the plane of greatest peripheral view so they can see who breaks outside. X4 and X5 can help them. X4 and X5 split the two attackers. 3 comes off the double screen, hoping to get a pass and a quick jump shot or dump the ball off inside. X3 sees the cut away; so he knows he will have the attacker left on that side, 5, the first man right of X1. X5 follows the inside cut, and X3 follows the outside cut. On the other side, X2 follows the outside cut, and X4 follows the inside cut. X2, therefore, covers 3 as he cuts by the double screen. X5 takes the high man, "releasing" X4 to the low man.

2 screens the high defender, X5, hoping to free 4 at the low post (Diagram 8-10). X4 and X5 shift men. 2 goes back to activate the double stack on the right side. 3 passes to 1 and goes to double stack on the left side. 1 dribbles to the other side, and 3 breaks off the double stack on the right side. The offense begins again.

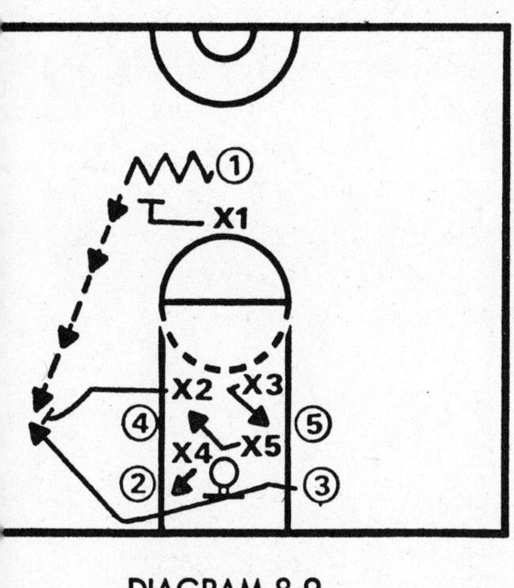

DIAGRAM 8-9

DIAGRAM 8-10

Summary

These maneuvers represent some techniques that will be used against your 1-3-1 match-up. A good scouting report will allow you to pre-plan, pre-drill. But even without a scouting report, mastery of the defensive fundamentals of the match-up and knowledge of the coverage and cutter rules will allow your players to respond solidly.

You may think this is too much for your players to learn, too many variations of offenses. That is true if you try to memorize all the different variations. A careful check of every diagram will show you that the coverages of all the offenses are the same. They all depend on the cutter and the coverage rules. And that is not too much to know. You merely apply those rules, drilled under the fundamentals of Chapter 3, and your 1-3-1 match-up will amaze you. A good scouting report merely adds confidence and preparation to your solid defensive plans.

PART THREE

THE 2-1-2 MATCH-UP

9 UNDERSTANDING THE BASIC 2-1-2 ZONE

You do not think your personnel is suited for the 1-3-1 zone and its companion match-up. But you believe your players would fit perfectly into a 2-1-2 mold. The next four chapters added to Chapters 1 through 4 would comprise your containing 2-1-2 match-up zone. Chapter 9 is to the 2-1-2 match-up what Chapter 5 was to the 1-3-1.

Your choice of zone is most important. You must run it long enough to get your opponent into his zone offense. And sometimes your opponent might try his man-to-man offense against your match-up. You might counter with your standard zone defense.

"Home" keys our defenders to come out of their match-up and play straight zone. When teams run an offense which we have not seen or drilled against and which might confuse our players, we might respond with "home." And on some nights, no matter what you try, your defenders will not react quickly and instinctively: "Home" is a good response.

So there are many reasons to choose the best zone for your personnel. That is why this portion of the book has three parallel parts. Where Part II developed the 1-3-1 zone and match-up, Part III will give you what you need to teach the 2-1-2 zone and its accompanying match-up.

Areas of Strength

Three defensive rebounders near the basket is a primary strength of the basic 2-1-2 zone. The guard alleys and the corner alleys offer almost no shooting room. The high post area can be shut off by the inside post defender with help from the weakside guard. Baseline offenses cannot penetrate the three big defensive players who station themselves collinear with the ball and the basket.

It is difficult to gain advantages near the big blocks (a primary scoring area). A defensive forward can front a post man stationed there with the assurance that the center can stop any lob pass. The weakside forward has perfect rebounding positioning.

The big center can front any cutter into the lane, knowing he has help from the defensive forwards on the big blocks behind him. He can stay home on perimeter shots, becoming the primary rebounder.

Areas of Weakness

The 2-1-2 zone grants the point guard a shot or a dribbling penetration every trip down floor. This zone is also very weak at the wings.

2-1-2 zones ask too much from their guards. The guards must cover the point, guards, and wings positions. Sometimes this amounts to covering three or four attackers with two defenders. Two hustlers at guard, therefore, is a prerequisite for any team wishing to employ the 2-1-2.

When defensive forwards come out to help the guards cover a wing, they open a seam inside only six to eight feet from the basket. A pass there results in a high percentage shot or draws the defensive center away from the basket area. When the center extends his coverage too far from the goal, a lay-up usually results.

The area between the bankboard and the baseline can be exploited from the corner or wing passing positions when the center covers a side or high post. The only defender who could cover that area is the weakside forward. But his coverage eliminates one of the strengths of the 2-1-2 zone: strong weakside defensive rebounding.

Selecting and Positioning of Personnel

There are many ways you can play your 2-1-2 match-up. Positioning of your personnel as well as what you ask them to do (your rules) will determine to the largest degree the success or failure of your match-up.

With this zone you can have one matcher or two. If you have more players who can become matchers, it will just make your match-up that much tougher. So first evaluate your personnel. How many men do you want to trust as a matcher? If you choose two, are both of them forwards? That makes the best 2-1-2 match-up alignment. But if one of them is a forward and the other a guard, you can still use two matchers. Because most teams attack the 2-1-2 match-up with a 1-3-1 alignment, the matchers as a forward and a guard can be a blessing in disguise. (More details on this concept will be illustrated as adjustments in Chapters 10 and 11.) Ideally, you will want a forward—X4 in this book—as your matcher; and if you have two, you will want the other forward, X3, as the second matcher.

X1, in Diagram 9-1, should be your offensive ball handler, usually your point guard. The bigger he is, the better; but don't sacrifice quickness for height. All the other defenders will key their positioning off X1.

So your first decision: Where to play your point guard? Because most teams are right handed and because most point guards are quick, able defenders, you might want to place X1 where X2 is located in Diagram 9-1. But because X1 is your point guard and ball handler and you want to fast break, it would be best to have him on the defensive right side. If you prefer, because of the personnel you have, that X1 and X2 exchange places, then exchange their duties and positioning in all the diagrams in the next three chapters.

X1, when we use the 2-1-2 match-up, plays the point guard or the attacker out front on the right side of the court. These offensive players do not have to have the ball. X1 should quickly point to and call out the number of the man he is guarding. If his man does not have the ball, X2

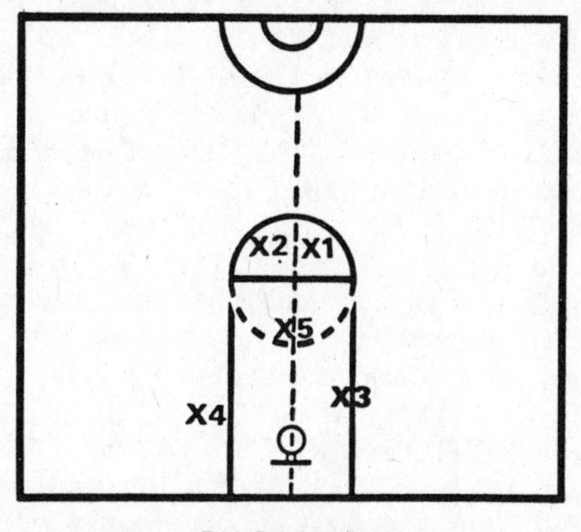

DIAGRAM 9-1

would probably be picking up the dribbler. X1 must be able to move laterally. He must never permit his man to drive by the front line of the zone. He will cover the high post area when the ball is at a wing or the corner. He must help X2 and X3 close the gap should X2's or X3's man drive to the middle. It helps if this man is a talkative type, a "hot dog." He can keep everyone informed, inspired.

X2, the other guard, must be a good defender if you plan to use the two guard front match-up. He must be able to control a dribbler laterally, never letting him penetrate with a dribble. X1 and X4 can help him close the gaps: X1 on drives to the middle and X4 on drives to the outside. If the ball is at the low wing or corner areas, X2 will help close off the inside post area unless the attackers have rotated to a one guard front. Then X2 would have the left wing or corner himself. X2 does not have to be as big in the 2-1-2 as he did in the 1-3-1 zone. X2 will not have to worry about inside rebounding as long as you run your basic 2-1-2 zone. But when you match-up, he must be able to get weakside rebounding position and hold it (see Chapter 4 for weakside rebounding). He will always have the first attacker to the left of X1.

Both guards, X1 and X2, begin their basic 2-1-2 positioning about one step above the free throw line (Diagram 9-1). Both players should begin inside the circle. Both guards initially, before matching-up, have the same duties: They stop the point penetration, and the guard on the weakside, once that is determined by a pass or a dribble out of the point alley, defends the passing lane into the high post area. They match or stay "home" from this placement.

X3, your smallest forward, can be your weakest defender if you use only one matcher. If you use two matchers, X3 must be an excellent inside defender. Whether you use one or two matchers, X3 must be a rebounder. Most weakside rebounds will be his responsibility. He must be able to turn all drives away from the baseline. He would receive help on drives toward the middle. This man, like X2 and X4, must become adept at accepting and releasing cutters. (See Chapter 3.) X3 can frequently see all potential attackers. Because of this, if X3 is a communicator, he will help your team defense. If he is big and slow, he will not hurt your team defense.

X4, your matcher if you have only one, must be a leader, a sound, basketball-wise, fundamental defender. He will be your tallest perimeter player who can defense the inside adequately. He will tell his teammates when to "home," when to trap, when to stunt. He must know what is expected of the team defensively. He must be a defensive coach on the floor. He will have to play the corners, defend the baseline, defend inside men, rebound, and play the wings. This man must be a gifted defender. His greatest asset will be his knowledge of basketball. He must shift and move as the offense shifts and moves. He must be able to recognize when his teammates are in trouble and come to their aid. He must recognize when the team defense is in trouble and call "home" or some other previously determined key.

Both forwards, X3 and X4, begin with their backs to the baseline and their feet on the big blocks (Diagram 9-1). These forwards can come out and cover an open wing attacker, but they must retreat quickly to the big blocks when the guard "releases" them (Penn State Sliding Zone Maneuver). From this positioning, they can match or stay "home."

X5, the defensive center, must be the best rebounder on the team. In the 2-1-2 zone, he will not need to be as quick as he would in the 1-3-1. But he must be more rugged, for he will get banged around frequently. He must be taught how to fundamentally guard a pivot man, both at the high and the low posts. He must know how to three-quarter any pivot player located along the lane line. He should be an aggressive individual who can stay in the game without fouling out. He must possess the ability to appear big because he will constantly have to help on cutters yet play the center attacker. Of course, he will have weakside forward and guard help. He is the last stopper on an attacker who is driving the baseline. If he can block shots, that is an added plus.

X5, the center in the standard 2-1-2 zone, starts each possession with his behind foot on the broken circle (Diagram 9-1). Not only does this give the impression of a standard zone, but the center can easily match from this placement.

So if you have one matcher (or two), a good defensive center, and an excellent guard defender (X2), this is your zone. Throughout the next three chapters we will describe adjustments you might make if you had two matchers (both forwards, or one forward and one guard). This, we hope, will lead you to establishing rules to govern the personnel you have on hand. Otherwise, we will limit explanations to X4 as the lone matcher.

The 2-1-2 Works Best Against Which Personnel

Teams with two excellent guards or two outstanding corner men will not cherish facing the 2-1-2 zone. Teams with two outstanding jump shooting wing men, or even one, might defeat the standard 2-1-2 zone handily. Teams with good guard penetrators, especially at the point, could demolish the basic 2-1-2 zone.

Good passing post men will not hurt this zone as much as the 1-3-1 or 1-2-2. Inside drivers should find little room to maneuver against the 2-1-2.

Teams whose offenses feature reverse passes from wing to point to wing or who skip a pass from wing to wing can get easy jump shots against the hustling outside guards. When the defensive forwards offer help against these offensive wings, the inside shot becomes available. And the inside defensive rebounding is reduced.

The 2-1-2 Zone Forces the Opponents into What Offenses

Most teams, when they see the 2-1-2, immediately adjust into their 1-3-1 offense. This puts a point guard in the hole between the defensive guards, and it places both offensive wingmen in the holes between the defensive guards and the defensive forwards. It also places an attacker behind the back line of the zone. The pivot attacker keeps the post defender occupied.

Some teams move into a 1-2-2 alignment. This gives them a point penetrator between the two defensive guards and two wingmen behind the defensive guards. These three shooters can bombard the defense from those holes. Making things worse for the defense is the back two of the 1-2-2. This base line duo lines up behind the defense, often cutting along the baseline unnoticed. These two men can post at the low post for a pass from the wing when a defensive forward goes out to stop the wing's jump shot. Or they can locate in the corners if they are good perimeter shooters. This puts too much of a burden on the defensive forward. Sooner or later an easy shot is obtained. Or the two deep attackers can line up on the same side of the court, in an overload: one in the corner and one at low post, for example. The 1-2-2 offense leaves the middle man of the basic 2-1-2 guarding space: he has no attacker to defend.

There is always that coach who believes the 1-4 cures all zone coverages as well as the match-up. So he faces the 2-1-2 with his 1-4. But the 1-4 is not a very good attacking formation until movement begins. And once motion commences, players cut into a 1-3-1, a 1-2-2, a 2-1-2, or a triangular, box, or diamond overload. Without cutting, no attacker would ever get closer than fifteen feet to the goal and the offense would never be a problem; but with cutting, the 1-4 becomes another array moving players nearer to the basket and becoming a problem.

Some teams give up trying to outmaneuver the match-up. They line up in the match-up's alignment and try to go one-on-one. But one-on-one play is not championship basketball. One-on-one tactics are poor substitutes for team offenses.

10 DEVELOPING THE COVERAGE RULE FOR THE 2-1-2 MATCH-UP

Chapter 10 parallels Chapter 6. Where Chapter 6 detailed the coverage rule as it related to the 1-3-1 zone, this chapter will explain the coverage rule as it applies to the 2-1-2 zone.

Offenses normally used against the 2-1-2 receive the greatest attention. Every effort is made to thoroughly and succinctly present the coverage rule against the more popular offenses against the 2-1-2. Also, this chapter elaborates on the coverage rule using two matchers as well as one. All adjustments are fully discussed and diagramed.

Coverage Rule Using One Matcher

Match-ups are easier to teach and simpler to use when you consider only one matcher. It is also easier for the offense to recognize and to attack. So if you have two possible matchers, it might be worthwhile to rule them both into your defense. It certainly would be more confusing to the offense.

Your lone matcher should be a forward because he will have some inside responsibilities. But if your personnel dictates that a guard would make the more natural matcher, this zone can supply it. Your center may even be slow in the 2-1-2 match-up, just as long as he is also big.

Because the other four defenders use X1 as their guide, he must play outside where those defenders can see him. X1 plays the initial attacker with or without the ball in the point alley. If no attacker locates in the point alley, he takes the player with or without the ball in the right guard alley.

X2 uses X1 as his key, covering the first attacker to the left of X1. That usually is the other attacking guard whether he lines up initially in the left guard alley or in the left wing corridor.

But if you intend to use a guard (point or second guard) as your lone matcher, he must be labeled X2. If you think your point guard is to be your matcher, assign him as X2 and your second guard as X1. But if you can, you want to leave X1 as your point guard type.

If you have scouted your opponent and they rigidly send a guard through as the initial cutter, assign X2 to that cutter. With that defensive move, you would not only have your matcher on the baseline but he would be defensing a guard. If your guard is your matcher, then X4 must take the first player left of X1 after X2 cuts to the baseline (see Diagram 10-3). Some of the diagrams in this chapter will use X2 as the matcher. Each will indicate the guard as the matcher where applicable.

When you deduce that your matcher should be your guard, X2, and you do not know your opponent's offense, you would want to start this defender at the high post (Diagram 10-1). The defense appears to be a 1-1-3 alignment; but actually it will most often take the form of the 2-1-2 because most offenses attack an odd front zone with two guards. X1, the defensive key, picks up the dribbler at midcourt. X1 can push the ball to one side of the court or let the offense choose a side. If the dribbler

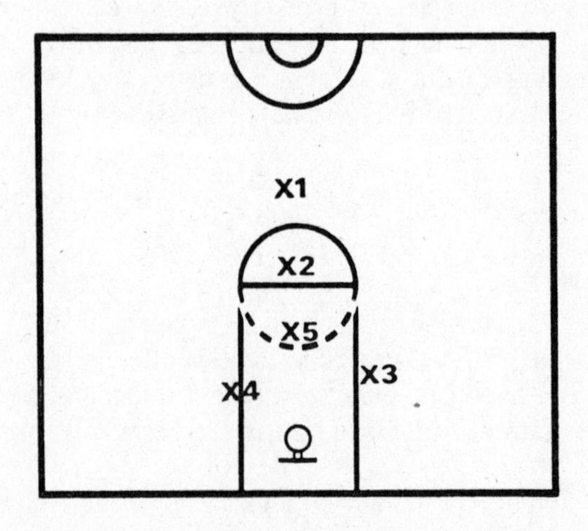

DIAGRAM 10-1

dribbles past the fore court marker, X1 stays with him. If the offense has a two guard front and if the dribbler passes to a wing or a guard stationed near the fore court marker, X2 can move out to cover the pass receiver. This means that the second guard (offensively) and not the point guard probably will have possession of the ball.

Most point guards have instructions to stay outside and handle the ball and provide defensive balance. Most second guards do the cutting. So the man X2 is guarding will pass the ball either to the corner alley or back to the point guard. This second guard then will cut if the offense intends to use a guard as a cutter. This puts X2, your matcher, on or near the baseline where you want him.

Even if the offense does not intend to cut a guard and you know that from scouting, you can still begin your defensive alignment as shown in Diagram 10-1. You rule: X4 takes the first player left of X1, and X3 covers first player right of X1. X5 takes the post man and X2 finds the second player left or right of X1 as the ball reaches midcourt.

But let's let the forward be the original matcher for the remainder of this section. X3 would, therefore, cover the first attacker to the right of X1. This man can be your weakest defender. He can even be big and slow.

X4, the matcher, takes the second attacker to the left or right of X1. Because most teams attack the 2-1-2 with a 1-3-1 set, X4 usually has the baseline man. If the offense is in the five perimeter set, X4 takes the second player left of X1. If the offense is in the three perimeter set, X4 covers the left high post.

X5 covers the offensive center: usually against the 2-1-2 the pivot man is at the high post. If there is no high post (five perimeter), X5 takes the second attacker to the right of X1. If there are two high post players (three perimeter), X5 takes the right high post. The 2-1-2 is your zone choice if X5 is a big but very weak defender. He must be taught to appear big even if he is slow. He must be an excellent defender if you use the 1-2-2 and an adequate defender if you use the 1-3-1.

Coverage Rule Using Two Matchers

Two possible combinations of two matchers are available from the 2-1-2 match-up. Two forwards make the best mixture; but a guard and a forward supply another possible blend.

When X3 and X4 are the matchers, you change your rules somewhat. X1 is still the key. He takes the point alley or the right guard alley initially. X2, the other guard, covers the first player left of X1. X5 still takes the center; and X4 still covers the second player left or right of X1. Although X3 still covers the first player right of X1, he adds the responsibility of covering the third player around the perimeter left of X1 when X2 covers the point attacker. (X4 always covers the second player left of X1.) This coverage occurs when 2 dribbles into the point alley and 1 rotates down to the right wing, bringing X1 with him. An overload on the left side of the court would put X4 at the wing and X3 covering the left baseline. In other words, X3 is defensing the left side of the court exactly as X4 has defensed the right side in all the previous diagrams in this book.

When you have two matchers, X3 and X4, frequently locating on the same side of the court, they both operate under one set of rules. Their duties interchange from one side of the court to the other: What X3 does on the right side, X4 accomplishes on the left side of the court.

Another adjustment involves a guard and a forward as matchers. When attacking teams line up in a 2-1-2 and send the guard through to the baseline, you can send the guard matcher with the cutter. Many teams run this type of attack to get into a 1-3-1 offense (see Chapter 12) from a 2-1-2 array. Since all defenders respond to X1, X2 must be the guard matcher. This coverage gives the attacking team trouble deciding the type of defense they are facing (more about that in Chapter 12). X2 begins as the first defender left of X1 but changes to assume X4's responsibilities, covering the second player left or right of X1. X3 still takes first player right of X1, and X5 still covers the center. X4 begins as matcher, taking second player left of X1. But when X2 cuts through, assuming X4's role, X4 becomes the new X2, taking the first player left of X1. When no offensive guard cuts, X4 remains the matcher.

When both guards can operate as matchers, the one going with the cutter is designated X2. The other guard remains named X1.

Coverage involving two matchers requires adjustments. And adaptations mean that you change your rules slightly. But then, our rules are different than Coach Ward's or Coach Green's or almost any coach who runs a match-up. By necessity, the defensive coach must adopt rules that best fit his personnel and his own coaching personality. All discussions in the next three chapters will involve X4 as the lone matcher. From time to time, X2 and X3 will be included as a matcher. When that happens, that evolution will be mentioned and fully discussed.

A Drill to Teach the Coverage Rule

Procedure:

1. Allow five offensive players to bring the ball downcourt while the defense shows a 2-1-2 zone.

2. Start the drill by having the offense set up in a typical or basic set used against the 2-1-2. Check to see if the match-ups are correct according to who covers whom and according to positioning (peripheral view and three-step drills).
3. After you are comfortable with the original matching, you allow passing but no offensive player movement.
4. If you intend to use two matchers, drill the matchers on their dual responsibilities.
5. You can advance the drill to allowing drives, forcing defenders to close the gaps. You still should not allow cutter movement.
6. Repeat the first four steps by having the attackers start in an overload alignment (triangle, box, and diamond).
7. Repeat the first four steps by having the attackers start in any free-lance array they wish.
8. Repeat the first four steps by having the attackers use the formations of your next opponent.

Objectives:

1. To teach closing the gap.
2. To teach the coverage rule, including the use of two matchers.
3. To teach the three-step drill.
4. To teach playing on the plane of the greatest peripheral view.
5. To teach defenders to respond to the next offense you will face.

Matching the Basic Sets Used Against the 2-1-2

The 1-3-1 offense is the most used alignment against the 2-1-2 (Diagram 10-2). There are four basic ways the attackers shift into this formation. A minimum of cutting will be shown because that gets into the cutter's rule (Chapter 11). Most often teams just line up in the 1-3-1 attack. 1, the point guard, tries to split the two guard front of the 2-1-2 zone. This guard, 1, either has the high percentage shot at the head of the circle or he can penetrate with a drive between the two zone guards. X1, in the match-up, picks up 1, neither giving 1 a shot nor letting him penetrate. Containment is X1's order. 2 and 3 line up in the area behind the guards and in front of the forwards of the 2-1-2 zone. Against the standard 2-1-2, 2 and 3 would have excellent jumpers. But against the match-up, neither 2 nor 3 should be initially open. X2 covers 2, the first man left of X1; and X3 covers 3, the first attacker right of X1. X4 takes 4, whichever side he lines up on, the second player left or right of X1. And X5 covers 5, the pivot man.

Some teams line up in the formation of the defense and go one-on-one. Some of these teams, from time to time, cut into the 1-3-1 (Diagram 10-3). They frequently send the guard through to the baseline, accomplishing the shift to the 1-3-1. Even if you basically use X4 as a lone matcher, you could sometimes send X2 with this guard cutter and confuse the offense. (See explanation of Diagram 11-3 for our basic coverage of this cut.) X2 guards 2 through to the baseline in this adjustment. X2 now becomes the matcher. You can run this adjustment when X2 is capable of being a matcher. He must tell X4 that he, X2, will now be the matcher. X3 covers first man right of X1, and X4 now covers first man left of X1. X2 covers the second man left and right of X1. X5 has 5.

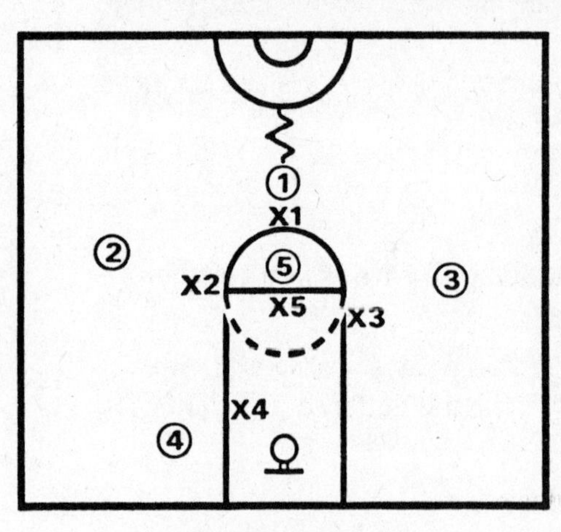

DIAGRAM 10-2

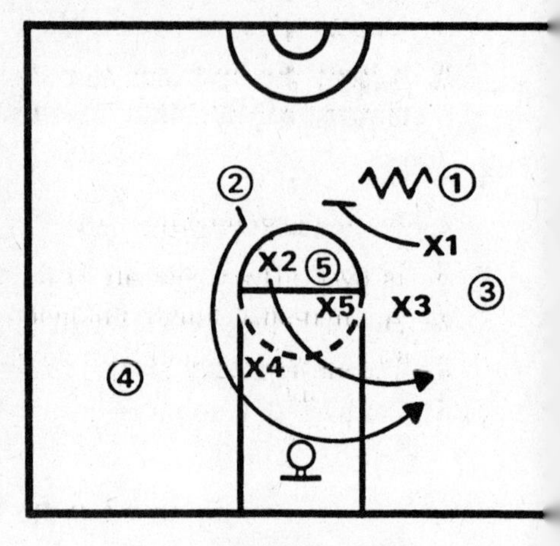

DIAGRAM 10-3

As long as the offense stays in the 2-1-2, the match-ups are as shown in Diagram 10-3. When cutting begins, defenders may play their regular match-up (X4 as the lone matcher) or by the above adjustments (X2 as the second matcher).

Some teams attack the 2-1-2 zone by beginning in a 1-2-2 alignment and adjusting into the 1-3-1 (Diagram 10-4). X1 takes the point guard, 1. X2 takes 2, the first player left of X1, and X3 takes the first player right of X1, 3. This formation represents a five perimeter form (Chapter 1). As a five perimeter offense, there are no high post men. X4 takes the second player left of X1, 4; X5 takes the second player right of X1, 5. To get into the 1-3-1, 4 or 5 would break to the high post. It is easy for X5 to cover either player to the high post. If 5 breaks, it is man-to-man. If 4 breaks to the high post, X4 shifts to X5's "release" call.

The last of the four major ways to get into the 1-3-1 is shown in Diagram 10-5. It starts in a 1-4 and rotates with the post man on the ball side rotating to the low post as 1 passes to either 2 or 3. The off-side high post man rolls to high post ball side. These are individual cuts, covered man-to-man. Notice in Diagram 10-5 that X1 takes the point guard, 1. X2 follows his rule and covers the first man left of X1. X3 covers, according to the rule, the first player right of X1. Because this is a three perimeter offense (two high post men), X4 takes the pivot on the left, and X5 covers the post on the right.

Now let's match-up the basic overloads before we get into ball movement. Chapter 11 will cover the cutter movements.

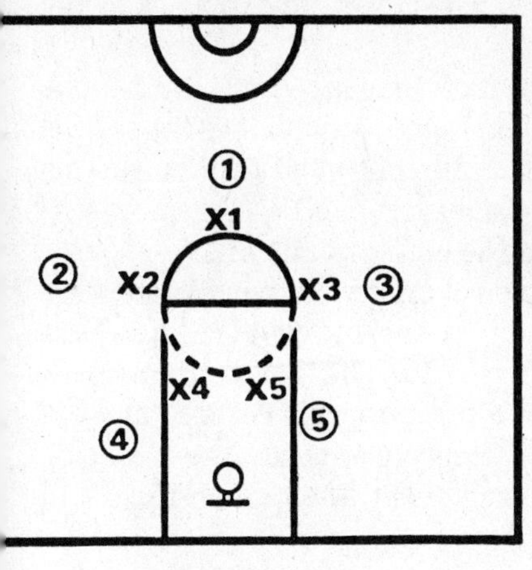

DIAGRAM 10-4

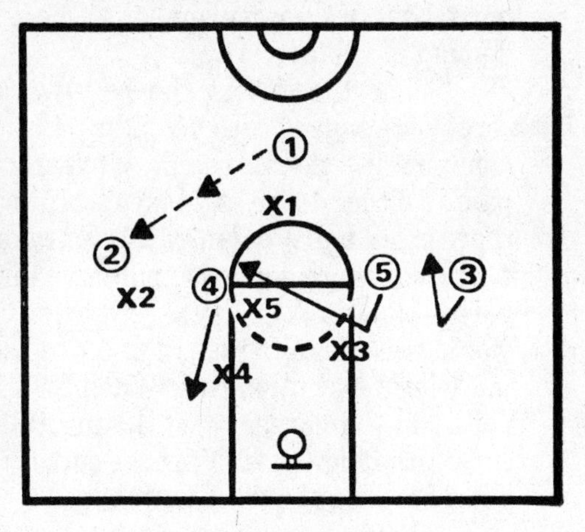

DIAGRAM 10-5

Matching the Overloads Used Against the 2-1-2

There are two methods of getting into an overload: line up in an overload when you come down the floor or line up in an attacking formation and cut into the overloads. This cutting can be continuous. The three basic overloads are the same against all zones: triangular, box, and diamond. The static overloads will be discussed in this section; overloads from cutting maneuvers will be discussed in Chapter 11.

Against the 2-1-2 zone most coaches run the 1-3-1 offense. The 1-3-1 offense is a constant triangular overload. (See Diagram 10-2.)

Diagram 10-6 discloses a very popular triangular overload used against the basic 2-1-2 zone. X1 has 1. X2 takes the first player left of X1, 2. X3 covers first potential cutter right of X1, 3. X4, the matcher, covers 4, the second player left of X1 in Diagram 10-6. X5 covers 5, the offensive center.

This popular overload starts with 2 trying to draw the defensive forward out to a wing. When the defensive forward of the standard 2-1-2 approaches 2, he dumps the pass off to 4. Only the center of the basic 2-1-2 zone could prevent 4's jumper. But if the center covers 4, 4 passes to 5 who rolls to the basket for the lay-up. 4 tries to locate on the baseline as close to the basket as he can and still receive the pass from 2. But as you can see, the match-up plays this deadly overload with man-to-man matching principles (Diagram 10-6). And the offense cannot even throw the lob pass to 5. X3 has perfect positioning to steal the lob pass from 2. More help is available inside: When 2 has the ball, X4 can sink and help; and when 4 has the ball, X2 can sag into the passing lanes inside. This offense must have cutter movement to become a problem, and that is in the domain of Chapter 11.

2 has the ball in the box overload of Diagram 10-7. Notice the three-step sags of each defender. X1 takes 1, and he must know that he is alone on one side of the floor (clearout). Also, X1 must help on the lob pass to either 4 or 5. X2 takes the first player left of X1 if there is one. If there is not a player left of X1, X2 takes the high post, 5, or the low post, 4. His coverage depends upon X5's initial coverage. X3 takes 3, the first player right of X1. X4 takes the second player right or left of X1. That would be 2. And X5 takes 4 or 5. (In Diagram 10-7, he took 4.) Remember the wing's exception rule: When X5 has a low post man covered and the ball is in the corner or at a wing, the defensive wing on the weakside covers the high post. Without cutting maneuvers, the box overload will not dismantle the 2-1-2 match-up.

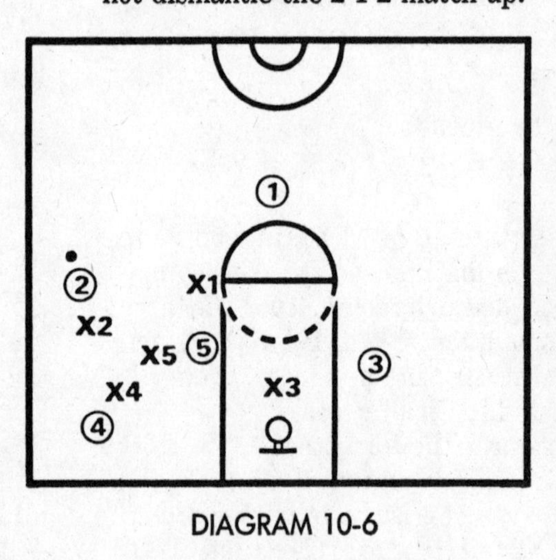

DIAGRAM 10-6

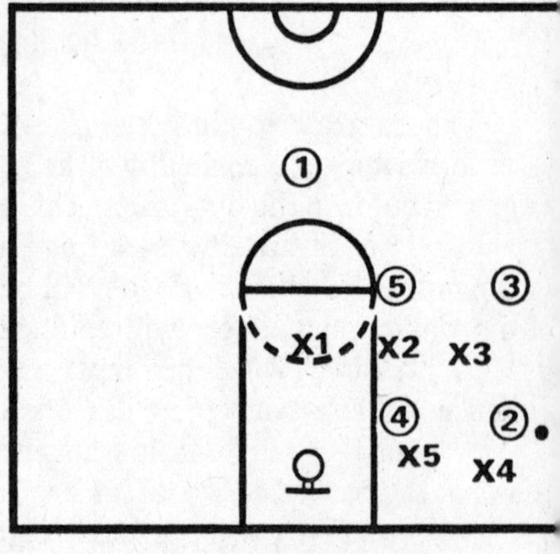

DIAGRAM 10-7

Diagram 10-8 displays the diamond overload. Again, notice the proper sags. X2, this time, is alone and must become aware of it. X1 takes 1. X3 takes 3, the first player right of X1. X4 covers 4, the second player right or left of X1. X5 covers the center.

The offense plans to force a defensive forward of the 2-1-2 zone to come out to cover the wing. The wing would then dump the pass to 4 on the baseline. 4 has the easy jumper unless the defensive center covers him. But the center can't come out without letting 4 hit 5 for the lay-up. All of this works wonderfully well against the 2-1-2 standard zone, especially if 3 is an excellent outside shooter. But against the match-up, the offense encounters a one-to-one coverage. There are no seams on the baseline. There is no successful overload unless the defense becomes confused by player movement. And the match-up, when played properly, leaves no cutters open. (See Chapter 11.)

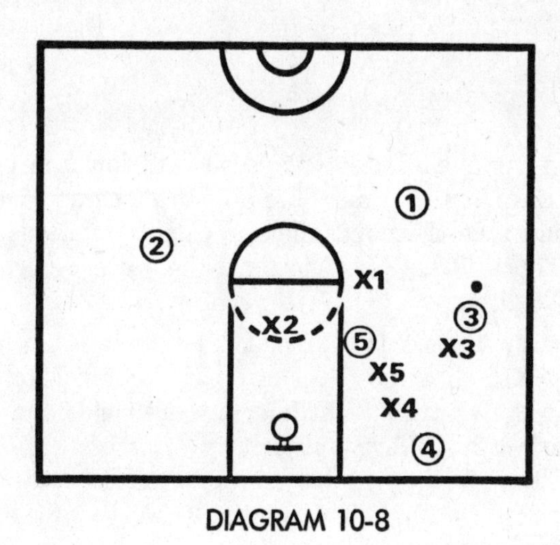

DIAGRAM 10-8

Defensing Ball Movement

By drilling on defensing teams that attack with ball movement, you can observe and correct the basic match-up fundamentals. Playing on the plane of greatest peripheral view and the three-step drills are the two most important. If these fundamentals are executed properly, your team defense will handle cutting and driving expertly. And, after all, the match-up is in the broadest sense a superb team defense.

A Basic 1-3-1 Offense Versus 2-1-2 Match-Up Drill (Diagrams 10-9 and 10-10). The lines in the diagrams show the approximate shoulder-to-shoulder line of each defender.

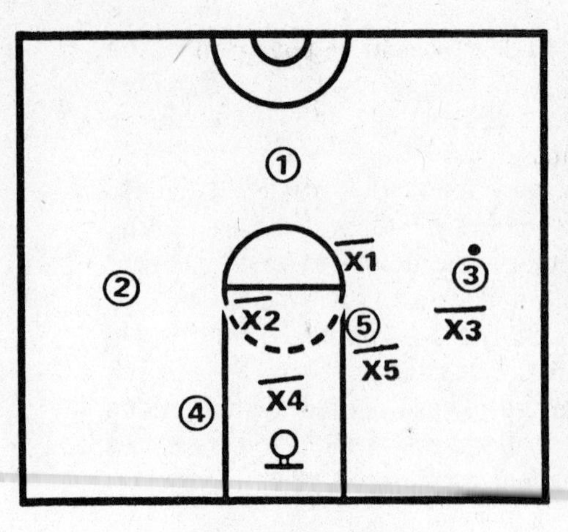

DIAGRAM 10-9

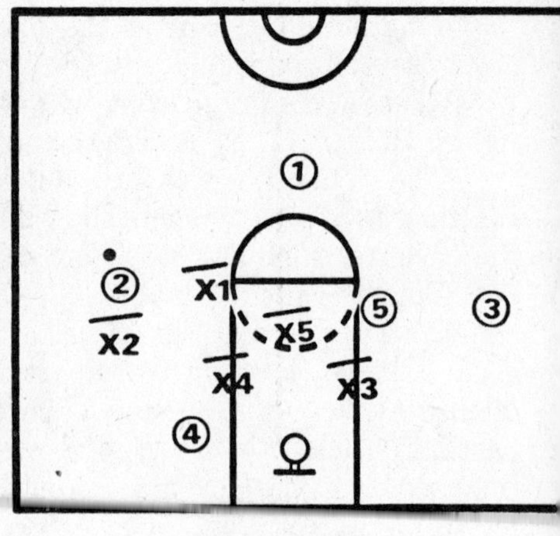

DIAGRAM 10-10

Procedure:

1. First let the five offensive players break downcourt and set up. See if the defense executes the proper match-up coverage rules. X1 would take the point alley on each trip because there is a player there. It does not matter if the player in the point alley has the ball.
2. In Diagram 10-9, 3 has the ball. X1 sags into the passing lane leading to the high post. X1 can play the interception stance if that is your desire for team defense. He should have view of 3, 1, and possibly 2. He should intuitively know or should be informed by X5 where 5 is. When drives are permitted, X1 must stop the drive across the middle. Diagram 10-10 shows the pass being made around the horn or skipped. Diagram 10-10 shows the necessary defensive slides.
3. X2 can see 2, 1, 3, and 5 (Diagram 10-9). He knows when cuts begin. He can see the ball passed or the man with the ball dribbling. He could be in the interception stance, but he must use the three-step drill, two steps off of his man and four steps toward the basket. As the ball is passed around the horn, X2 must cover the ball, and X3 would see 1, 2, 3, 4, and 5 (Diagram 10-10).
4. X3 begins covering 3 (Diagram 10-9) and ends with a weakside sluff of four steps to the basket and two steps off his man (Diagram 10-10). X3 starts with front foot to pivot foot stance and can end in the interception stance (see Chapter 3) or in a basic sagging stance (Diagram 10-10).

5. X5 plays the center, sluffing, and appearing big. He always has help from X1, except when 1 has the ball. But if 1 is not a shooter—and many point guards are not—X1 would sink and help 5 as the ball is reversed. X5's stance allows him to peripherally view the outside three, 1, 2, and 3, and his man, 5.
6. X4, the matcher, sees the entire court (Diagram 10-9). He plays his interception stance or sags, playing on the plane where he sees everyone. When the ball comes around to 2, X4 denies 4 the ball; but his stance still should allow him to spot peripheral movement, even from 3. X4 closes the gap on a baseline drive by 2 (Diagram 10-10).

Objectives:

1. To teach the match-up coverage rule.
2. To teach the interception stance.
3. To teach proper positioning of the body so it will be on the plane of greatest peripheral view.
4. To teach proper weakside sags.
5. To teach the three-step drill.

How well you can make up drills to teach your match-up will play a large part in the success of your defense. This book tries to present drills in an orderly fashion for those young, inexperienced drill creators.

After your players learn proper sags and helping stances from an ordinary set, you should drill the defense just on ball movement from an overload set. The next drill covers that. After covering positioning from basic sets and basic overloads (this chapter), you should develop drills covering movements from basic sets into overloads (next chapter).

A Box Overload Against the 2-1-2 Match-Up, a Drill (Diagrams 10-7 and 10-11). Diagram 10-7 shows the box overload with the ball in the corner. This is how the offense would look if 2 cut through to the corner, if cutting were allowed in this drill, as 1 passed the ball to 3. Diagram 10-11 will show the coverage as the ball is passed back out to 3.

Procedure:

1. Let the attackers bring the ball up floor and get into their overload formation. See if the defenders can properly match the overload.
2. X4 takes the cornerman 2, the second attacker right of X1. X4 must prevent the initial baseline drive of 2. When 2 passes to 3, X4 jumps his three steps (two toward the basket and one toward the ball).

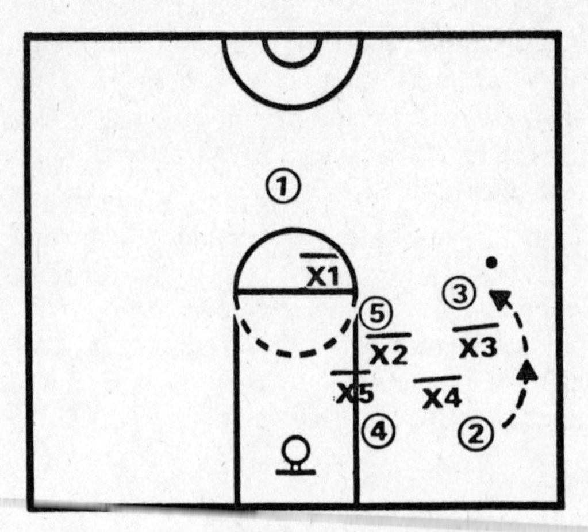

DIAGRAM 10-11

3. X1 sags four steps to the basket when the ball is in the corner. As the ball comes out to 3, X1 moves back out to cover the high post passing lane, two step sag and one step toward the ball. X1 must always be alert for 1 cutting backdoor. If he does not see the weakside being opened for 1, his teammates must warn him.
4. X2 would cover 5, because there is no attacker to the left of X1. X2 would play the passing lane from the corner to the high post. X2 would adjust to the three quarter position when the ball goes out to 3. X2 should be able to see 1, 2, 3, and 5 at all times. If X5 had taken the high post, he would play on the same plane described for X2. X2 would then cover the low post as described for X5 in section 6 of this drill.
5. X3 must help on the inside drive from the corner. He would be two steps toward the basket and one step toward the ball. When 3 receives the pass from 2, X3 should reach 3 as the ball does. X3 can expect help from X1 on the inside drive and from X4 on the outside drive. You as a coach can have either X3 or X4 play the drive in only one direction if your defender is slow.
6. X5 would play the low post, 4. X5 would front when the ball is in the corner. If X5 fronts, X1 must cover the lob. This is consistent with our rule: If the defensive center has the low post man on the ballside, then the weakside man (either X2, X3, or X4) takes the high post. This is the one exception to X5 always covering the high post. By playing it this way, X2 is in better position to play the first attacker left of X1. Of course, an easy adjustment, should you prefer it, is to let X2 take the low post, leaving X5

always covering the high post. This way X2 could see all cutters, and he could get back to his position (first player left of X1) on the first cutter. Most cutters cut near the basket and through to the weakside, helping X2 switch and get back to the weakside. But you give up your big man near the basket with this adjustment. X2, usually a guard type, might have to play a much taller opponent on the baseline. X5, on the other hand, could force a pass receiver near the basket to raise his shot, or X5 could block shots from the low post. X2 could outquick the high post receiver. So we feel our regular match-up rule far outweighs what might on the surface seem to be a more logical rule.

Objectives:

1. To teach match-up coverage rule.
2. To teach proper weakside sags when everything is on the strongside (overload).
3. To teach the interception stance, fronting, denial, and three-quartering inside.
4. To teach proper positioning of the body so it will always be on the plane of greatest peripheral view.
5. To teach the sagging three-step drill.

Defensing the Offense That Penetrates the Holes and Seams

Many coaches want their perimeter players to line up in the holes of the zone defense. Diagram 10-12 graphically displays why the 1-3-1 and 1-2-2 are popular offenses against the 2-1-2 zone. These holes, however, are not available against the match-up.

When X5 must play on a high post, a seam appears near the basket. And when X3 or X4 has to come out to hole #2 or hole #3 to cover an excellent wing shooter, seam #1 or seam #3 opens up. But, again, this does not occur in the match-up which covers men and not areas while a zone is played.

Attackers line up in the holes, intending to penetrate with a drive. When another defender offers help, the driver passes to his open teammate, either the area the defender just left or to a cutter cutting into the inside seams. To eliminate the advantage of these drives into the pockets, you should use the closing the gap drill in Chapter 3. The more your players drill on this, the better your team defense becomes. You can do this drill in two ways: line players up in the regular zone (2-1-2) and close

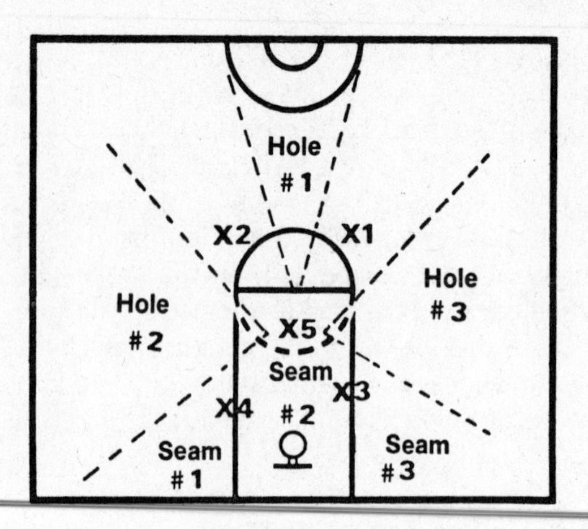

DIAGRAM 10-12

the gaps—you need to drill on this because you will run your basic zone many times during the year; and line players up in the match-up and close the gap. In the first drill, your players will be defensing an area. In the match-up drill, your players will be playing a man. (More will be presented at the end of this chapter on breakaway dribblers.)

An added adjustment: If some of your players cannot cover a driver because of the difference in speed, quickness, and anticipation, order those players to cover their man's drive in only one direction. This negates the advantage of quickness. The defender can concentrate his coverage in only one direction. He can overplay half a man. But when you do order this coverage, be sure all defenders who must help close the gap know their added responsibilities. Sometimes it is wise to cut all dribblers in one direction. Sometimes you can more easily defeat a team by cutting all dribblers on the right side inside and cutting all dribblers on the left side baseline or vice-versa. At other times with other teams you might want to cut all dribblers from the point or guard alleys outside, all dribblers rom the wing alleys inside, and all dribblers from the corner alleys inside—or any combination you prefer. This shows another adjustability of the match-up zone coverage. You, as coach, must decide what strategy will help your team the most. But drilling and drilling and drilling is the only way such coverage will become instinctive with your players. Telling them is not enough. (See Chapter 3 and Chapter 6 for more details on this strategy.)

Any cutter breaking to the seams should pay for the cut. The defender should body check the cutter. If the cutter continues his cut without changing his direction, it constitutes charging. Proper sags, the three-step drill, and body checking should prevent any cutter from reaching any seam.

Inside stationary attackers can be fronted, three-quartered, or denied the ball. Fronted attackers will face double coverage on the lob—a weakside defender helps the fronter. Three-quarters or denial defenders should deflect passes into the center of the court where the defender's teammates will recover the deflected ball.

That leaves only one possible open area: The spot where releasing and accepting cutters sometimes create an opening. But constant drilling on the correct fundamental techniques of Chapter 3 will make this coverage instinctive. Such instinctive play rarely, if ever, leaves an opening. Drilling makes this maneuver, called shifting in our vernacular, smooth, quick, and second nature.

There should be no holes, and seams—which drilling eliminates—won't exist against the match-up. Attackers must use ball and player movement to present problems to the defense.

"Bust Out" and "Bust Over"

"Bust Over" eliminates two perimeter defensive men from guarding the same attacker. It occurs after a cut, usually by a guard or a wing. Let's explain "Bust Over" by allowing the offense to match the defensive array, the 2-1-2, and cut into the popular 1-3-1 formation. This happens frequently to the 2-1-2 match-up (Diagram 10-13).

Because we will explain two coverages, defensive men have been eliminated from the diagram. So begin with X1 covering 1, X2 guarding 2, X3 blanketing 3, X4 taking 4, and X5 guarding the post, 5.

Coverage in Diagram 10-13 can take two forms; and without "Bust Over," X1 would get confused on his assignment. The Penn State Sliding Zone maneuver should be worked if X4 is your only matcher. X2 would "release" X4, allowing X4 to sink to the big block and cover 2's cut to the weakside corner. X5 would help on 2's cut until X4 dropped to the big block, and X1 would sag into the high post passing lane until X5 gets back. X2, therefore, has 4. X1 picks up 1. X3 keeps 3. X4 takes 2.

But let's use both forwards as matchers. Now X2 would follow 2 to the free throw lane area where X5 would "release" him. A step or two into the lane by 2 would be greeted with X3 "releasing" X5. When X2 looks opposite the ball to find his next assignment, he might find X1 and 1. So X2 declares "Bust Over," cueing X1 to take the next attacker around the perimeter. This puts X2 on 1, X1 on 3, and X3 on 2. X4 has 4, and X5 covers 5.

"Bust Out" is used whenever an inside defender must hurry outside to cover what seemed to be an open attacker. This happens when the offense skips a pass and the perimeter defenders have assignments other than the new receiver. Diagram 10-14 shows an inside attacker breaking

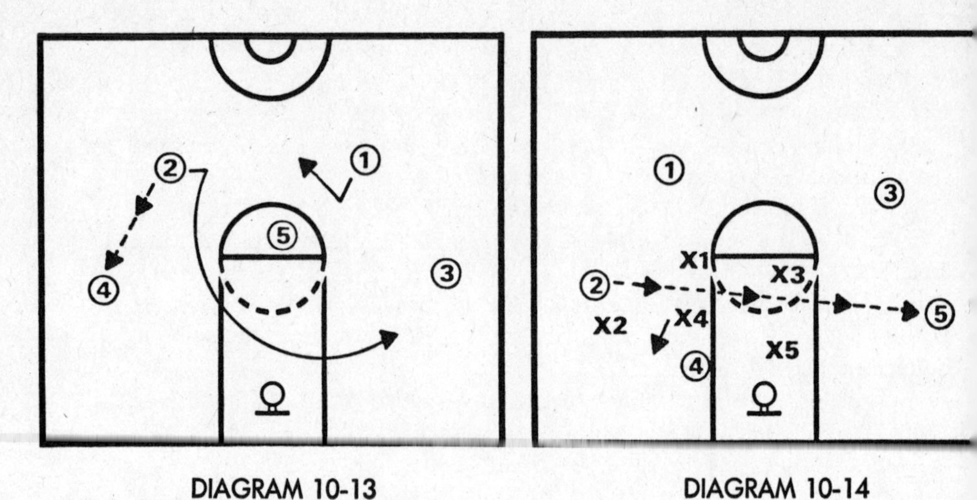

DIAGRAM 10-13 DIAGRAM 10-14

outside and receiving a skip pass. Every perimeter defender has his assignment, but you don't want X5 staying on the perimeter. And you don't want 5 shooting an uncontested jumper. So X5 declares "Bust Out" to let everyone know he is vacating the area near the basket. This can also cue X3, if you want to keep X5 near the goal, to use the Penn State Sliding Zone move to release X5. As X3 uses the Penn State Sliding Zone maneuver and "releases" X5, each perimeter defender would slide over one assignment.

Stopping the Breakaway Dribbler

No matter how much we drill on closing the gap, we ultimately face a clever dribbler who breaks through a pocket for what seems to be a defensive breakdown. We still don't concede the easy shot. As 2 drives by X1, who should have closed the pocket, X4 reacts to pick up the dribbler, 2, near the foul lane line. X3 rotates down to 4. X1 moves over to 3, and X2 looks opposite the dribble to find his new assignment, 1. Once X4 converges on 2, it is impossible for 2 to dribble further. X2 or X1 would steal the next bounce. And X4 would draw the charge if 2 continued. X4 races at the dribbling shoulder of 2. This overplay prevents 2's continuing. 2 cannot cross the ball over to the other hand. His original defender would steal the dribble. X4 should, if possible, get to 2 before 2 reaches the foul lane. X3 must rotate quickly, and X1 must leave when he sees 2 touch the ball with both hands. 2 would probably pass out to 1. The defense adjusts, and the temporary defensive breakdown costs the defense nothing but time.

11 DEVELOPING THE CUTTER'S RULE FOR THE 2-1-2 MATCH-UP

Most teams employ both ball movement and man movement when they attack a match-up zone. Ball movement against the 2-1-2 match-up was discussed in Chapter 10. Player movement will be defensed in this chapter. They will be combined in Chapter 12.

Sections in this chapter parallel Chapter 7, but all diagrams will demonstrate different alignments, different cuts, different passes. This will enable you to have, at the end of Chapter 16, a complete detailed defensive explanation of all possible alignments, cuts, and passes against the three basic match-ups.

The Cutter's Rule for the 2-1-2 Match-Up

There are two ways your 2-1-2 match-up can initiate coverage: using a guard and/or forward as the matcher(s), or using the two forwards (Chapter 10). Many cutter rule variations can be invented from these two concepts.

If you intend to use a guard as a matcher, he needs to be of above average size. Quickness can be sacrificed for height. This guard-matcher would be called upon to cover inside attackers many times during a game.

The guard-matcher begins at a disadvantage because he cannot see the action behind him. He begins by lining himself up one step above the free throw line if your teams intend to employ the basic 2-1-2 zone. He could, however, be at high post in the center of the lane if you propose to match out of the tandem guard alignment (Diagram 10-1). This latter defense is best if you designate a particular guard as your matcher. If you leave the choice to whichever defender's man cuts first, then the standard 2-1-2 would best confuse the offense.

In either case, usually the first cutter through is the guard who initially passed the ball. The opposing coach wants this cutter to break to the baseline so he can determine the defense his team is facing. If the defensive guard goes with him, it naturally appears to be man to man. And because the cut is usually to the baseline, the matcher now is able to see the entire attacking formation, the cuts of all offensive performers. But when you employ this defensive guard as your matcher, you must make sure your forwards cover the first attackers left and right of X1, the other guard. X1 would naturally take the other attacker who is out front. Your guard-matcher and your defensive center would match the remaining two attackers. The center would take the center if there were only one, or the center on his right if there were two.

Using a guard as a matcher usually means that the opponents will use more player movement because they frequently figure man defense. And most opponents' man-to-man attacks feature more player movement than their zone attacks. If you know your opponent's man offense and have drilled your zone defense against it, you can certainly confuse the opposition whether they surmise man or guess zone.

Employing either one or both forwards as your matcher(s) offers the best initial coverage and the best deception when cuts begin. Because most attacking teams would suppose zone coverage when no defender followed the guard who initially cut through the zone, the defense would face less personnel movement. And player movement gives the match-up its most difficult moments.

To use only one forward as a matcher is less desirable because the 1-3-1 zone would probably have suited your personnel more. But to use both forwards as matchers means you must have two above average players in both basketball intellect and physical size to fill those positions. You must also have a center, but he can be much slower and less of a jumper in the 2-1-2 than he would be in the 1-3-1.

When you use two forwards as matchers, your initial coverage results from the defender who guards the ball as it crossed a predetermined area (such as a half court line). The guard on the ball becomes X1. The other guard takes the first attacker to the right or left of X1, whichever side the defensive guard is stationed on. It would change from possession to possession depending upon which guard assumed the roll of X1. The forward on the side of the ball takes the first attacker on that side away from X1. The weakside forward would always be the matcher; weakside also changes from possession to possession depending upon where the ball crossed the designated area. The center covers the center. If there were two offensive centers, the defensive center takes the attacker on his right.

Coverage with two forwards as matchers naturally offers more deception in the 2-1-2 match-up. But your personnel must dictate which type of coverage and cutter rules you will employ. The 2-1-2 match-up, as you have noticed, offers much more versatility than the 1-3-1 and the 1-2-2 match-ups. Our aim is to get you to think match-up according to your personnel and personality. In all the diagrams that follow we will assume you will use only one forward as a matcher, X4. But that X4 could in reality be either forward (if you use two forwards as matchers) or a guard who followed the first cutter through to the baseline. From time to time, we will deviate from these rules by considering adjustments to this coverage. When we do adjust, both the basic ruled coverage and the adjustment coverage will be explored and explained.

Regardless of how many or which men you use as matchers, matchers will frequently begin their coverage of team movement from a baseline placement. If they are on the strongside, they must follow the cutter to the free throw lane line where they will hear a weakside defender call "release." This strongside defender, whether matcher or not, should look opposite the cut for his new assignment. He must help defense the inside, but he must also reach his new assignment by the time a pass arrives.

The weakside acceptor of the cutter should sag his three-step drill prior to movement by the strongside or the weakside cutter. From this plane of greatest peripheral view, this weakside defender, many times the matcher, has full view of the court. He can make instant decisions as to when to shift and where. A weakside acceptor may have to cover the cutter and his own man momentarily while the other defenders adjust. He does this by physically stepping toward the cutter, appearing big, but staying in the passing lane between the passer and his original man. Because this action takes place on the weakside with an attacker moving away from the ball, it usually offers no problems.

Weakside defenders of cutters should body check all flashes toward the ball, directing the cutter away from the most advantageous position with respect to the ball. Weakside defenders may have to carry cutters to the ballside of the free throw lane lines before releasing them.

A Drill to Teach the Cutter's Rule

Diagram 11-1 shows the most popular single offensive pattern rotation used by teams to attack the 2-1-2 zone. It offers the best opportunity to drill your defenders on their cutter rule. It happens to be a four perimeter set. Chapter 7 explained a popular five perimeter set against the 1-3-1 zone, and Chapter 15 will disclose a popular three perimeter set against the 1-2-2. When taught separately, these sections will fulfill all the drill your players will need to learn a particular cutter rule; and when they are read concurrently, they will allow you to see all the different options you have available to establish and to teach a cutter's rule.

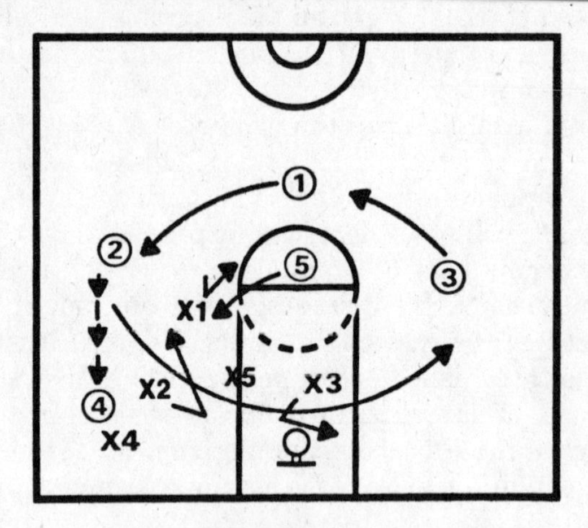

DIAGRAM 11-1

Procedure:

1. Line up five players against five defenders as shown in Diagram 11-1.
2. The coach should number his offensive positions and call out the numbers as he wants that position to cut. He can also call out the type of cut. He can begin by allowing his players to walk through the defense and offense, but he can quickly expand into full speed movement. The coach can require the cutter to go to the baseline near the basket before breaking back out weakside or strongside. Or he can call flash pivots, give and goes, weakside to strongside, or any move he wishes. Or, of course, he could let the players decide.
3. The other offensive players must fill a hole vacated by the cutter. This means each player must move over one position as shown in Diagram 11-1.

4. Diagram 11-1 depicts the popular 1-3-1 offensive rotation against the 2-1-2 zone. X5 naturally opens his defense on 5. As 5 rolls low, X5 plays him man-to-man, trying to prevent the pass inside. He can front 5 because X3 provides weakside lob help. X1 starts on 1, but slides into high post passing lane (three-step drill) as 2 receives the ball. When 2 passes to 4, X1 can drop yet another three steps.
5. X2 begins on 2, the first man left of X1. When 2 passes to 4 and cuts, X2 goes to the area of the free throw lane line on the ballside, staying between the cutter, 2, and the passer, 4. When X2 hears X3 call, "Release," X2 hurries back outside to cover 1, who has filled 2's vacant spot. As X2 hurries out on 1, he should tell X1 to "bust over." X2 has the option, if you so ruled, of covering 4, releasing X4 as in the Penn State Sliding Zone. In that case, X1 would cover 1. Because the ball has been passed to the corner, instead of dribbled there, it is best that X2 rotates out on 1 and calls for X1 to "bust over" on 3. 3 has rotated to the point.
6. X3 ends up on 2 as the ball is reversed.
7. Other cutting options are available. If X3 has had trouble covering a flash pivot from the four perimeter set, let 3 initially flash pivot, then run the rotation. You can run and defend any cut that the opponent might use from the four perimeter set.
8. If you plan on using two matchers, a guard and a forward—for example, X2 and X4—you could allow X2 to continue with 2's cut man-to-man. This puts X2 on the weakside and in the best of positions to read the entire court as a matcher must. But your opposition might read man defense and run their man offense against you.
9. If you use two forwards as matchers, you could alternate your coverage by having X2 play the point guard, X1 play 3, and X4 defend against 2. Then line 4 up on the other side of the court in the corner, forcing X3 to cover him. By having the same cuts, you give X4 opportunities to be a weakside matcher and you drill X3 on strongside matching.

Objectives:

1. To teach the coverage of cutters.
2. To teach the cutter's rule.
3. To teach accepting and releasing cutters.
4. To teach the three-step drill.
5. To teach closing the gaps (by letting dribblers drive while players cut).

6. To teach body checking (on cutters from the weakside).
7. To teach the interception stance.
8. To teach playing on the plane of greatest peripheral view.

The Passer as a Cutter from the Point, Guard, Wing, and Corner

Point. The 1-3-1 array is the favorite offensive alignment against the standard 2-1-2 zone. As 1, the point guard, brings the ball into front court, he passes to the wing, 2, and cuts off the high post (Diagram 11-2). After he reaches the low foul lane area, 1 can cut off of 4 to the strongside; or he can cut to the weakside, allowing 4 to post his defender low.

X1, the defender on 1, would jump the three steps toward the ball and basket, preventing 1 from receiving a quick return pass and helping X5 cover the passing lane inside to the high post area. As 1 cuts, X1 would follow him to the area of the foul line where X5 would "release" X1. X1 covers the high post area, but he begins to look opposite his drop for his next assignment. Someone must rotate high, or 2 has no way to swing the ball. 3 would probably rotate high, or 2 could dribble toward the center of the court. If 2 dribbles, X1 would have more than enough time to "bust over" and find 3. In either case, 3 is X1's next assignment, but X1 covers the high post passing lane until X5 "releases" 1.

If 1 continues his cut weakside, X3 could pick him up. If 1 darts out into the strongside corner, X4 could take 1 as he receives the ball. X3 could cover 4; or X5 could shift with X4, forcing X3 to take 5. This type of coverage must be drilled upon until the rules become instinctive.

You could count 5 as a flash pivot cutter with X5 already covering a low post strongside attacker (as our rules do). This would put X3 on 5.

Or you could rule, especially if you have two forwards as matchers, that the high post must be covered by the center, and the weakside forward, X3 in this diagram, would always receive and release cutters. Under that condition, X3 would cover 4. And if you feel that this latter case best suits your personnel, you must make X1 aware of the potential backdoor layups and relieve X1 of his coverage of the high post passing lanes. If you don't, 3 could sneak backdoor for an easy lob pass.

Guard. As 2 has crossed the keyed area with the dribble, he passes to 1 (Diagram 11-3). X1 would cover 1 according to our basic coverage rule regardless of who was our matcher. X2 would go with 2's cut if we were using a guard as our matcher (not shown in Diagram 11-3). X3 and X4, the defensive forwards, would cover 3 and 4 respectively. X5 would cover 5, and X2 would have 2. From there the defenders would stay matched by shifting personnel as the attackers cross or cut into other areas.

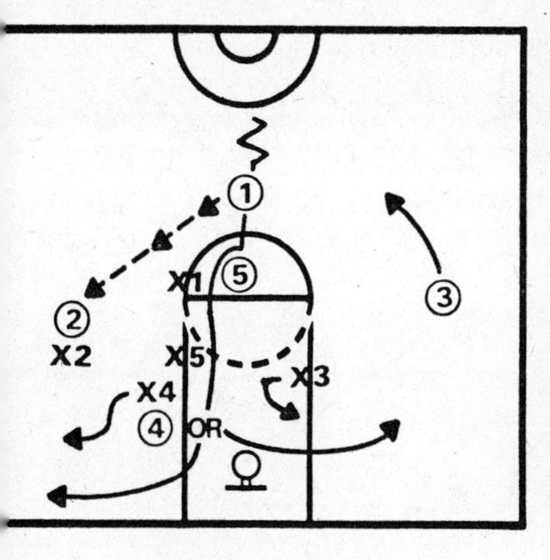

DIAGRAM 11-2

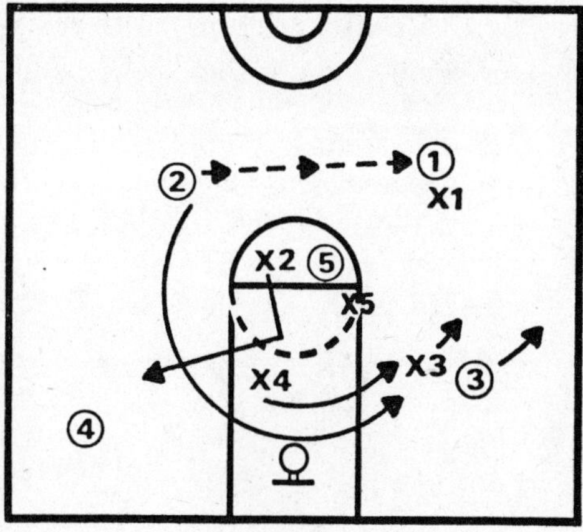

DIAGRAM 11-3

If your defense called for either forward to be the matcher, then X1 would have 1, X2 would drop on 2's cut and take 4, the first attacker left of X1. X3 would cover 3, the first attacker right of X1. X5 covers 5 the high post and X4 shifts onto 2 as he cuts through. It is easy to imagine the coverage from the other side if the ball is passed from 1 to 2 and 1 cuts. X3 becomes the matcher (the weakside forward is constantly becoming the matcher and covering all cutters toward the strongside almost man-to-man). The weakside forward must remember: the closer his man is to the basket, the more he plays him man-to-man; the farther his attacker moves away from the basket, the more he can sag and play the passing lanes. He must always shift with the nearest defender as his man moves farther outside (crossing paths with another attacker), and both forwards must keep each other informed, should they both be on the same side of the floor, as to who has the matcher's responsibilities. The matcher is always the defensive forward closest to the basket, X4 in Diagram 11-3.

Wing. Diagram 11-4 depicts a wing passing to a point and cutting through to overload the weakside. This occurs frequently during any game. And it is an extremely effective move against standard 2-1-2 zones, especially if 1 will fake a pass toward 4 before reversing the ball to 3. Fake passes opposite the direction of the intended pass frequently freeze the zone's defensive movement for that fraction of a second that the offense needs to get the good shot. But fake passes should not freeze a match-up zone which slides using man-to-man principles.

X1 has a hand in the high post passing lane but quickly slides out on 1 as 2 makes the pass. X1 moves while the ball is airborne, not after 1 has received the ball. X5 covers the high post, 5. X2 hears X4's "release," and the two defenders shift responsibilities. X3 covers 3, using the three-step drill and the plane of greatest peripheral view drill.

Corner. Diagram 11-5 shows a cornerman passing back out to a wing and then cutting baseline hoping to either "post up" low or break to overload triangularly the weakside. The coverages, according to match-up rules, would result in straight man-to-man defense. All off-the-ball defenders help by sagging, using their three-step drill. As long as the ball is at the wing, X4 covers high side or fronts the low post, 4. X3 has weakside lob help. If 4 cuts through to the weakside, X4 stops with both feet in the lane until the ball is reversed at least to the point, 1.

DIAGRAM 11-4

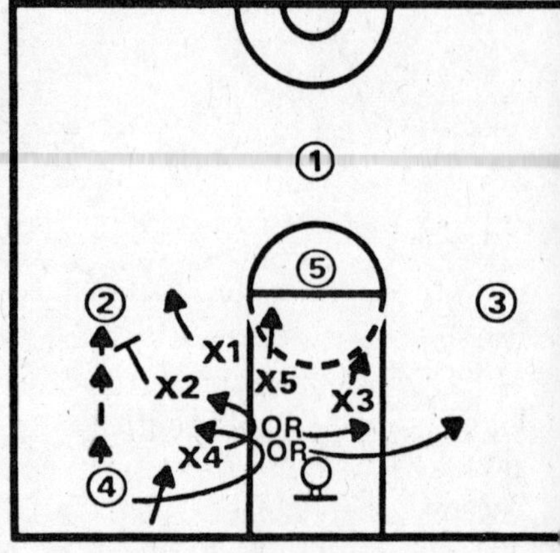

DIAGRAM 11-5

Strongside Guard Cutter

Many coaches attack all zones, including match-ups, by overloading one side of the court. The diamond overload, Diagram 11-6, represents one of the three methods of overloading.

When 1 passes to 2 and cuts through, 2 has many options. He can hit 5 for the high-low game between 5 and either 1 or 4. He can hit 4 who has four passing lanes available as well as a drive or a shot. Or he can hit 1 in a post up low. Or he can quickly reverse the ball to 3 and have players cut to the weakside for another overload there.

X1 would follow 1 to the free throw line extended area where he would hear "release" from X5. X2 pressures 2; and X1, who keeps an arm in the high post passing lane, looks away from the ball for his next assignment (3 moving to an area to receive a reverse pass). X4 denies 4 the ball. This leaves X5 and X3 to execute the cutter's rule. If you want X5 to always keep the high post when there is one, you must rule that X3 covers 1 at the low post. X1 must then be aware of the backdoor responsibilities. But if you allow X5 to cover the low post, then X3 takes 5 as if he were a flash pivot cutter. We prefer the latter because X1 stays in the high post passing lane as he would in the regular 2-1-2 zone and because X5, our tallest and most capable inside defender, can negate any posting by a guard on the big block. It also makes our inside coverage simpler to rule, easier to teach.

Strongside Wing Cutter

4 has the ball in Diagram 11-7, and 2 cuts to low post, either intending to post up or roll to the weakside for a reverse action. 1 and 3 must rotate offensively, providing passing avenues, if 4 is unable to shoot or drive quickly or the offense becomes stagnant. X2 follows 2 to the free throw lane area where X5 should release him. X2 looks opposite the ball for his next assignment (1 rotating over). X1 has used the three-step drill, preventing any penetrating pass into the lane area. If X5 overshadows 2 physically, he can play behind 2. If 2 keeps cutting toward the weakside, X5 releases 2 to X3. X1 continues to prevent the pass to the high post area while looking opposite the ball for his new assignment. When X2 goes outside to cover 1, he declares, "Bust over," indicating to X1 that he must find his new assignment (3 rotating outside). X3 has the high post, 5, if X5 takes 2 at the low post. X3 has 2 if he releases X5, leaving the high post 5 to X5. Both X2 and X1 sag, keeping the pass from the lane area when the ball is in the corner.

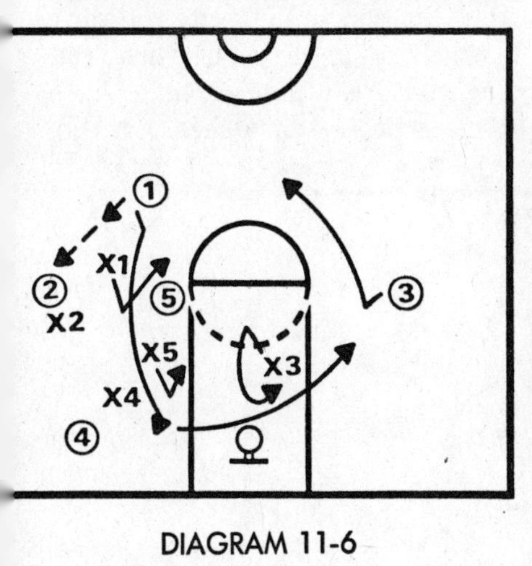

DIAGRAM 11-6

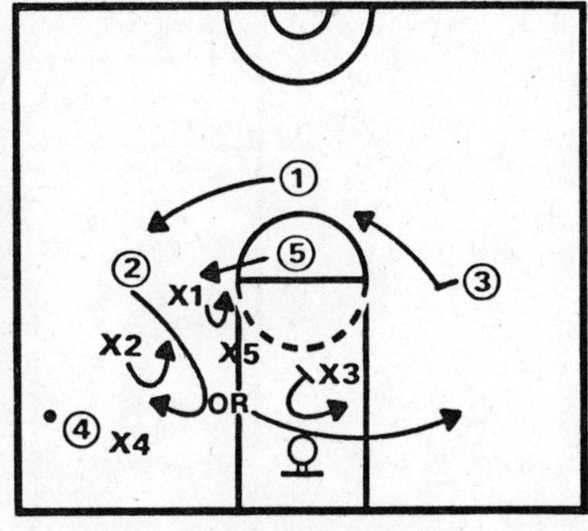

DIAGRAM 11-7

Strongside Corner Cutter

In order for there to be a strongside corner cutter, the ball must be at strongside wing or strongside guard and there must be a cornerman cutting. Diagram 11-5 showed such a movement preceded by a pass. But a pass could have been made from 1 to 2 with 4 cutting. In either case—a pass by the cornerman and a cut or just a cut by the strongside cornerman—the defense remains the same. It, in the final analysis, is just man-to-man coverage by the strongside defensive forward. He must be drilled to the point where he can handle this situation as one-on-one cutting.

Weakside Guard Cutter

All possible strongside cutting maneuvers that your team will face have been covered by the diagrams and sections previously presented in this chapter. Now we will consider the only possible action coming toward the ball (in other words, weakside cutters). They must come from the guard position, from the wing position, or from the corner area.

Diagram 11-8 exhibits not only a weakside guard cutter but a team movement from a 2-1-2 set into a 1-3-1 formation. Many teams use this offensive maneuver to rotate their offenses from a matched alignment to a triangular overload. We will use this diagram to illustrate the three different ways you might wish to formulate your match-up rules; consequently, defensive men have been omitted from the diagram.

First, you have decided on a guard as a potential matcher. You send

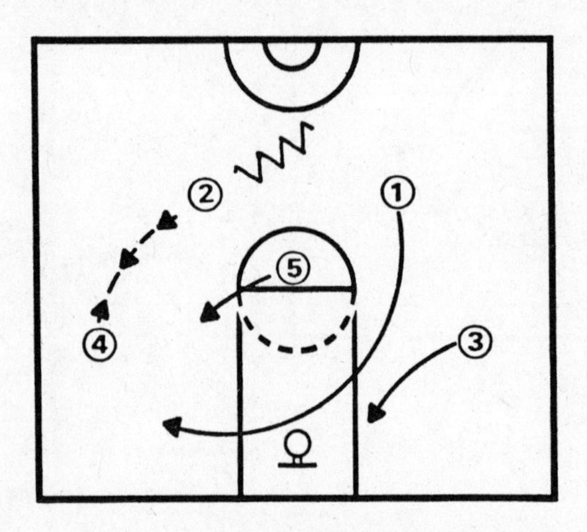

DIAGRAM 11-8

your guard through on 1's cut, covering him man-to-man. Now X1 has 2; X4 has 4; X3 covers 3; X2, your matcher, is on the baseline and covers 1; X5 stays with 5. Your problems: The other team might run their man offense, and your team might not have drilled against it; your guard must be able to handle 1 inside, and 1 doesn't necessarily have to be their guard—he is whoever cut from that guard alley. If you are satisfied, however, with a guard as a matcher, you now have your defense in position, with the first cut covered, and you are ready to accept and release cutters as they occur.

Secondly, you use two forwards or a forward and a guard as a matcher. In either case, X4 covers 4 unless you want to run the Penn State Sliding Zone maneuver between the guard covering 2 and the forward covering 4. You would not do this if you used two matchers. The other matcher is the weakside forward, X3, or the weakside guard, X2. (Remember: When we use a guard as a matcher, he is designated X2 because we key everyone off of a guard fixed as X1.) X2's coverage was discussed above. X3 would shift onto 1 as he cut,calling, "Release." This matches X1 with 3, X2 with 2, X4 with 4,and X3 with 1. X5 takes the high post. Of course, you could allow X5 to take 1 on the low post, and X3 to cover 5 as though he were a flash pivot cutter (an adjustment discussed in detail in Chapters 3 and 7).

Thirdly, you could be using the 2-1-2 with only one matcher, X4. In this case, you would use the Penn State Sliding Zone maneuver. X1 would have 1 initially, but would come and cover 2 as 1 cuts because X2 would be going to "release" X4 as 4 receives the pass. X1 would sink and cover the high post passing lane. X4 slides quickly to the big block and picks up 1 on his cut. X3 keeps 3. And X5, who sagged near the basket and fronted 1 as he cut by, comes back out on 5 as X4 picks up 1. Now X4, your matcher, has the cutter, and X2 and X3 are one player left and right of X1. And X1 has 2 while X5 has 5.

Under no circumstances would you teach all three coverages. That would confuse your defenders. First, you study your personnel. You decide on a matcher or two matchers. You write your rules, and keep them few and simple. Then you drill your players on the coverage you have adopted. The three coverages were offered to help you decide on the best possible coverage for your personnel. The 2-1-2 match-up, unlike the 1-3-1 and 1-2-2, can be adapted to almost any personnel. That is why it is the most popular match-up formation.

Weakside Wing Cutter

While 1 passes to 2, 3 cuts to a box overload on the strongside (Diagram 11-9). This offensive maneuver occurs frequently against the 2-1-2 zone.

X2 takes the first man left of X1, which is 2. X1 sags and helps on the pass into the high post area, a move he makes in any 2-1-2 coverage. X3 goes with 3 until X5 "releases" him. X3 then picks up the high post man, 5, who is the first player right of X1. As 3 passes by 4, X5 and X4 shift responsibilities and coverages. X4, of course, keeps a hand in the passing lane to 4. X4 would move out to cover 3 as the ball is airborne between 2 and 3. Each defender must constantly sag the three-step drill. X3 can, if he wishes, notify X1 that 1 might cut backdoor. But if 1 goes backdoor, X3 and X1 should shift responsibilities.

Weakside Corner Cutter

Weakside corner cutters are covered man-to-man using body checks to prevent them from reaching their most advantageous position. In Diagram 11-10, each man matches up according to the coverage and cutter rules. Then as 5 begins to cut toward the ball, X5 body checks 5 away from the ball. Each defender has sagged the three-step drill. But as 5 cuts and X5 defends, X3 must become aware of a potential lob pass to 5 should he decide to stop quickly and backdoor X5. X1 helps on the high post passing lane; and X4 keeps a hand in the low post passing lane (Diagram 11-10).

DIAGRAM 11-9

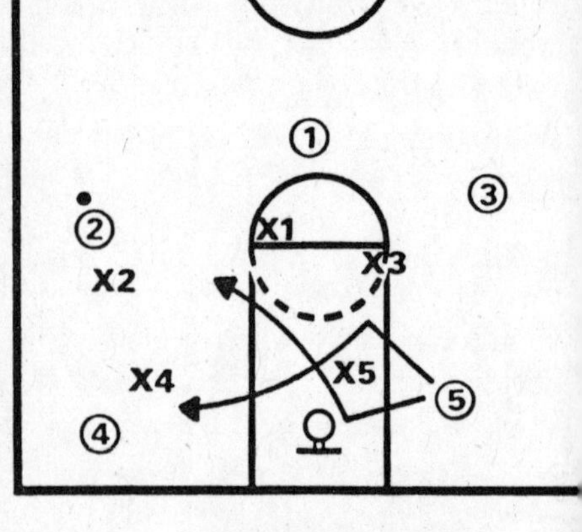

DIAGRAM 11-10

Combination of Two Cutters

In Chapter 10, all alignments were initially matched by the coverage rule. In Chapter 11, all possible cuts have been covered from all possible alleys. But many teams do not cut one person at a time. Instead, they cut two and sometimes three. The next two sections will show how such plural cuts should be handled. Other multiple cuts were shown in parallel sections in Chapter 7.

2 has control of the ball in Diagram 11-11 while the two big men, 5 and 4, cut to try to free themselves inside. X1 sags the three-step drill into the high post passing lane. X2 covers the ball handler with aggressive man-to-man play, no further away from 2 than an arm's distance as long as 2 is in shooting range, channelling 2 in a pre-determined direction. X3 has weakside rebounding and lob pass responsibility. X5 and X4 shift men and responsibilities as the attackers cross, regardless of which attacker cuts first or if they cut simultaneously.

Combination of Three Cutters

Frequently during the course of a season, expecially after you become known as a match-up zone club, your defense will face multiple movement by three or more offensive players at a single instance. Many offensive coaches believe mass movement of players will confuse and ultimately defeat a match-up. In fact, many teams run their man-to-man offenses against it.

Again, we will begin with 2 having possession of the ball while 3, 4, and 5 cut from the popular 1-3-1 alignment into a box overload (Diagram 11-12). X2 must pressure 2, using man-to-man coverage, inviting or encouraging 2 to move in only one pre-determined direction. X1 sags into the high post passing lane, activating his three-step drill. Only X3, X4, and X5 must make adjustments, and that is usually the number of de-

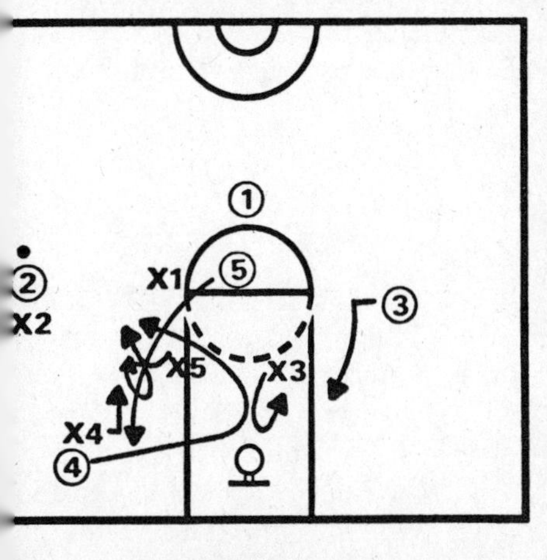

DIAGRAM 11-11

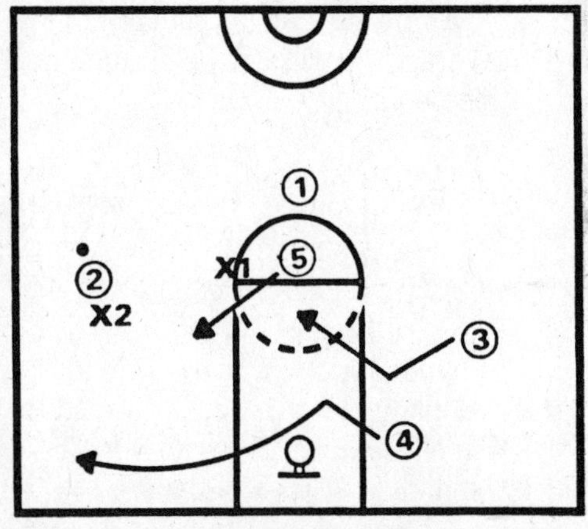

DIAGRAM 11-12

fenders who must apply the cutter's rule. Two attackers, the one with the ball and the one responsible for defense and providing an escape route for the ball, can easily be located, defended. That helps any match-up defense: We rule that X1, who usually has the responsibility for the first player away from the ball when it is at the wing, must play the passing lane into the high post area. X1 knows where his next assignment will appear.

The sequence of the cuts and the number of matchers you have could determine who shifts to whom in Diagram 11-12. Defensive players have been omitted from Diagram 11-12 because of the possible order of offensive cuts: consider X4 on 4, X3 on 3, and X5 on 5 before cutting begins.

If 4 cuts first, X4 would cover him man-to-man. If 5 cuts next, X5 must follow him man-to-man, and that would leave X3 to cover 3's flash pivot cut man-to-man. But if 5 cuts first, followed by 3 then 4, your match-up responsibilities change slightly. When 5 cuts, X4 could release X5. In that case, X5 would drop onto 4 or cover 3's cut to the high post, depending on which attacker cut first. But should X5 cover 5's cut man-to-man, X4 would "release" X3 on 3's cut. This would put X3 on 4. But as 4 cuts by 5 on the baseline, the defender on 5, either X4 or X5, would release the defender on 4 if it were X3. On this last cut, the defender on 3 at the high post must notify X1 of the potential backdoor cut by 1. If 1 cut backdoor, however, the defender on 3 would "release" X1, letting X1 pick up 3.

These coverage possibilities all exist and all can be ruled, depending upon your personnel and personality. By no means should you use any two of them: two different ways to cover these moves would confuse your defenders. You decide on the number of matchers you have and the way you want to cover this popular move and then drill, drill, drill on it. Soon it will be instinctive coverage. The next section will discuss our ruled coverage, which will be consistent to all our other coverages throughout this book.

Matching Cutter Movements into Overloads

Diagram 11-12 features the popular 1-3-1 alignment with three cutters moving into a box overload. In our match-up rules, X2 would harass and channel 2 using man-to-man tactics. X1 looks away from his drop to find his next assignment. But while doing this, he maintains a presence in the high post passing lane.

Because we prefer to have X5 high if possible and because of our three-step sag, we would have X4 cover 5 on his cut to the low post, unless 4 had cut first. But if 4 cut first, all the moves would have been covered with straight man-to-man coverage. So let's let 4 cut second or third. X4 has 5 low, "releasing" X5 to cover 4 low if 3 has not cut. If 3 has cut high, X3 would have 4 low and X5 would take 3's flash pivot cut. Now if 4 cuts second, X4 "releases" X5 as 4 cuts around 5. This puts X4 on 4, X5 on 5, and X3 on 3's flash pivot cut. If 4 cut last, that puts X4 on 4, X3 on 5, and X5 on 3. This is all consistent with our rule: (a) if the center has a low post attacker on strongside, then the weakside wing covers a flash pivot to the high post, and (b) if there are two low posts, X4 takes the one on the left and X5 takes the one on the right.

Defensing Dribbling Moves

Coaches constantly originate methods of defeating their opposition. They can be quite creative. There used to be an axiom that dribbling around the perimeter against a zone was taboo. Recently, however, offensive minded coaches have found that clever movement with a dribble can be a powerful weapon against all zones. Diagram 11-13 offers one such use of the dribble.

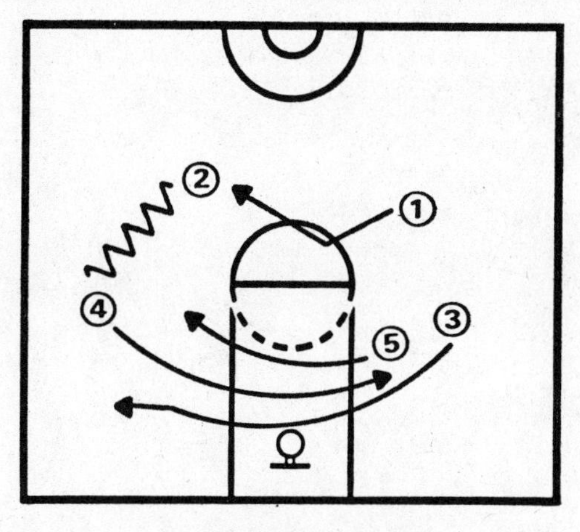

DIAGRAM 11-13

2 starts his dribble at a guard alley and moves into a wing area (Diagram 11-13). This cues 4 to move to the weakside big block for offensive rebounding (the primary rebounding area against a zone). 5 breaks to the ball,and 3 cuts baseline to the strongside cornerman's position. 1 dips and comes to the top of the circle for defensive balance and for providing 2 with a passing avenue. The offense now has moved into triangular overloads and aligned into the popular 1-3-1 attack against the 2-1-2 zone.

X2 covers 2, taking away one driving alley. All his defensive teammates would know which driving lane has been eliminated by the predetermined team defense. X2 also is within arm's length of the ball handler, discouraging the shot attempt. X1 has 1, and X1 has sagged his three steps into the high post passing lane.

X5 covers 5's flash pivot cut man-to-man. X5 body checks 5 away from the most advantageous area. X4 and X3 shift as 4 and 3 cross. If 4 and 3 cut at different times, X4 and X3 "release" the attackers using our guidelines to stay within our match-up rules.

12 DEFENSING BASIC CONTINUITIES WITH THE 2-1-2 MATCH-UP

Offensive continuities that periodically overload offer the most popular attacks against zones. To defeat good zones, a team must provide movement of the ball, movement of the players, overloads (triangular, box, or diamond), post play, penetration by the dribble, penetration by passing, and offside rebounding. Screening, outside shooting, balance, and fast breaking are taken for granted. These parts of an offense don't happen haphazardly. They are pre-planned, pre-drilled. Players know their responsibilities, and they rapidly and skillfully perform them.

The 1-3-1 set is the most popular alignment against the 2-1-2 zone, but some coaches begin from the 3-2 and the 1-4. And a big minority believes in matching the match-up's array, in this case a 2-1-2. A popular play from each of these sets will be presented and defensed in this chapter. That defense will correspond to the fundamentals of Chapters 1–4, including a mastery of the cutter (Chapter 11) and the coverage (Chapter 10) rules. From time to time, an explanation of two matchers will be offered.

A 1-3-1 Offense Defensed

Undoubtedly the most popular zone attack against the 2-1-2 is the offense shown in Diagram 12-1. Not only is it simple and easily taught, but it can be tremendously effective. Many teams run different variations of this pet pattern, but over the span of a quarter-century of basketball, this seems to be the favorite 1-3-1 part play.

This attack is easily matched initially: X1 takes the guard in the point alley; X2 covers 2, the first player left of X1; X3 takes the first player right of X1, 3; X5 covers the high post, 5; and X4 guards the second player left or right of X1, 4.

If you intend to use the two forwards as matchers, X3 might sometimes have 4. If that happens, X4 would have 2, with X2 on 1 and X1 covering 3. This occurs when X2 steps out to get 1 (see Chapter 9 for guard's initial positioning), or when you run the Penn State Sliding Zone maneuver.

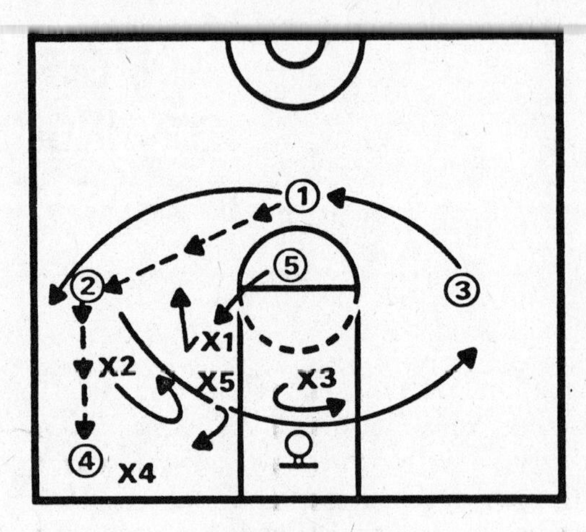

DIAGRAM 12-1

As 2 passes to 4, 5 rolls to the ballside, but 5 stays near the side high post area. This clears the low post area for 2 to receive a pass or post up as he cuts. 1 fills the spot vacated by 2, and 3 takes the point for defensive balance and for reversal of the ball. This offense increases in difficulty for the defense in direct porportion to 1's outside shooting ability.

X4 covers 4 when he receives the pass in the corner (Diagram 12-1). X2 jumps his three-step drill while the pass is in the air from 2 to 4. This prevents 2 from receiving a direct return pass for an easy jumper or the lay-up. 5 is covered by X5. But X5 appears big, helping on any lob pass to 2 as he cuts. X2 follows 2 to the free throw lane area and he "releases" 2 to X3 upon X3's beckon. X2 must then hurry back out on 1, especially if 1 is an adept outside shooter.

When 2 had the ball, X1 covered the high post area. As 2 passes to 4, X1 drops yet another three steps. All the time, however, X1 is cognizant of his new responsibility, 3's cut to the point alley. This drop by X1 and the corresponding drop by X5 provide more than adequate protection to the vital inside area. So if 1 is an exceptional outside shooter, X3 can release X2 earlier, and X1 and X5 can provide quicker and concentrated help inside. Adjustments from the match-up are easily made, but facing this offense with regular 2-1-2 zone slides relinquishes the advantage to the attackers.

A 3-2 Offense Defensed

Many coaches believe in opening up the middle against the match-up. And if those coaches have excellent perimeter personnel, they can hurt the match-up with exceptional outside shooting.

Diagram 12-2 shows an excellent offensive decoy movement which works well for teams with remarkable outside personnel. 1 passes to 2 and exchanges with 3. 5 flash pivots to high post, and 2 checks 5 for an open pass. If 5 gets the pass from 2, he looks inside to 4 for high-low possibilities. If that option is not available, 5 passes to the opposite wing, 1. 4 continues along the baseline for the pass from 1. Either 1 or 4 can shoot, with 5 and 2 hitting the boards against the lone weakside rebounder if the defense exhibits a standard zone.

If 2 cannot hit 5, 2 passes to 3, who reverses the ball to 1. Or 2 can skip the pass to 3, hitting 1 directly. 3 and 2 exchange. 5 drops to the big block for weakside rebounding. If 1 or 4 does not shoot, 5 breaks to the ballside high post area and 4 runs the baseline again. This pattern provides continuity. And if 4 is a deadly shooter, this offense can easily defeat the standard 2-1-2 zone.

But the match-up will not only handle the player and ball movement, it will also prevent the double-team rebounding on the weakside. Remember: the match-up will have a man assigned to each weakside rebounder where all standard zones have a lone weakside rebounder (a real weakness of all basic zones).

X1 matches 1. X2 and X3 take the first attacker left and right of X1 respectively. X5, according to the coverage rule, covers the second player right of X1 when there is no high post (five perimeter rule); X4, the matcher, chases the second player left of X1.

When 1 passes to 2, X1 sags his three steps, helping cover the high post area. X1 shifts men with X3 as 1 and 3 exchange. When 5 breaks to the ball, X5 covers him as a flash pivot cutter, body checking him, turning him away from the high post area if possible. Because the ball is above the free throw line, X5 covers 5 on his low side. This gives him coverage on 5's cut, and this prevents the weakside alley-oop as 5 steps his cut and breaks backdoor for the lob. X3 must be alert to help on this play. Also, this low side coverage will enable an alert X1 to steal some passes directed to the (non-defensive) side of 5.

As 4 cuts baseline, X4 plays between 4 and the ball. This denial positioning prevents the high-low maneuver. And it prevents any direct pass from 2 to 4 at the low post initially. X4 must never, however, give 4 the baseline drive once 4 has received the ball.

Against this type of attack, the match-up virtually plays a three-man zone outside and a two-man man-to-man inside. A strong part of the offense is lost to the match-up. When a shot is taken, block outs occur as in normal man-to-man defenses, eliminating the two-on-one weakside rebounding attack.

A 1-4 Offense Defensed

Diagram 12-2 depicts a 1-4 alignment breaking into a box overload. When the ball is reversed (3 passing to 1), 3 swings through the lane, and 5 races along the baseline before returning to high post. (Or 5 could go directly to high post.) And 2 would fill 3's vacated wing spot. The offense continues from 1-4 into box overload into 1-4 into box as the ball swings from one side of the court to the other.

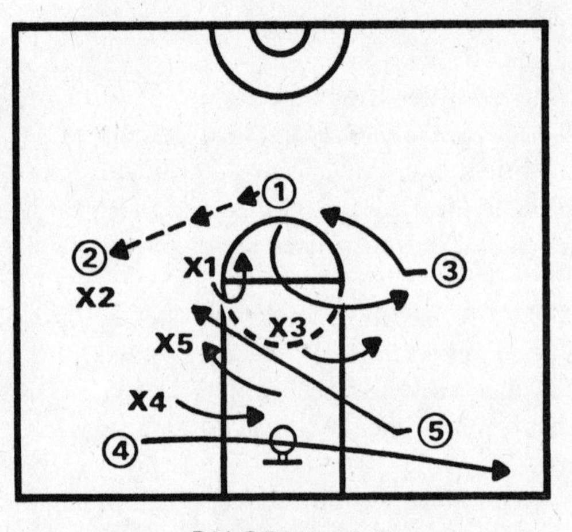

DIAGRAM 12-2

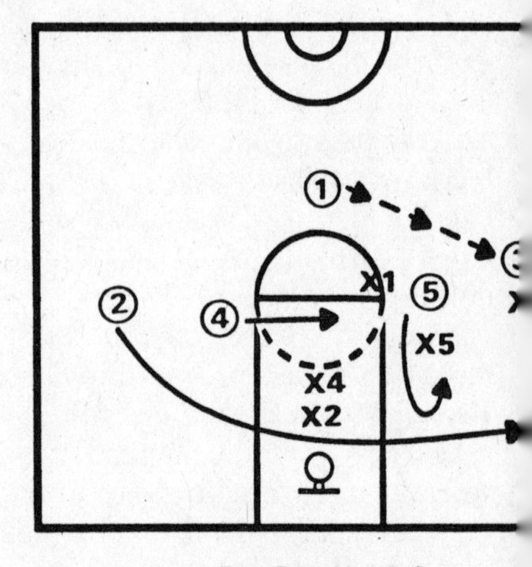

DIAGRAM 12-3

4 could go low initially, letting 5 stay at the high post. This offensive adjustment is not as popular as 4, the weakside high post, filling the vacuum created by 5's inaugural movement to the low post. Sometimes 2 will not cut through, creating the popular 1-3-1 attack.

According to the coverage rule, X1 covers 1. X2 and X3 take the first attackers left and right of X1 respectively. Under the three perimeter rule (Chapter 1), X5 takes the high post to the right and X4 covers the high post to the left of X1.

When player movement begins, team coverage can take several forms. We will explain two. You determine which is best for your personnel. But don't teach both. That would confuse your athletes. Make your rules; then see that your coverage is consistent with those rules.

But before we explain the two forms, let's defense the inside cuts. X4 and X5 could cover their assignments as individual man-to-man cuts. This places X5 on 5 at the low post and X4 on 4 at the side high post. We prefer, whenever possible, to keep X5 at the high post, so we favor X4 and X5 shifting responsibilities (see Center and Matcher's Coverage, Chapter 3). In either case, X1 would help at the high post, preventing the quick pass inside, using his three-step drill. Let's let X4 cover 5 low and X5 stay at the high post. X5, at first, appears big and puts an arm into the low post lane. X4, who has sagged three steps on the pass from 1 to 3, can easily get to 5 before a pass from 3 to 5. X5 helps on the low post while X4 is cutting across the lane. And X1 helps on the high post until X5 gets back. These are basic zone slides. X3 covers 3 man-to-man, cutting him to the center. X1 must be aware that he will be alone on the weakside when 2 cuts.

When 2 cuts, the two different team coverages can occur. X2 and X4 can shift responsibilities as 2 cuts by 5. This must occur when X4 is your only matcher. However, if X2 is also a matcher (X3 if the pass initially went to the left side), he can cover the cutter man-to-man all the way into the corner. This would put the matcher on the baseline where he would have the greatest peripheral view of the court.

Or you could rule that on any pass to a wing the guard and the forward should activate the Penn State Sliding Zone maneuver. X1, therefore, would hurry to "release" X3. X3 would drop toward the big block upon being released, picking up 2 if 3 throws a pass to 2, covering the big block area until such a pass is airborne. X2 would now have 1. X2, as the weakside guard, offers help in the passing lane to the high post (see Chapter 9). X4 has 5. X5 has 4. When 3 reverse passes to 1, 3 cuts through the lane. As 3 cuts, 2 steps up to the wing 3 vacated. X4 picks up 3 with "release." X1 takes 2, and X3 moves up with 5. Now the forwards and guards are ready to perform the Penn State Sliding Zone maneuver again, regardless of the wing 1 favors with another pass: X2 and X4 on a pass to 3; X1 stays with 2 on a pass to 2.

Let's say you have only one matcher, X4. X4 is in the corner and X2 has 5. As the ball is reversed from 3 to 1, 3 cuts from the box formation back into the 1-4 array by cutting across the lane to the opposite wing. As 3 cuts, X3 shifts off onto 5 at the low post, and X2 takes 3 on his cut. Because the ball is out front, X4 will have sagged his six steps (three per alley—and he is two alleys away) into the lane. X3 and X4 then trade responsibilities, with X4 covering 5's move back to the high post.

If you had two matchers, let's say X3 and X4, the two forwards, your coverage could be ruled differently. For example, as 3 cuts, X2 would pick him up and go to the weakside wing with him. X3 would have 5. When 5 cuts to high post, X3 would stay with him. X4 would keep 2.

Your rules must always adapt to your personnel. The better you evaluate your personnel, the tighter and more solid your match-up will be. But always keep your rules simple and consistent with a minimum of basic rule adjustments.

A 2-1-2 Offense Defensed

Match-up defenses scare some offensive coaches. Some run their man-to-man attacks against it. Some give up and free-lance. These latter coaches usually beat themselves. They have little or no control over what happens on the court.

Still other coaches believe the best method to defeat the match-up is to match its alignment. They know there will be no initial holes—so why try to find them. From this initial match, they cut their players into what they hope will be unfamiliar areas for the defenders. They reason that this might confuse the rules with long, complicated slides.

Diagram 12-4 shows a 2-1-2 offense matching the 2-1-2 match-up. The guard, 2, cuts to strongside, creating the popular 1-3-1 attack. We will again show two coverages: our regular coverage with one matcher, and a coverage if you use a guard and a forward as matchers.

According to the coverage rule, X1 takes 1. X2 and X3 take the first attackers left and right respectively of X1. X4 covers second player left or right, and X5 takes 5.

When 2 cuts, X2 and X4 shift responsibilities if we had only X4 as a matcher. X2 follows 2 to the area near the free throw line, where he hears X4's "release." X2 takes 4, and X4 covers 2's cut.

But if X2 was a guard matcher, X2 could cover 2's cut to the corner man-to-man. Remember: if you use a guard as a matcher, he must be X2. X1 must be the key for your other defenders. So always have X1 cover the point guard and X2 line up at high post initially (see Chapters 10 and 11). This way you can rule your defense so X2 will almost always cover the cutter and X1 cover the ball handler. If X2 is a matcher, he is now in the corner where he has the greatest peripheral view. Now you are ready to match the next movements of the offense. A disadvantage of the guard as a matcher is that your opponents may read the coverage as man-to-man. They would then run their man attack, which would be no disadvantage if you had pre-drilled against it.

A Special Gimmick Offense Defensed

Special gimmick offenses will not a season make. Coaches who use them frequently experience losing seasons because they overcoach: They give their players too many offenses to learn.

Diagram 12-5 shows a gimmick offense that can be incorporated into the regular 1-3-1 pattern. 1 can pass to a wing, either 2 or 3. In Diagram 12-5, 1 hits 3. 5 rolls opposite to set a double screen with 4, the low post attacker. 3 intends to lob pass to 2 for the jumper over the double screen. But X2 has 2 covered man-to-man. X3 must be made aware that he has a one-on-one clearout.

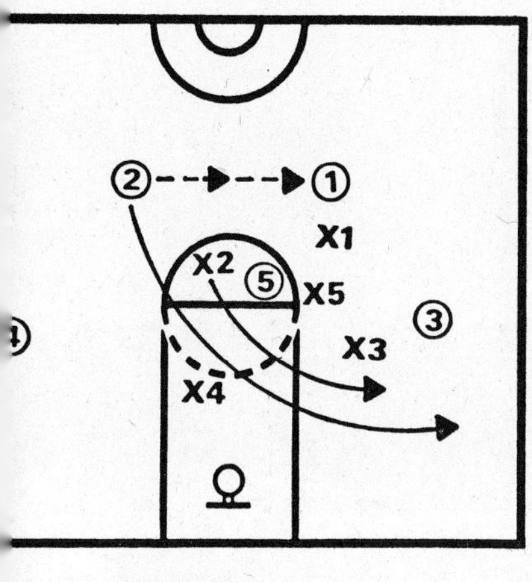

DIAGRAM 12-4

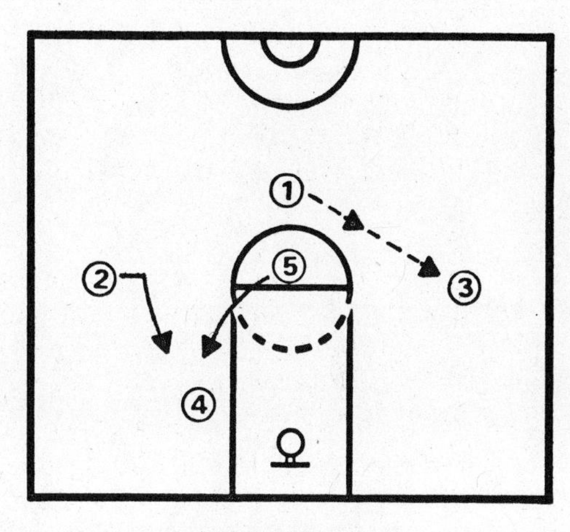

DIAGRAM 12-5

2 could continue by breaking toward the ball off of the double screen. When 2 cuts by the double screen, X4 "releases" X2. And we still have perfect match-up coverage: X2 on 4, X4 on 2, X1 on 1, X3 on 3, and X5 on 5. 5 could flash to the strongside high post which X5 would cover man-to-man. X2 would then have 4 if he breaks outside as the ball is reversed.

Summary

The fourteen fundamental ways that teams use to defeat the 2-1-2 zone have been presented and defensed in this section of the book. Coverages using two matchers as well as coverages using one matcher have been presented, explored, and explained. Mastery of the fundamentals (Chapters 1–4), of the coverage rule (Chapter 10), and of the cutter rule (Chapter 11) should eliminate any advantage the offense might enjoy with a sudden cut or a surprise offense. Couple this with your knowledge of your personnel (in case you want two matchers—a guard and a forward or two forwards), so you can make the placements to the best advantage of the defense, and your 2-1-2 match-up should be unbeatable.

PART FOUR

THE 1-2-2 OR 3-2 MATCH-UP

13 UNDERSTANDING THE BASIC 1-2-2 ZONE

If you have two big center-types, both of whom can become matchers, and if you have three perimeter defenders, the 1-2-2 is the perfect match-up and zone alignment. You would probably want to run a 1-4, a 1-2-2, or a 1-3-1 array on offense. You should fit your defense and offense to your personnel unless you coach where you can recruit.

Jack Kraft, head coach at Rhode Island University, popularized the 1-2-2 match-up when he took his Villanova club to the final four of the NCAA. Television coverage showed the solid effectiveness of Villanova's defense. Before long, their 1-2-2 match-up zone was being emulated by high school teams throughout the United States. Teams differed in their coverage assignments somewhat, displaying how those coaches changed their rules minutely to harmonize with their personnel. But the basic principles remained constant, much like the 1-3-1 match-up, because of the specific personnel needed to effectively execute the 1-2-2 match-up. This chapter will illustrate and explain those guidelines necessary to successfully apply the 1-2-2 match-up zone.

Areas of Strength

The greatest strength of the jug zone, as the basic 1-2-2 zone is called, is its adaptability. For instance, if your opponent exhibits excellent perimeter shooters, the defense can spread, still keeping good interior defense while covering all perimeter shooting areas. However, if a team does not have the excellent perimeter attack, the three perimeter defenders can sag inside, completely closing off the area near the basket.

Poor outside ball handling clubs and poor passing teams cannot consistently defeat the jug defense. Trapping and doubling ball handlers are integral parts of this zone. Playing in the passing lanes can force the dribble from opponents who prefer not to dribble. But proper sags inside and closing the gap maneuvers outside will prevent dribbling penetration from those clubs who want to use the dribble.

Two large, slow inside defenders can be used. If they also possess bulk, the interior defense can become superior to any opponent's inside offensive attack.

The 1-2-2 is ideal for the fast breaking ball club if the interior two can control the defensive boards. This already gives the fast break three perimeter defenders to fill the three fast break lanes.

Areas of Weakness

The entire lane area is an open seam. Penetration there—and it is easy to pass into the lane without proper defensive coverage—results in a high percentage shot or a pass out which leads to a high percentage shot.

Great corner shooters can force the big men to concede the corner shot or open another high percentage area inside (the seam near the basket and the big block region, known as the short corner), especially when the offense operates with a high side post man.

The jug zone can be overloaded in the deep and very dangerous scoring area. Two big attackers, stationed on the big blocks, and a great scorer-passer, breaking from the baseline toward the high post, give the offensive team an unstoppable triangular overload directly in the heart of the team defense.

Good offensive rebounding teams will get many second shots. With only two dependable defensive rebounders, an attacking team that plans overloads in the primary rebounding areas will obtain enough extra shots to defeat the 1-2-2 zone. But this will not be a weakness to the match-up zone which checks off the defensive boards with man-to-man block-out principles (see Chapter 4).

Selecting and Positioning of Personnel

1-2-2 zones blend themselves toward several coverages. Those coverages and the rules of your match-up dictate what type of personnel you will need.

There are three theoretical types of jug zone coverage (Diagram 13-1). X1 can sag into the center as the ball goes to a wing, and he could cover the low post strongside when the ball is passed to a corner (see Yo-Yoing section in Chapter 2). This occurs when you use X1 as a tall defender, capable of defensing the inside as well as the perimeter.

Or the wings, X2 and X3, would have coverage of the guards, wings, and corner areas. This forces X2 and X3 to cover a large area, but it leaves your two top rebounders, X4 and X5, near the basket; and rebounding is a major weakness of the regular 1-2-2 zone. An alternate coverage is to let X4 and X5 go to the corner and X2 and X3 cover the strongside low post. This removes a perimeter alley from the defensive wing's coverage, but it also means that your wings must be capable of defensing the inside low post with the ball in the corner. It does leave the opposite low defender in the primary rebounding area. In both cases, X2 and X3 must be extremely quick and fast to cover the area assigned to them.

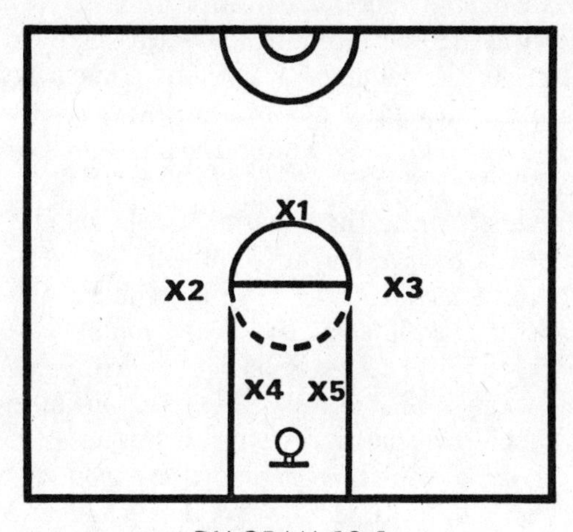

DIAGRAM 13-1

Probably the most popular coverage is the third theory. As the ball moves to the corner, the low defenders operate on a string: as one of them moves to the corner to cover the pass receiver, the other low defender comes to cover the strongside low post. The weakside wing drops immediately for weakside rebounding. This means your wings don't have to be quick, but they must be capable weakside rebounders. This is the most popular slide because it requires less specialization of skills from each defender. While it fits the personnel of most teams, it does have the disadvantage of utilizing those principles against which most teams drill daily.

But if you intend to match up, your players must possess added characteristics. These skills must be kept in mind for your match-up to operate at maximum effectiveness. The slides of your basic zone and your match-up will depend therefore on your evaluation of your personnel. How well you fill those spots will ultimately mark the success or the failure of your match-up zone defense.

X1, for example, must be your best perimeter defender. He must be a quick, pepper-pot type of leader. On most teams the point guard fits this mold. He has to channel the offense in a pre-determined direction. Once having done that, X1 must prevent lateral penetration. Quickness, therefore, is more a premium than size. If X1 also has size, it'll just make your zone and match-up that much tougher. X1, when channelling, should initiate his coverage at midcourt; and, when not channelling, should line up at the top of the foul circle.

X2 should be your second best perimeter defender. Because many teams use a two guard offense against the 1-2-2, X2 will frequently cover the other guard. He must cover any quick moving attacker laterally without allowing dribbling penetration. In the match-up, size takes a back seat to quickness. If you intend to have this man cover weakside rebounding or inside in the regular 1-2-2, then he must have some size. Because most teams attack the right side of the court the majority of time, X2 should be left of X1. If you intend to fast break, this is an ideal position for a left handed shooter.

X3 is the weakest of the three perimeter defenders. In fact, you could place your best offensive player—on many teams the weakest defensive player—in this spot without drastically reducing the effectiveness of your defense. He can be big and slow. When you match-up, he usually gets the weakest wing or corner attacker. And when you run your basic zone, he frequently has weakside rebounding responsibilities.

X2 and X3 should station themselves about three feet outside the free throw lane line extended. Of course, if your opponents are excellent outside shooters, you could extend these beginning spots a few feet. But, on the other hand, if they are weak outside, you could sag X2 and X3 to the corner of the free throw line and drop X1 back to the middle of the free throw line, shutting off the entire lane area, a weak seam of the jug zone.

X4 and X5 can be slow, but they must be talented inside defenders. They are the reason you choose the 1-2-2 match-up. They are your matchers. The bigger they are the better. They must be adept defensive rebounders. X4 can be a little smaller than X5. X5 should be the better high post defender. X4 might have to cover perimeter players more often than X5. X5 must be a better inside defender, a better rebounder. He can be a little less mobile than X4.

X4 and X5 begin about two to three feet inside the lane and between the first and second foul lane spaces. Often an attacker will break to the high post area or be stationary there. You, as coach, can determine which of two coverages you prefer. X4 can always keep the low attacker, and X5 can cover the high post. Or, if there is a break from low post to high post, you can cover the cut man-to-man, letting the opposite deep defender cover the low post. We prefer the latter in the 1-2-2 match-up and the former in the 1-3-1 match-up. You had a center-type and a matcher-type in the 1-3-1, but you have two center-matcher types in the 1-2-2. Of course, if the offense lines up initially in the 1-3-1 alignment,we would define definite responsibilities, such as X5 takes the high post and X4 takes the low post. Whichever guideline you choose will work wonderfully well for you if you drill, drill, drill until it is instinctive to your defenders. But don't confuse your players with both rules. Select the best rule for your personnel.

X4 and X5 must be astute basketball players. They have the responsibility of accepting and releasing cutters all game long (the defender on the weakside). They must know when to "bust out" on an open attacker. They must quickly trade responsibilities so they can return inside. They see the entire court most of the time. They are your matchers.

The Jug Zone Works Best Against Which Personnel

Good outside shooters, except in the corners, will have a difficult time finding the open shot. Good driving-passing penetrators will find little area to drive through. This zone is perfectly aligned to close all the driving gaps, to stop all dribblers. Poor perimeter passing attacks will find no success against the jug. Trapping and playing the passing lanes will force the poor passing team into turnover after turnover.

Great offensive rebounding teams will destroy the jug. Excellent inside shooters and passers will hurt your 1-2-2 zone. So you would want to match-up quicker against the good inside game. You might not want to run your "home" zone more than a few possessions each quarter.

The Jug Zone Forces the Opponents into What Offenses

Most teams will face the 1-2-2 zone with a 1-3-1 or a 2-1-2 attack. Triangular overloads seem more popular than the box or the diamond. A few teams will begin in the "cure-all" 1-4 offense. The 1-2-2 is rarely matched by a 1-2-2 offense. And there are still those coaches who design special gimmick offenses to defeat the different defenses they will face. All these offenses will be presented and defensed in Chapter 16.

14 DEVELOPING THE COVERAGE RULE FOR THE 1-2-2 MATCH-UP

First you show your zone. The offense recognizes it. They begin their attack, usually from a specified formation. This attack alignment could be symmetrical, an overload, or free-lance. Most coaches know that victory comes from pre-planning and pre-drilling; so even if they free-lance there is method to what appears as random play.

After showing your zone and the opponent's responding with their offensive array, you match their set-up by predetermined guidelines known as your coverage rule. That is the subject of this chapter, which supplements the discussion of Chapter 1. The offense will not defeat your match-up by setting in a formation and passing the ball. Their players must move. And defensing player movement requires a cutter's rule, which will be the subject of Chapter 15.

Coverage Rule Using One Matcher

You chose the jug zone because you have two relatively big men who can become matchers. If you feel that only one of those pivot-type defenders would make a good matcher, then you should employ the 1-3-1 zone and related match-up. By placing your big matcher on the baseline and your other big defender at high post, you have an excellent match-up beginning. But if both can defend high post attackers and if both are capable matchers, then start both defenders low and match from the 1-2-2. Your match-up will be that much tougher, that much more confusing to the attackers.

Having two matchers low, both of whom can cover the high post more than adequately, does not mean that you cannot designate one of them as a high post defender if the offense consistently shows a 1-3-1 or a 2-1-2 alignment. Although both matchers might appear equal in coverage of the high post, one of them probably does it a little better. We designate that post defender as X5 in this book. That leaves X4 as the lone matcher. Otherwise, you should not use the 1-2-2 defense with one matcher. You should utilize your strength, two matchers and two post defenders.

Coverage Rule Using Two Matchers

X1, as in all our match-ups, tells the other defenders who they cover. He does this by choosing an attacker. He is stationed where all defenders can see him and key off of him. He takes the attacker in the point alley with or without the ball if there is one. If the offense shows a two guard front, X1 covers the attacker with or without the ball in the right guard alley.

X1 must possess lateral quickness. He must never permit dribbling penetration. If he is quick enough to pressure, to harass, and to channel the dribbler without allowing penetration, your defense will be superb, almost unbeatable.

X1, when the ball is passed, would cover the high post passing lane. Yet, X1 must know where his next assignment is. Teams must attack the basket to win, but they must keep a player back for defensing the fast break. This attacker-defender, responsible for defensive balance, forever changing during any game, is X1's new assignment.

When teams hurt your match-up by quickly reversing the ball around the horn, X1 can lane the pass back to the point alley. This delays the quick ball reversal, slows down the offense, ruins the timing of the next several cuts, and often forces the offense to find a new avenue of attack (more on this in Chapters 17 and 18).

X2, your second guard or offensive wing, covers the first attacker left of X1. X2 should be your second quickest perimeter defender. He, too, must prevent dribbling penetration. He should possess excellent lateral defensive quickness.

X3, your other offensive wing, or your small forward, defenses the first attacker to the right of X1. This attacker is usually a cornerman or a wing. He also is probably the weakest offensive attacker because most teams attack the other side of the court. So X3 can be your weakest defender, but he should be an adequate weakside rebounder. He can be big or medium-sized. He can even be slow. But he must be able to defense the baseline drive.

There are several ways you can utilize X4 and X5, your matchers. Their duties depend mainly on their athletic abilities. If both are equally adept at matching and at coverage of the high post, then let them cover the flash pivots from their side of the court to high post man-to-man. If one of them is slightly more advanced at covering the high post, you could designate him X5 (see Chapter 13). X5 would then go high regardless of the side from which the flash pivot originates. This would require X4 to remain at low post. He may have to move opposite the ball or opposite the side he initially lined up on. This second coverage, to us, is weaker than the first coverage. But you must make your guidelines match the skills of your personnel.

X4 begins his coverage of the second player left of X1. X5 initially covers the second perimeter player right of X1. If there is no second attacker either left or right of X1, then the defender (X4 or X5) responsible for that area will find his man at the high post. This happens when you face a 1-3-1 or a 2-1-2 offensive alignment.

Sometimes offensive teams employ the 1-4 formation. This means both X4 and X5 will cover high post men. X4 takes the attacker on the left, and X5 takes the high post on the right.

Some teams race downcourt into an offensive overload. When that happens and there is no high post, X4 takes the third player around the perimeter right of X1 and X5 takes the third player around the perimeter left of X1. Remember, we count the low post as a perimeter. So, for example, an overload to the right side of the court would find X3 covering the wing, X5 covering the corner, and X4 covering the low post, the third player right of X1. An ordinary 1-2-2 formation shows both X4 and X5 guarding low post men: both X4 and X5 are covering the second and the third attacker right and left respectively around the perimeter from X1, but both are also covering the low post. In other words, X5 is covering the second attacker around the perimeter right of X1 and the third attacker around the perimeter left of X1. The second attacker right of X1 and the third attacker left of X1 is the same player.

Sometimes your matchers might get confused, and you might have to rule that one of them always covers the low post and the other covers the corner. That would resemble the 1-3-1 match-up. But you chose the 1-2-2 because you have faith in your two matchers. So drill them and drill them until your match-up is perfected instinctively. The 1-2-2 match-up's greatest advantage over the 1-3-1 is that your inside defenders, near the dangerous scoring area, can guard the area man-to-man. Your outside men offer zone help. This defensive advantage is difficult to overcome offensively. So, if possible, use both X4 and X5 as matchers and as high post defenders. The remainder of this Chapter and Chapters 15 and 16 will use both X4 and X5 as matchers and as high post defenders. If you wish only one as a primary matcher and the other as a primary high post defender, you should re-read Chapters 5 through 8.

A Drill to Teach the Coverage Rule

Procedure:

1. Allow five offensive players to bring the ball downcourt while the defense sets in a standard 1-2-2 zone.
2. art by requiring that the offense line up in a typical or basic alignment used against the 1-2-2. Check to see if the match-ups are correct accor g to who has whom and according to positioning (three-step drill and the plane of greatest peripheral view).
3. You may then allow passing with no offensive player movement.
4. You can advance to allowing drives, forcing defenders to close the gap, but still no man movement.
5. Allow cutters after you teach the cutter's rule (next chapt
6. Repeat the first four steps by having the attackers start in an overload alignment.
7. Repeat the first four steps by having the attackers start in any free-lance array they wish.
8. Repeat the first four steps by having the attackers use the formation of your next opponent.

Objectives:

1. To teach closing the gap.
2. To teach the coverage rule.
3. To teach the three-step drill.
4. To teach defenders to respond to the next offense you will face.
5. To teach playing on the plane of greatest peripheral view.

Matching the Basic Sets Used Against the 1-2-2

Most teams attack one guard defensive fronts with a two guard offense. These teams employ their personnel in a 2-1-2 or a 2-2-1 array.

By teaching your jug zone how to match these alignments, you have successfully begun tutoring your match-up coverage rule.

There is a seam along the foul lane area in the 1-2-2; so many teams place an offensive shooter-passer at the high post or break one there. The seam vanishes when you employ your match-up.

Prior to the matching up, you will run your basic zone, the 1-2-2. The opposition questions with a 2-1-2 array with the player at the high post being a passer-shooter. You answer with your match-up (Diagram 14-1).

X1 takes the attacker in the point alley. There isn't one. X1 then takes the player with or without the ball in the right guard alley or the right wing alley, 1 in this case. X2 covers the first player around the perimeter left of X1, 2. X3 guards the first attacker around the perimeter right of X1: 3 in Diagram 14-1. X4 takes the second player left of X1, 4. And X5 guards the post, 5.

Because of the versatility of the two matchers, X4 and X5, you could allow X1 to take 2, putting X2 on 4 and X3 on 1. According to the jug match-up rules, X5 takes second player around the perimeter right of X1, namely 3 in Diagram 14-1. Now X4 has the post 5. We call this "rotation left," because X1 covers the left guard alley instead of the right. This strategy or adjustment works best when you do not want X4 to cover a quick cornerman. For example, maybe 4 is an extremely quick, agile driver with a great jump shot. Maybe your X2 could cover him better. The rules of the match-up do not change, but this simple adjustment can cause trouble to offensive forwards who are quicker than your matcher X4 (for more adjustments see Chapters 17 and 18).

Diagram 14-2 depicts the 2-2-1 array some teams will use against your 1-2-2. X1 covers 1. X2, according to his rule, would get 2; and X3

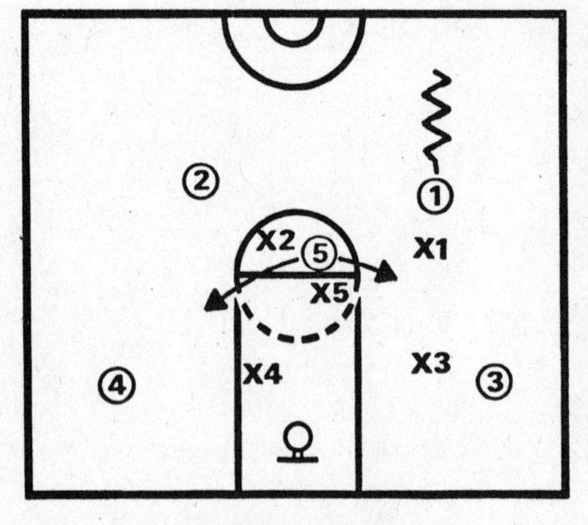

DIAGRAM 14-1

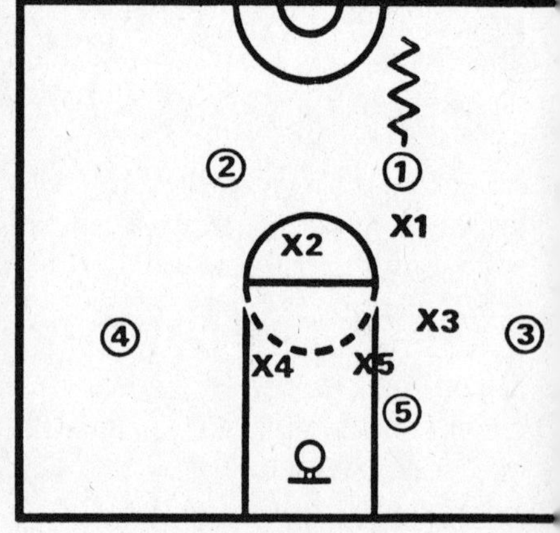

DIAGRAM 14-2

would guard 3. X4 covers second player around the perimeter left of X1, 4. And X5 covers 5, the second player around the perimeter right of X1.

You could use the "rotation left" adjustment by letting X1 cover 2. This places X2 on 4, X3 on 1, X5 on 3, and X4 on 5.

The 1-3-1 offense is popular against all zone defenses, the jug zone being no exception. Because 1 is in the point alley, X1 would cover him whether he has the ball or not. X2 would guard 2 while X3 would pick up 3, according to their coverage rule. X4 covers second player around the perimeter left of X1, 4. X5 takes 5.

If 4 had been at the right low post instead of the left, X5 would have covered him because 4 would have been the second player around the perimeter right of X1. In this case, X4 would have had 5 at the high post.

You could decree, however, that X5 always covers the high post if there is one. That would leave X4 as the lone matcher. But two matchers are better than one when you use the 1-2-2 zone.

Some teams attack the 1-2-2 zone with the 1-4 or the 1-2-2 alignments. Both formations match the defensive set. Teams that employ either array usually cut into the 1-3-1. From the 1-4, one post will break low while the other stays high on passes from the point to either wing. From the 1-2-2, one low post will flash to high post either on passes from the point to a wing or as the ball is dribbled downcourt. A simple man-to-man flash pivot coverage would deny the post cutter the ball in either case. But if your rules demand only one defender on the high post, X5, and one matcher, X4, you must teach them proper shifting methods. (See Center and Matcher Coverage section in Chapter 3 for these techniques.)

Matching the Overloads Used Against the 1-2-2

There are three basic overloads against all zones: the triangular, the diamond, and the box. There are two ways for an offensive team to achieve an overload: line up in the overload when they come downfloor, or cut into the overload from their basic sets. The former is a static overload, the subject of this section; the latter is a continuous overload, the subject of a parallel section in Chapter 15.

Diagram 14-3 shows a triangular overload on the left side of the court. A triangular overload on the right side of the court would place X4 at the high post and X5 at the low post if you use both big men as matchers. If you use only one matcher, your rule would leave X5 at the high post and X4 covering both the left and the right low post positions. Your zone, with only one matcher, would be better from the 1-3-1.

Diagram 14-4 depicts the classic diamond overload. X1 contains 1, preventing dribbling penetration. X2 has the lone weakside attacker,

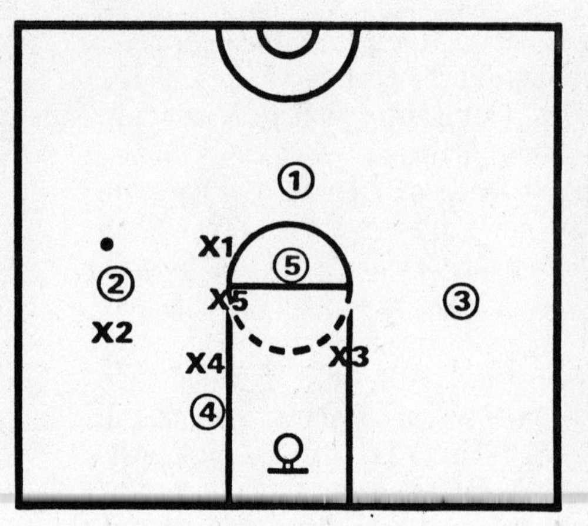

DIAGRAM 14-3

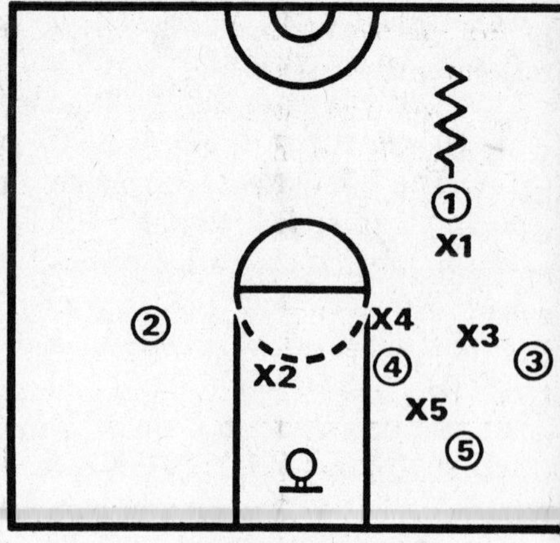

DIAGRAM 14-4

using his three-step and peripheral view drills. X3 plays ballside of 3, eliminating the middle cut, and helping X1 on outside drives. X2 has coverage on the first attacker left of X1 and X3 defends the first attacker right of X1. X5 guards 5, the second attacker around the perimeter from X1. X5 sags his three-step drill, one toward the ball and two toward the basket. This gives him good help position on 4. X4 takes the second player left around the perimeter from X1. This attacker also happens to be the third player right around the perimeter from X1. These coverages obey the five perimeter rule using two matchers.

Both offensive shooters, wingmen 2 and 3, have overloaded (box) the left side of the court in Diagram 14-5. This happens frequently during

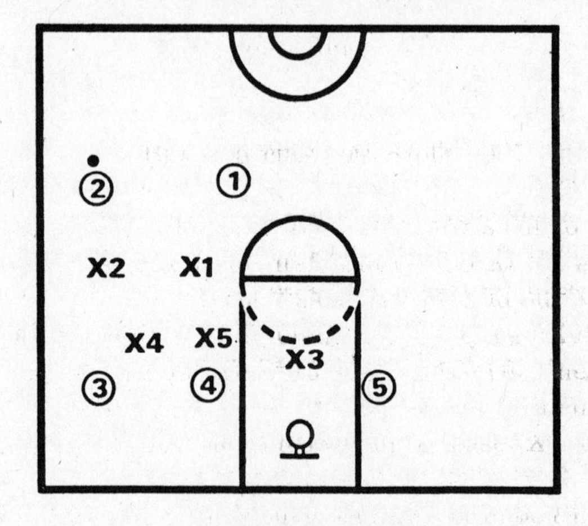

DIAGRAM 14-5

games when wingmen (shooters) are cutters. But in this section, we are matching static overloads, leaving cutting maneuvers for Chapter 15.

2 has the ball, and X2 prevents an unencumbered shot by playing within arm's length of the ball. X1 sags three steps, covering the high post and helping X2 close the gap on drives to the middle. X2 obeys his coverage rule: covering first player around the perimeter left of X1. X3, applying his coverage rule, defends the post player, 5, the first attacker around the perimeter right of X1. X4 covers 3, the second player around the perimeter left of X1 or the third player right of X1. X4 sags his three-step drill, helping on 4 inside and helping X2 close the gap on outside drives by 2. X5 covers the high side of 4 as long as the ball is at a wing. X5 guards 4, the second player around the perimeter right of X1 or the third player left of X1. X3 has lob pass responsibility.

Defensing Ball Movement

Many teams attack a zone by getting into their overload and passing until they get the good perimeter shot or penetrate the inside with a pass. The match-up is a primary team defense. As such, the defenders must help inside, yet force the hurried perimeter shot.

By drilling against ball movement from a basic array and an overload alignment, you can accomplish two objectives at once. You can observe the application of the match-up fundamentals (playing on the plane of greatest peripheral view and the three-step drill being the two most important), and you can drill against teams which use ball movement as a primary attack. When ball movement and overloading fail, cutting will become the next offensive objective. That will be met and defensed in Chapter 15.

A Basic 2-3 Baseline Offense Versus the 1-2-2 Match-Up, a Drill (Diagrams 14-6 and 14-7). The lines in the diagrams show the approximate shoulder-to-shoulder alignment of each defender.

Procedure:

1. First let the five offensive players break downcourt and set up. See if the defense knows the proper match-up coverage rules. X1 would take the point alley or the right guard alley each trip (Diagram 14-6).
2. In Diagram 14-6, 3 begins with the ball. X3 covers the baseline side of 3. X3 is within arm's length of 3, discouraging the jump shot.
3. X1 sags his three-step drill (two toward the basket and one toward the ball), using the plane of greatest peripheral view. He

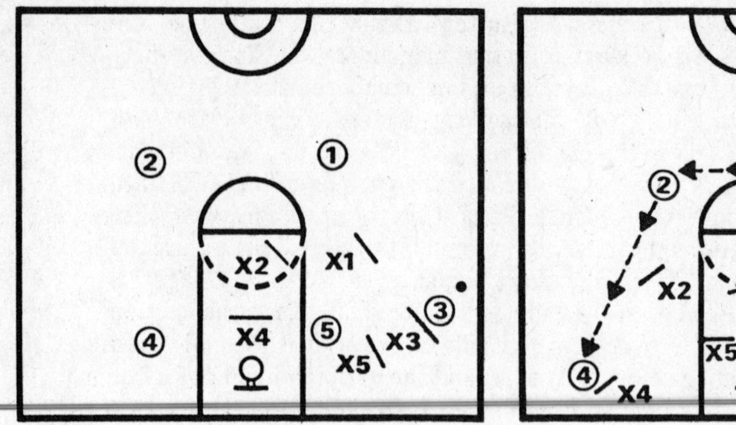

DIAGRAM 14-6

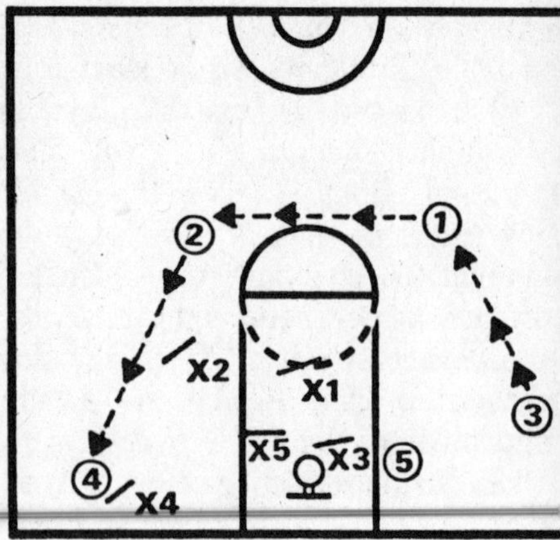

DIAGRAM 14-7

should see 1, 2, and 3. He should intuitively know or feel 5's presence. X1 must help defense the upper side of 5 if 3 directs a pass inside. X1 must help X3 close the gap if 3 drives inside. If 3 completes a pass inside to 5, X1 must sag and force 5 to pass back outside, stealing any dribble if 5 puts the ball on the floor. If X5 and X3 can handle 5 and 3 respectively and we are laning (Chapter 18), X1 would use his interception stance (Chapter 3), forcing the offense further outside, slowing the pass from 3 to 1.

4. X5, with the ball in the corner, plays the low side of 5 in a three-quarter stance. This forces all passes to 5's upper side where an alert X1 can deflect or steal the pass. If X1 is laning, X5 would front 5. X5 should see all players except 4 clearly with proper use of the plane of greatest peripheral view.
5. X2, with the ball in the corner, can see 1, 2, 3, and 5. He has sagged four steps to the basket and two toward the ball. His body should be even with a line through both baskets. He can see a cut by any attacker except 4.
6. X4 guards 4, the second player around the perimeter left of X1. X4 sees every player on the court. He has lob pass responsibility. As the deepest weakside defender, X4 would stop 3's drive if 3 got by X1. X2 would have to sink to cover 4 if X4 had to stop 3's drive. X4 would be even with the basket and a step or two off the line between 3 and 4.

Objectives:

1. To teach the match-up coverage rules.
2. To teach proper weakside sags.

3. To teach the interception stance.
4. To teach proper positioning of the body so it will be on the plane of greatest peripheral view.
5. To teach the three-step drill.

As the ball is reversed (Diagram 14-7), each perimeter defender would jump toward the pass. Defenders react as the pass is in flight, not after it has been received. Each man readjusts his plane of greatest peripheral view, using his three-step drill, as the ball is passed from one attacker to another.

While the ball is in flight to 1, X5 moves over the top of 5 and X3 sags to a position nearer the lane. X3 can help on 5. X2 moves nearer his man, 2. 4 breaks outside to receive the pass in the other corner. X4 guards him.

With 4 having the ball in the corner, X4 covers baseline side. X4 is within arm's length of 4. X2 sags to the line between 4 and the high post. X2 is on the ballside of 2 where he can prevent a direct middle cut by 2. X2 helps X4 close the gap on an inside drive. X2 sees 4, 2, and 1.

X1 sags even with the basket. He can see 1, 2, and 4. X1 jams the middle, preventing any pass there.

X5 has used his three-step slides to the basket area. He plays on the plane where he can peripherally view every player on the court. He would stop 4's breakaway drive on the baseline. He must be aware of 5's potential flash pivot cut. And he must be aware that 3 might cut.

X3 slides over the top of 5 as the ball goes into the corner to 4. X3 plays on a plane where he, too, can see all the other attackers and defenders. He must be alert to box 3 off the boards should 4 manage a shot (see Chapter 4).

Diamond Overload Against the 1-2-2 Match-Up, a Drill (Diagrams 14-4 and 14-8). Diagram 14-4 shows the ball at the right guard alley, and Diagram 14-8 continues the overload with a pass to 3.

Procedure:

1. Let the attackers bring the ball up the court and get into their diamond overload. See if the defenders can match the line-up using the coverage rules.
2. As the ball is passed from 1 to 3, X1 uses his three-step drill. He hurries inside, preventing a pass to the upper side of 4. He can see 1, 3, 4, and 5.
3. While the ball is airborne, X4 steps over the top of 4, using the three-quartering stance, preventing a pass to the low side of 4. X4 sees 1, 3, 4, and 5.

4. X3 plays within arm's length of 3. X3 could even channel 3 if that is your wish and the design of your team defense. X1 can help X3 close the gap inside, and X5 can help X3 close the gap outside.
5. X5 denies 5 the ball. 5 must not be allowed to receive the ball in the diamond overload. From his position, 5 could pick the defense apart with passes.
6. X2 plays on a line between 3 and 2. X2 sags to the line between the two baskets. X2 plays on the plane so there can never be a direct pass between 2 and 3. He must force the semi-lob skip pass. He might pick it off, or, failing that, the semi-lob gives the defenders time to slide to their new responsibilities. X2 has lob pass duties. X2 can see every player on the court.

Objectives:

1. To teach the match-up coverage rule.
2. To teach the proper weakside sag when everything is on the strongside (overload).
3. To teach interception, fronting, denial, and three-quartering stances.
4. To teach proper positioning of the body so it will be on the plane of greatest peripheral view.
5. To teach the sagging three-step drill.

Defensing the Offenses That Penetrate the Holes and Seams. Holes are the areas between the perimeter defenders. Seams are the regions within the interior of the defense where there is no defender.

Most teams attack the zone defense by stationing their perimeter men in the holes of the zone and putting a stationary passer-shooter in the seams. Some teams penetrate with the dribble into the holes of the zone, and some teams break a cutter into the seams.

The 1-2-2 zone presents four holes and one seam, perfect for a 2-1-2 attack (Diagram 14-9). Some coaches feel that the area near where the foul line meets the baseline is a seam (known as the "short corner").

But against the match-up, there will be no holes to defend. Each perimeter attacker is matched up with a defender. Inside defenders receive help from perimeter defenders, and inside defenders are matched with inside attackers, leaving no seams available. Sometimes as the offense forces the defense to slide (ball movement), an opening appears inside for cutters to take advantage of (man movement). Proper execution of match-up fundamentals should eliminate these defensive mistakes, however.

There are no holes to defend in the match-up. But a dribbler can

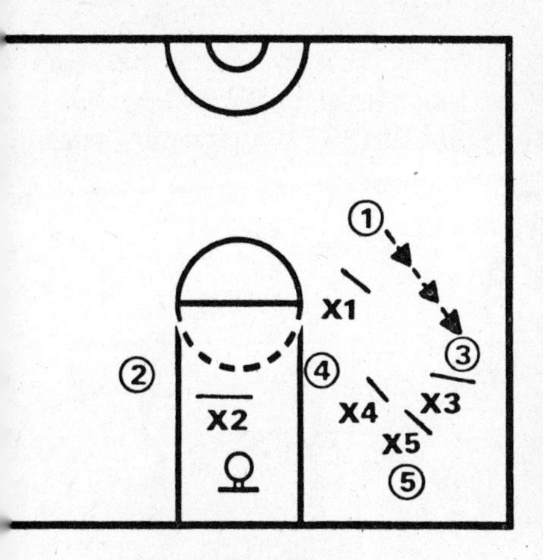

DIAGRAM 14-8

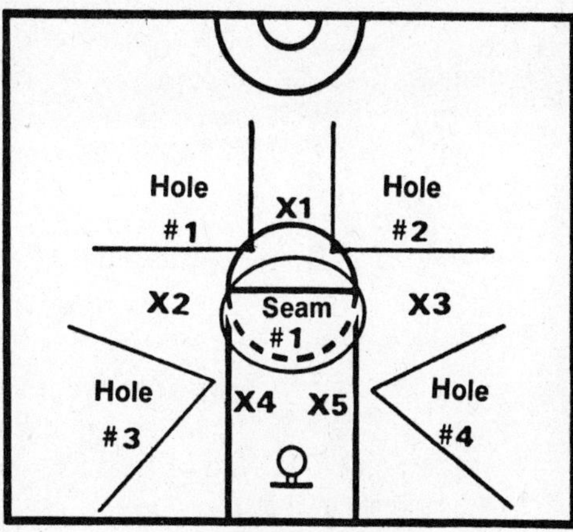

DIAGRAM 14-9

occasionally drive into a pocket. To reduce the effectiveness of these drives, defenders can be drilled on closing the gaps (see Chapter 3). The more you drill your players the better they reduce pocket jump shots.

When an attacker is quicker than his defender, the attacker frequently can drive until he encounters another defender (the pocket helper). To eliminate this mismatch of speed and quickness, we instruct the defender to overplay his assignment. He denies any drive in a predetermined direction. His teammates know that direction. They cheat toward that pocket. The team defense closes it more quickly and the individual defender can cover one direction and the jump shot better. He can concentrate on only that direction. And although he may be slower, the defender has regained the advantage. He is dictating.

A good scouting report would reduce this driver's effectiveness even further. For example, does he drive better left or right? Will he pass off of the drive? Or does he shoot? Can he pull up and shoot the jumper? Is he better doing this going right or going left? Does he have a favorite maneuver once in the pocket?

Stationary seam attackers should be denied the ball. Three-quartering usually is enough. But fronting is mandatory if three-quartering is ineffective. Remember, inside defenders do not need to intercept passes. Getting a hand on them, deflecting them, enables your teammates to recover the loose ball.

Attackers who break to the seams must be body checked, turned away from their proposed route. Because the defenders away from the ball use the three-step drill, they are in perfect pre-position to deny the cut. They must never allow a cutter between themselves and the ball, and they must never permit a cutter the direct route to the ball.

Releasing and accepting cutters might create an opening in a seam unless executed properly. Drilling on this technique (see Chapter 3) would make this exchange instinctive, eliminating even momentary openings.

"Bust Out" and "Bust Over"

Because you employ two matchers and two post defenders in your jug match-up, more "busting out" will occur. For example, a simple maneuver (see Diagram 14-2), such as passing from 1 to 2 to 4, would require X4 to proclaim loudly, "Bust out." This lets all of X4's teammates know that he must leave his inside coverage area. X5, in particular, must now become more aware of inside responsibilities.

"Bust over," as in the other match-up zone alignments, occurs mainly when a perimeter attacker cuts through the zone to the weakside. If no attacker fills the spot vacated by the cutter, the cutter's defender must pick up the next attacker around the perimeter (Diagram 14-10). 1 passes to 2. X1 follows 1 on the ballside to the free throw lane line and maybe a step beyond where X4 would pick him up. As 1 looks opposite the cut to find his new assignment, he and X3 could become confused. So X1 declares, "Bust over," telling X3 to drop to the next attacker around the perimeter. This places X3 on 1, X4 on 4, and X1 on 3. X2 keeps 2, and X5 guards 5.

"Bust out" and "bust over" prevent confusion. They enable the defense to keep in the coverage rule and still not allow an opening outside. They can be used in conjunction with the Penn State Sliding Zone maneuver (see Chapter 6) or the traps and stunts of Chapter 18.

Stopping the Breakaway Dribbler

No matter how sound your defense is or how great your individual defenders are, occasional breakdowns occur. One such occurence is the breakaway dribbler. You can recognize this fact and drill on a method to stop it, or you can ignore it and concede the lay-up. We prefer to make it difficult for our opposition to score even when we make a defensive mistake.

Our rule, in all our defenses, demands that the weakside deep defender stop the dribble penetration and that the weakside high defender (the next defender around the perimeter) drop to the area near the bas-

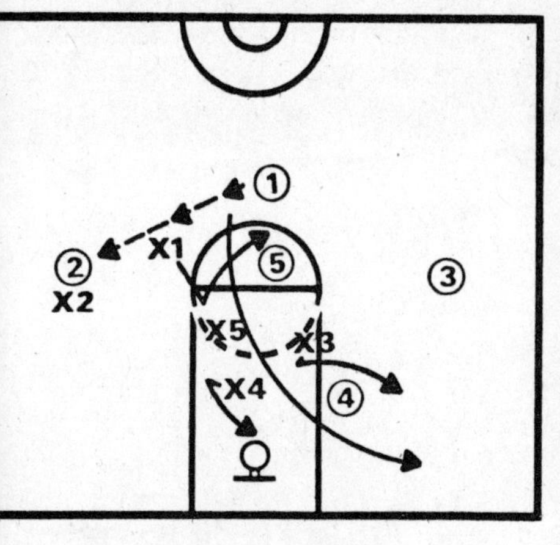

DIAGRAM 14-10

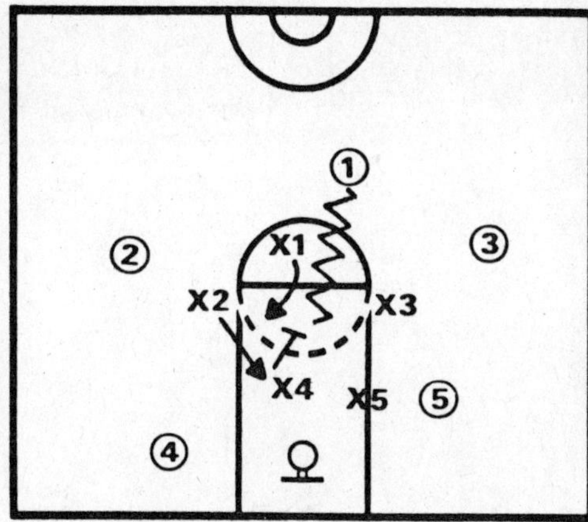

DIAGRAM 14-11

ket. This enables us to stop the drive immediately and to stop the lay-up. A pass back to the open attacker might grant the jump shot. And this coverage avoids confusion—only two defenders must hurry back to their assignments. The simpler you keep your rule, the easier it is for your team to recover from a bad situation.

1 drives around the right side of X1. X1 commits the defensive sin of not stopping dribbling penetration. Maybe X1's lateral slides are not as quick as 1's first step. X3 should have closed the pocket, but he does not get there in time. Our rule would require X4 to pick up 1 as high as X4 can. X4 races at the dribbling arm of 1. 1 cannot cross the ball over; X1 would steal it. 1 cannot continue; he would charge. If 1 can, 1 would pass to 4. But the second part of our rule requires X2 to drop on X4's man (near the basket). This pass from 1 to 4 is frequently stolen. If 1 passes to 3 or to 5, those attackers are easily covered by their assigned defenders. Most likely 1 will pass to 2. X1 can make 1 work to make this pass. If X1 can force 1 to bounce or lob pass to 2, X2 can slide back on 2 and X4 back on 4. X1 keeps 1 (Diagram 14-11).

You can, if you wish, allow X1 to rotate to 2 and X2 to keep 4 and X4 to stay with 1. But remember that the more people involved in the rotation, the less likely the rotation will function at maximum effectiveness.

If 1 had driven by the left side of X1, X5 would have stopped the dribble and X3 would have rotated down. The same coverage by X5 and X3 would result if either 2 or 4 drove through a pocket. This coverage rule would have required X4 to stop the dribble penetration of 3 or 5 and X2 to rotate down onto 4.

15 DEVELOPING THE CUTTER'S RULE FOR THE 1-2-2 MATCH-UP

You have shown your zone. Your opponent sets his offense, preparing for the attack. You respond by using your coverage rule, matching your opponent's alignment. If he stays in his array, passing the ball around the perimeter looking for the jumper, or penetrating what he thought were holes in the zone with a dribble before dishing off a pass or shooting, your coverage rule would be all the defense you would need.

But your opponents will begin cutting. You must have guidelines which will keep you in your coverage rule yet match up all cutter movement with man-to-man principles. That is the subject of this chapter.

The Cutter's Rule for the 1-2-2 Match-Up

First you must decide if you intend to use two matchers or one. Because one matcher and one post defender was covered in detail in Chapter 7, we will limit our discussion here to two matchers.

Weakside deep defenders accept the cutters coming from the strongside moving toward the weakside. Many times this becomes the responsibility of the matcher. Sometimes it is the duty of the wings. This means that X2, X3, X4, and X5 must all drill, drill, drill on accepting and releasing cutters (see Chapter 3). Whoever accepts and releases a cutter must be on the plane of greatest peripheral view so he can read the offense's intentions. The matchers become weakside acceptors when one of them is at the high post and the other is covering a man in the weakside corner. Otherwise, the weakside wings will be the acceptors.

Strongside perimeter defenders maintain the coverage rule by switching to cutters coming from the weakside to the strongside. But sometimes weakside perimeter defenders may have to cover the weakside cutter flashing to the strongside high post. Although it is best for the defensive center, either X4 or X5, to always cover the high post attacker, there is one condition where such a shift is impracticable. If the ball is in the corner, covered by X4 or X5 as matchers, and there is a low post attacker, covered by X5 or X4 as post defenders, the weakside wing must cover the flash pivot cutter to the strongside high post. This exception to the cutter's rule allows the perimeter defenders to maintain their coverage rule, and this exception prevents the momentary opening to the low post which would occur if the defensive wingman (X2 or X3) and the defender on the low post (X4 or X5) tried to shift.

All cutting through the zone is body checked, preventing any direct route to the ball. An opponent who tries to continue his direct cut will charge, a turnover-foul we want to draw because of its double-penalty value.

If a cutter makes it to the high post with the ball at a wing, the defender on the high post three-quarters the high post on his low side. If the ball is in the corner, the defender on the high post sags two steps toward the basket and one step toward the ball (three-step drill). He can three-step safely because the outside guards will have sagged into the passing lane into the high post.

If a cutter makes it to a low post strongside position with the ball at a wing, the defender on the low post three-quarters from the high side. A weakside defender has lob pass responsibility. A corner defender, if there is one, has low side help responsibility. With the ball in the corner and a strongside low post attacker, the defender on the low post three-quarters on the low side. The wing alley or the guard alley defender, if there is one, sinks and covers the low post's high side. If there is little help available from the guard or wing alley, you can front the low post. But if this condition exists, the offense will have no way to reverse the ball except by a cross-court semi-lob. This placement of offensive personnel gives the defense an opportunity to exaggerate a sag or go trap the corner (see Chapter 18).

Releases should occur as near the foul lane line on the ballside as possible. This frees the ballside defender guarding the cutter to get back to his new assignment before his new man can get an unmolested shot. And it means there is greater denial coverage on a cutter coming from the weakside. But no defender should release a cutter until he hears "release."

Defenders guarding cutters must always be between the cutter and the ball. These defenders should open to the ball around the foul lane area, making themselves appear big, as they would in any zone coverage. Defenders on the strongside to weakside cutter begin zoning it at the foul lane area, waiting to hear "release," and peripherally glancing away from the ball to find their new assignments.

An acceptor of a cutter should, by his three-step drill and playing on the plane of greatest peripheral view, see the cutter coming. He must momentarily cover his man and the cutter. He does this by physically stepping toward the cutter, appearing big, but staying in the passing lane between the passer and his original man. Proper defensive pressure on the ball handler will prevent him from momentarily spotting any open receiver.

Drill to Teach Cutter Rule

Procedure:

1. Line up five attackers and five defenders as shown in Diagram 15-1. You can switch from five perimeter to four perimeter to three perimeter as you feel you need to drill against whichever formation: Chapter 7 showed a five perimeter set; Chapter 11 displayed a four perimeter set; and Chapter 15 will detail a three perimeter array.

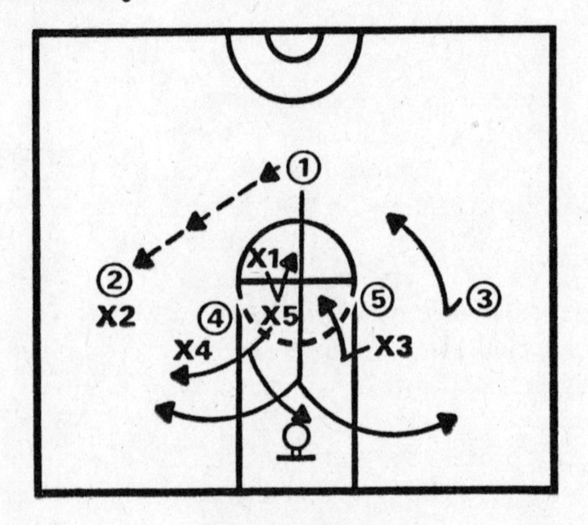

DIAGRAM 15-1

2. The coach can number offensive positions and call out the numbers when he wants a cutter. You can order the cutter to go baseline strongside, baseline weakside, or wherever you want him. Or you can let the cutter decide for himself.
3. The other offensive players fill the holes, keeping the continuity alive. For example, in Diagram 15-1, if 1 cuts baseline strongside, 2 would dribble to the point. 3 would drop to right wing while 1 moved to the left wing. If 1 cut weakside, 2 would pass to 3, and 1 would fill the right wing.
4. You could allow both posts to crisscross or one post to slide low and the other fill the vacant post spot. This would permit drilling on multiple cuts.
5. In Diagram 15-1, X1 follows 1 to free throw line. X5, the weakside matcher, calls "release." X5 has 1 regardless of 1's baseline cut. X1 looks opposite the ball for his next assignment, 3. X3 hears X5's "release" and shifts off onto the first man around the perimeter left of X1, namely 5. X2 covers 2, and X4 three-quarters low side of 4.
6. If 1 comes back out to the right wing, X5 and X3 would shift men as 1 and 5 cross a line parallel to the baseline through the ball. If 2 passed to 1 on the strongside baseline, for example, and 2 cut through the zone, X2 would follow to the free throw line where X3 would "release" him. X2 would then take 3, calling out, "Bust over," to let X1 know his intentions. X1 would cover 2 as 2 rotated back outside. X4 would sag his three-step drill with the ball in the corner.
7. You can make this drill continuous or as complicated as your needs demand. It can simulate your next opponent's offense. But whatever you decide, demand that proper fundamentals be executed. Therein lies the success or failure of your match-up zone.

Objectives:

1. To teach coverage of cutters.
2. To teach the cutter's rule.
3. To teach accepting and releasing cutters.
4. To teach the three-step drill.
5. To teach closing the gaps, by letting dribblers drive while other players cut.
6. To teach body checking.
7. To teach the interception stance (X1 could be in the interception

stance, helping inside on 4 but anticipating the pass back to 3 in Diagram 15-1).

8. To teach playing on the plane of greatest peripheral view.

The Passer As a Cutter from Point, Guard, Wing, and Corner

Your defense will face strongside cutters and weakside cutters. The strongside cutter can be a cutter near the ball trying to gain an advantage, or he can be a cutter who just passed the ball. Weakside cutters, of course, come toward the ball. This section investigates strongside cutters who just passed the ball. They must be cutting from the point alley, the guard alley, the wing alley, or the corner alley. The next two sections will examine the strongside cutters who do not pass the ball and the weakside cutters.

From the Point. Diagram 15-1 revealed coverage on one passer-cutter from the point. Diagram 15-2 displays another that the 1-2-2 zone frequently faces.

1 passes to 2 and cuts off 5 to low post (Diagram 15-2). 1 can continue his cut to the strongside corner or to the weakside. Because 4 initially lines up low on the right side, X5 takes him. X4 covers the high post, 5. X2 and X3 guard 2 and 3, the first attacker left and right of X1 respectively. As 1 cuts by 5, X4 "releases" X1. X1 covers the high post passing lane, looking opposite the ball for his next assignment (3 rotating up to the point). X5 "releases" X4, taking 1 regardless of his cutting direction. If 1 cuts to strongside, then X5 must tell X4 that they are switching sides of the floor from their original alignment. X5 should say "Scissors," to cue X4. If 2 passes to 1 in the strongside corner, X5 must declare, "Bust out," letting X4 know of the open area under the basket. X3 drops and covers 4, the first attacker right of X1. If X3 becomes confused, X1 should call out "Bust over," letting X3 know that X1 intends to cover 3 and X3 must look for the next player around the perimeter right of X1.

If you prefer, you could rule the center coverages differently. You may let X4 stay with 1's cut to either side. This would force X5 to move up and cover 5. But whatever guidelines you prefer, you must make your rules consistent throughout your match-up team defense. And you must keep them simple.

From the Guard. Diagram 15-3 shows a popular 2-3 set against the 1-2-2. 3 pops to a wing, receiving a pass from 1. 1 cuts down the middle for a return pass. 1 goes to the weakside for a baseline screen from 5 or a double screen from 5 and 4. The ball is quickly reversed from 3 to 2 to 1 for the jump shot behind the screens.

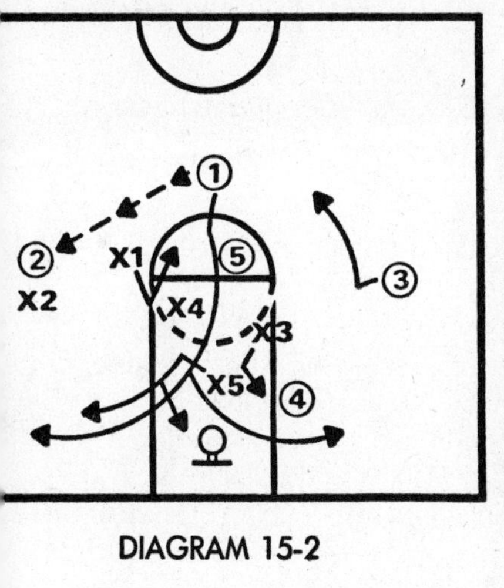

DIAGRAM 15-2

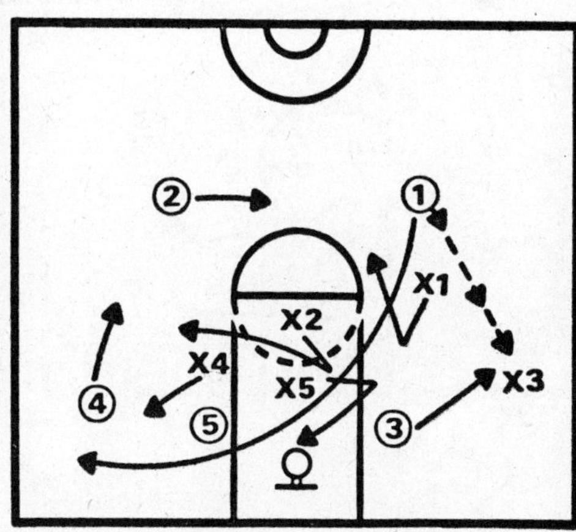

DIAGRAM 15-3

X1 jumps toward the pass from 1 to 3. This prevents the quick return pass to 1. X5 has sagged off 5 into the lane, as any zone defender would. X5 "releases" X1. X4 picks up 5. X1 looks opposite the ball for his new assignment while defensing the high post. He spots 2. He tells X2 to "bust over." X2 sags to pick up first attacker left of X1 around the perimeter. As 1 cuts by 5, X4 "releases" X5. X2 picks up 4 in Diagram 15-3 while X4 stays with 1. When 1 crosses the area where 4 is, as 1 breaks back out to the guard alley, X4 and X2 would again shift assignments.

From the Wing. 2 passes to 1 and cuts off 4's baseline screen for the short jumper (Diagram 15-4). Defenders have matched up according to the coverage rule. As 2 passes, X2 jumps in the direction of the pass, establishing his three-step drill, preventing the quick return pass to the cutting 2. X4 "releases" X2. X5 "releases" X4 as 2 cuts by 4. X2 has 5, X4 has 4, and X5 has 2. These releases keep the coverage rule in vogue while not disobeying the cutter rule.

From the Corner. Many teams attack the 1-2-2 with a 2-1-2. The high post is a passer-shooter. It is best to keep the ball from such a diversified and talented player. In Diagram 15-5, the weakside guard, X2, helps X5 keep the ball from 5. When 3 passes to 1, X3 jumps his three-steps, staying between 3 and the ball. Corner cutters are covered man-to-man; so X3 denies 3 the pass at the low post "posting-up" position. X4 offers weakside lob pass help. If 3 cuts by 4, X3 and X4 trade assignments as X4 calls, "Release." X1 must be made aware of the clearout.

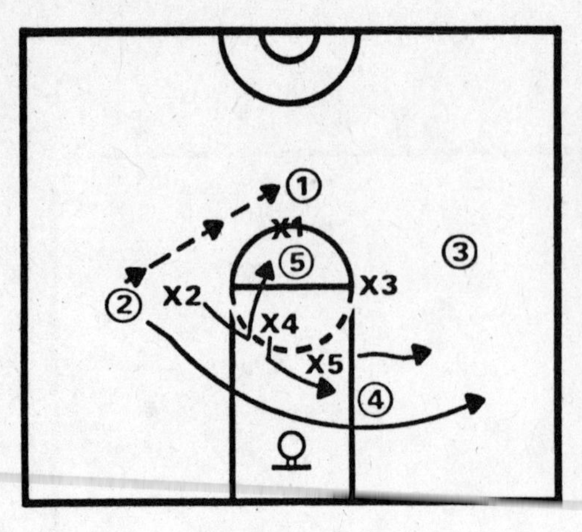

DIAGRAM 15-4

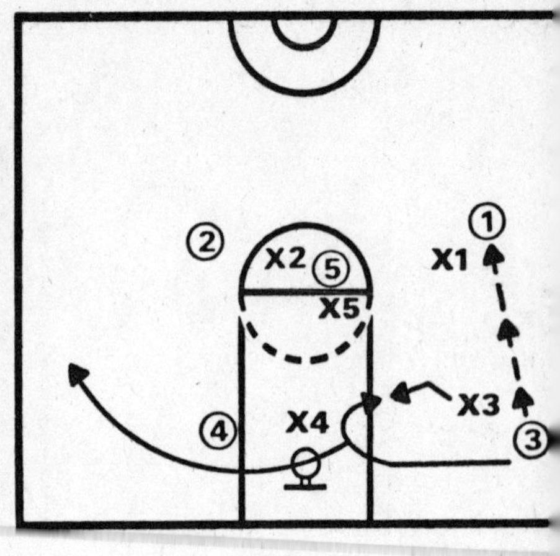

DIAGRAM 15-5

Strongside Guard Cutter

Attackers who cut after passing the ball can only come from four perimeter positions: point, guard, wing, and corner. Each has been diagramed, explained, and defensed in the section above and in the parallel sections in Chapters 7 and 11. Now let's move to perimeter attackers who cut without prior passing of the ball.

Some teams try to spread the containment match-up by spreading their offense. If defenders are not alert, they will extend beyond their ability to recover.

In Diagram 15-6, 4 has the ball. 2 cuts off high post, intending to post low, cut to the corner strongside, or cut to the weakside for quick reversal of the ball. X4 has 4 according to the coverage rule. As 2 cuts, X2 stays ballside of 2 until X2 sees 4. X2 then executes the Penn State Sliding Zone manuever with X4. X5 has made himself appear big, helping on 2 until X4 arrives. X1 helps on 5 at high post. X3 has weakside help. If 2 cuts to the weakside corner, X4 would follow, but X4 must let X5 know he has "scissored," changed sides of the court with X5 from their original alignment.

Strongside Wing Cutter

Diagram 15-7 begins from a basic triangular overload, used against all zones. 4 has the ball, and X4 prevents the baseline drive. X5 appears big, and X1 helps in the passing lane to the high post. X3 provides lob pass help and weakside rebounding defensively.

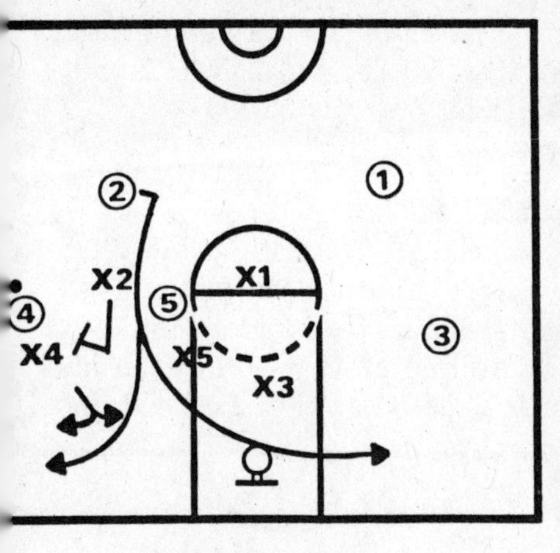

DIAGRAM 15-6

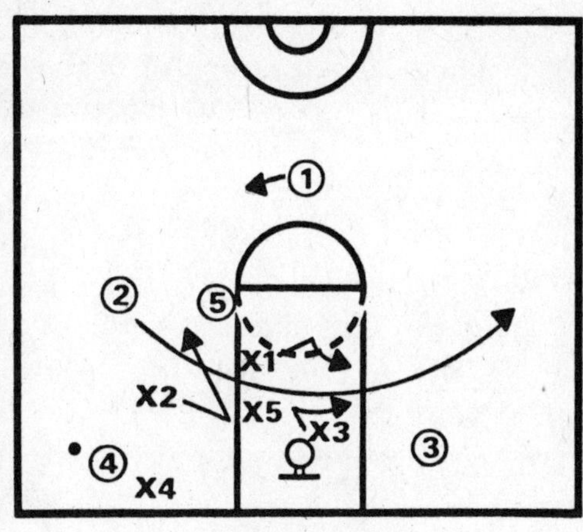

DIAGRAM 15-7

As 2 cuts, X2 prevents the direct pass by being between 2 and the ball. When X2 hears "release," he looks opposite the ball for his new assignment. He spots 1. He must tell X1 to "bust over." X2 now has the high post passing lane responsibility. X5 "releases" 2 to X3 as 2 cuts weakside. If 2 goes to the corner, he will be X1's responsibility as X3 remains on 3. If 3 breaks high on weakside, X3 would keep 2 and X1 would guard 3.

Strongside Corner Cutter

Strongside corner cutters are covered man-to-man. Let's use Diagram 15-6 to show this cutter's defender responsibility. If 2 has the ball and 4 cuts, X4 would cover him man-to-man regardless of where or how 4 cuts. If 4 breaks through the lane and out to a guard alley, X4 and X3 shift as 4 cuts by 3.

Weakside Guard Cutter

Cutters from weakside to strongside are more numerous than strongside to weakside cutters. They are not as dangerous because they usually are going away from the basket as they receive the ball.

As 2 passes to 4, 1 cuts through to the strongside corner (Diagram 15-8). X2 and X4 execute the Penn State Sliding Zone manuever. X1 sees this and goes over to cover 2. X1 helps defense the passing lane into the high post area. X3 "releases" X1; X5 appears big, temporarily releasing X3; and X4 completes the releasing when he "releases" X3. The key on defensing any guard to wing pass is the execution of the Penn State Sliding Zone maneuver. It must be drilled and drilled and drilled. It will make your weakside cutting releases stronger.

Weakside Wing Cutter

Diagram 15-9 depicts the same ending of the cut described in Diagram 15-8. The differences: the cut originates from the wing and the ball stays at the guard position. X5 and X3 still do exactly as they did in Diagram 15-8. Another difference: there has been no Penn State maneu-

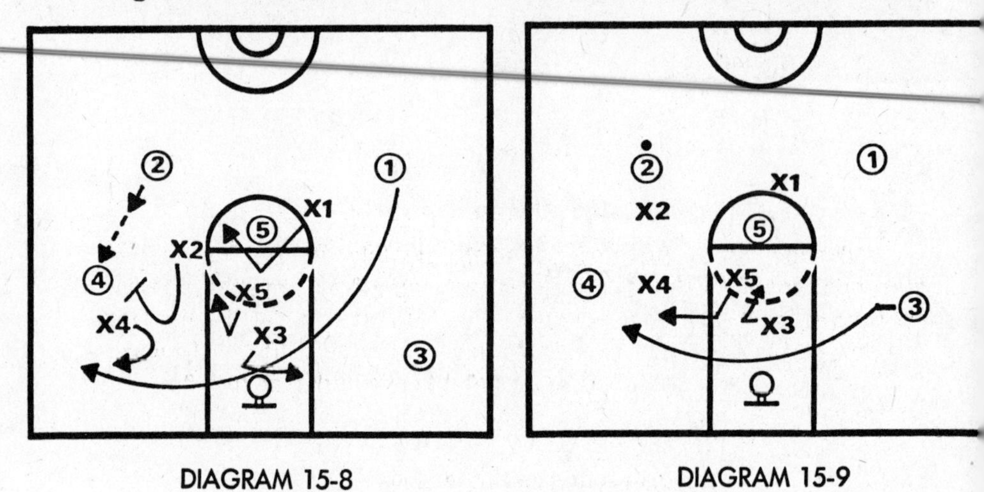

DIAGRAM 15-8 DIAGRAM 15-9

ver, and so there will be no X4 "release." X5 "releases" X3. X3 takes 5, the high post, and notifies X1 that 1 might try a backdoor. X5 keeps 3. X1 helps defense the high post passing lane until X3 arrives.

Weakside Corner Cutter

The baseline shuffle has become a popular offense against all defenses, including the match-up. Diagram 15-10 shows the first movment. 3 cuts off 5, going either low post or high post. X2 covers the ball, 2. X1 sags his three steps, helping at the high post. X4 uses his three steps, helping at the low post. X5 "releases" X3 as 3 cuts by 5.

Throughout this movement and all the other movements described above, defenders began coverage according to their coverage rule. They covered the cutters using man-to-man principles and ended still obeying their coverage rule.

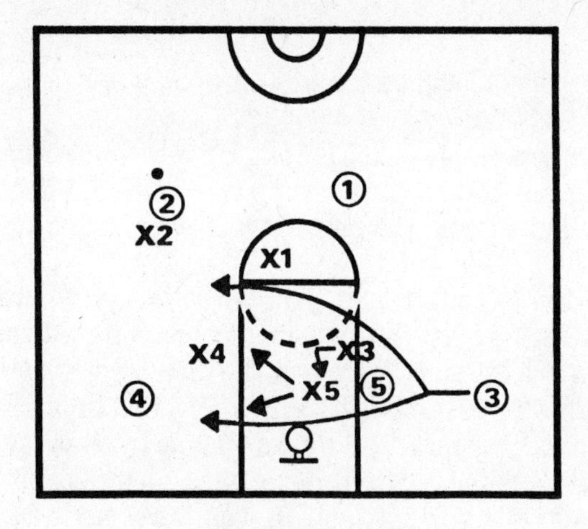

DIAGRAM 15-10

Combination of Two Cutters

Now that you have observed defense of single cuts through the match-up, let's move to the defense of plural cuts. Teams seldom use only one cutter, and they never use more than three: one man must handle the ball, and each team will have one player assigned to defensive balance. The other three players are the cutters. But armed with this knowledge, the coverage and cutter rules, and the defensing of singular cuts, plural cuts should offer minimum problems.

A few coaches will attack a match-up by lining up in the array of the zone before cutting into other formations or overloads. Diagram 15-11 shows such a move, featuring a combination of two cutters, breaking from a 1-2-2 into a 2-3. X4 takes 4, preventing the baseline drive. X2 goes with 2's cut to the free throw line where he hears X5's "release." X2 looks opposite the ball and finds 1 as his new assignment. X1 sags to congest the middle (his three-step drill). 4 has the ball, and 1 has defensive responsibility, leaving 2, 3, and 5 as potential cutters. Meanwhile, 3 has cut to the ball; so X5 again shifts assignments, "releasing" X3. X1's new assignment will be 2. When the offense completes its cuts, X4 will have 4, X2 will guard 1, X1 will cover 2, X5 will play baseline side of 3, and X3 will sag off of 5 to help in the middle. As long as the ball stays in the corner, X2 covers the high side of 3 (the low post). All cutters will be body checked, slowing down their cuts. X2 might have to tell X1 to "bust over" if X1 does not recognize the situation.

Combination of Three Cutters

Where Diagram 15-11 showed two cutters, one strongside and one weakside, Diagram 15-12 will present three cutters, one strongside and two weakside. Let's break the plural cutting into single cuts and defense them.

As 2 passes to 4 and cuts, X2 goes with 2, staying between 2 and the ball, until X2 sees 4. X2 then executes the Penn State Sliding Zone maneuver with X4. X5 sags to protect the middle, appearing big. X1 has sagged his double three-step drill (one when 2 had the ball and one more when 4 receives it), protecting the passing lane into the high post. Meanwhile, 1 has cut. X1 follows him ballside until X5 picks him up momentarily. X1 looks opposite for his man, 2, who must circle back outside for defensive purposes (he'll be the only defender for the offense—1 is in the corner strongside). X4 will pick up near the big block strongside. X3 has shifted to 2, calling, "Release." When 3 cuts to low post, X5 will call, "Release," picking up 3. 2 circles out front. X3, when he hears X5's "Release," will pick up 5. So X2 has 4, X1 has 2, X4 has 1, X3 has 5, and X5 has 3.

These are precisely the positions these defenders would have in the 1-2-2 zone slides with the ball in the corner. The match-up's advantage over the basic 1-2-2 zone is that each cut is covered by man-to-man principles while a zone is being played. Each cutter is body checked, slowing

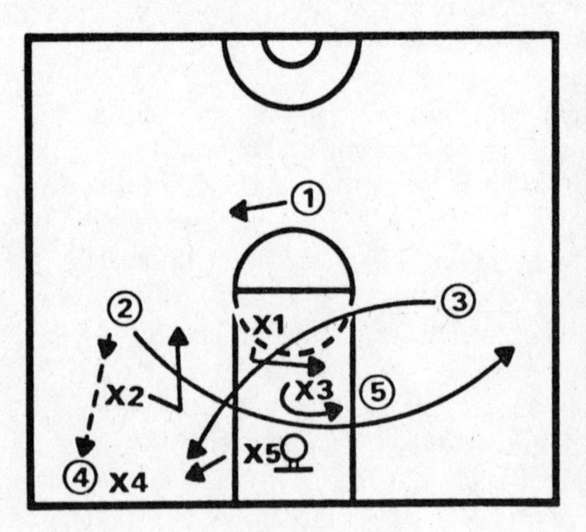

DIAGRAM 15-11

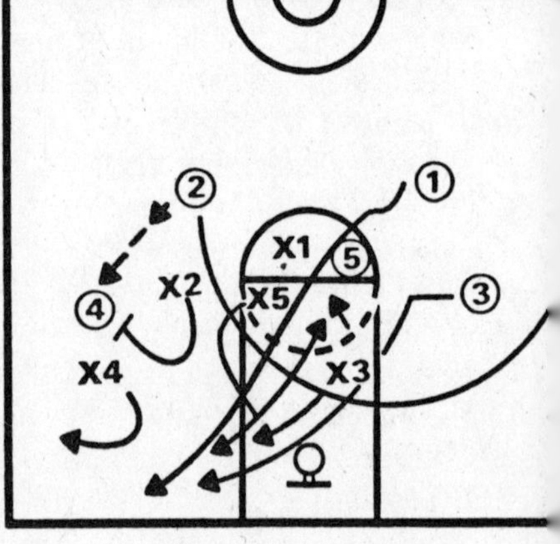

DIAGRAM 15-12

down the cutter's movement; and if patterned, slowing down the next several cuts of the offense. In case an attacker shoots, all offensive players can be blocked off the boards with individual blockout techniques (see Chapter 4).

Matching Cutter Movements into Overloads

Many teams attack zones by lining up in the holes of the zone and cutting into basic overloads. Diagram 15-13 begins from a 2-1-2 formation and cuts into a diamond overload.

When a guard, 2, passes to a wing, 4, it cues those defenders to run the Penn State Sliding Zone maneuver (Diagram 15-13). X2 sags to cover the high post passing lane before recognizing that a wing has the ball. X2 "releases" X4. X4 goes directly to the big block. 5 has followed 1's decoy cut to the "short corner," the baseline positioning of the diamond overload. X5 goes with 5 to the low post before X4 picks him up. X1, meanwhile, covers the high post passing lane. X1 knows he has 2. X3 picks up 1 on his decoy cut. 3 flash pivots. X5, after releasing 5 to X4, picks up 3's flash pivot cut. This puts X2 on 4, X4 on 5, X1 on 2, X5 on 3, and X3 on 1.

With the ball at a wing, this is the exact coverage slide of the regular 1-2-2 zone. It maintains the coverage rule while following the cutter's rule. Plus each cutter is body checked. A charge may be drawn, but, at worst, the cuts are slowed and checked man-to-man while a 1-2-2 zone is played—the basic theory of a true match-up zone.

Defensing Dribbling Moves

Dribbling against a zone, which used to be taboo, serves several offensive purposes. It can push a fellow attacker down an alley or two. It can force that fellow attacker to clear to the other side of the court. It can force the zone or the match-up into complicated, undrilled slides. It can free the dribbler for a shot while the zone defenders decide who covers whom.

To alleviate these offensive advantages, you should have your defenders on the dribblers stay with the driver until he has passed through three alleys unless he passes a teammate where a man-to-man switch can occur.

In Diagram 15-14, 1 drives by 3 into the corner. The offense has moved by dribbling from the popular 2-2-1 (against 1-2-2 zones) into the box overload. As 1 drives by 3, X3 switches to 1. X1 takes 3, jumping his

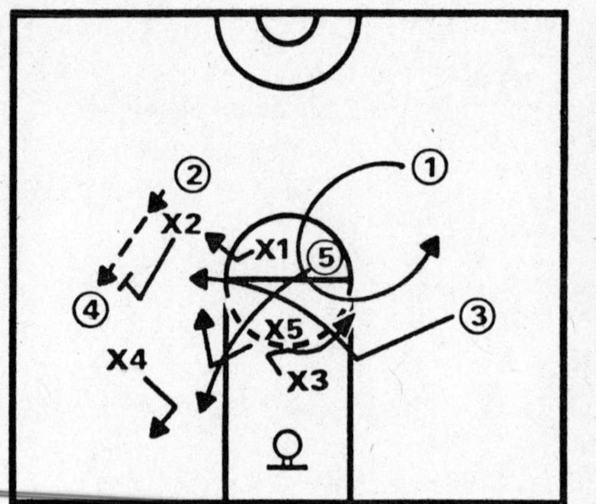

DIAGRAM 15-13

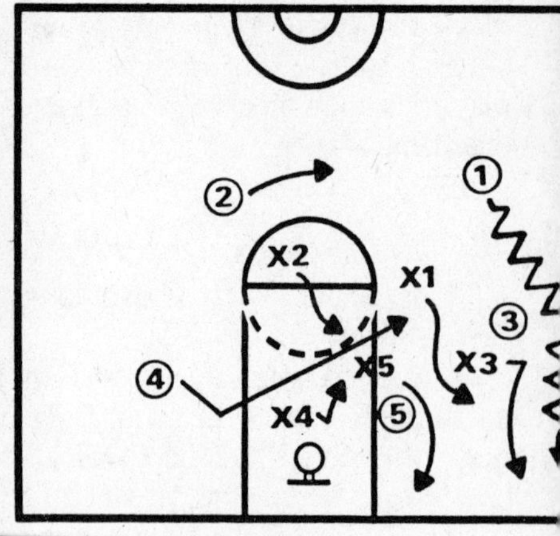

DIAGRAM 15-14

three-step drill, eliminating 3's direct cut toward the basket and the ball. X3 prevents 1's baseline drive. X5 steps over the top of 5 to get baseline three-quartering positioning. X1 helps on the upper side of 5. X2 sags his double three-step drill into the middle, vigilant of the lob pass to 5 and the backdoor to 2. X4 covers 4's cut man-to-man. X4 sags because he has plenty of help from X1 and X2.

If this is a major part of your opponent's offense, you could adjust defensively by requiring that X1 channel 1 into the middle of the court while he is dribbling. Or you could have X3 "jump switch" as 1 dribbles by 3. If 1 continued his dribble, he'd charge X3. Anything else that 1 does deviates from their patterned attack. But for the forcing of teams out of their pre-drilled attack, for adjustments inside the basic containment match-up, and for trapping and stunting, you will want to read Chapters 17 and 18.

16 DEFENSING BASIC CONTINUITIES WITH 1-2-2 MATCH-UP

Chapters 1 through 4 added to the last three chapters will make your 1-2-2 match-up and accompanying zone a defense of championship caliber. You have the breakdown drills, the coverage and cutter rules, and you will have the necessary adjustments (Chapters 17 and 18). By applying those rules, drills, and adjustments, your team will develop a cohesive defense.

Because this chapter combines all the previous ideas, techniques, slides, drills, and adjustments of the 1-2-2 zone and match-up into defensing basic continuities, it gives you an opportunity to see how those parts fit into the whole. Not only are the basic attack alignments presented, defensed, but a special gimmick offense will also be considered.

A 1-3-1 Offense Defensed

Diagram 16-1 portrays a 1-3-1 formation with movement into a box overload. Many seasons ago this type of movement convinced us that the adjustment phase of our cutter's rule was most logical: the weakside wing covers the high post when the post defender has a low post strongside attacker covered. An original adjustment must be made to the coverage rule to provide maximum coverage. But that is one of the beauties of the match-up. You can pre-plan adjustments when you have superior scouting reports.

This triple post alignment requires X1 to cover 1, X2 to cover 2, X4 to cover 4, X5 to cover 5, and X3 to cover 3. This might appear as a deviation to the coverage rule because the offensive alignment seems a three-perimeter array. But you can simply adjust your defense by decreeing that 3 is a wing and not a high post. This order allows the match-up coverage as illustrated in Diagram 16-1.

The pass from 1 to 2 initiates the offensive movement. All three attackers move concurrently. Each is covered man-to-man with X4 sagging, covering low side of 5, X5 covering high side, and X1 dropping his three steps into the high post passing lane. Because X5 has 5, the low post strongside, X3 covers 3, the flash pivot attacker at high post. X1 is told of the cleared side of the court, eliminating the surprise backdoor cut by 1. A backdoor cut, of course, would find X3 shifting responsibilities with X1.

Diagram 16-2 shows the offense changing sides of the court. Most zone offenses are continuous. 3 pops out from his high post position to the guard alley. When 2 passes to 3, 3 becomes X1's assignment. As 1 drifted

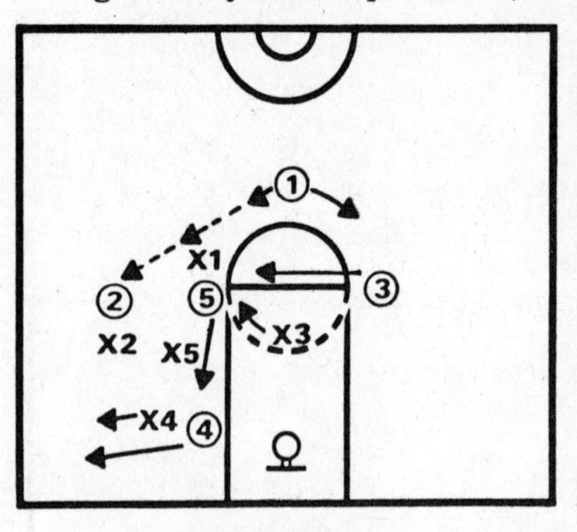

DIAGRAM 16-1

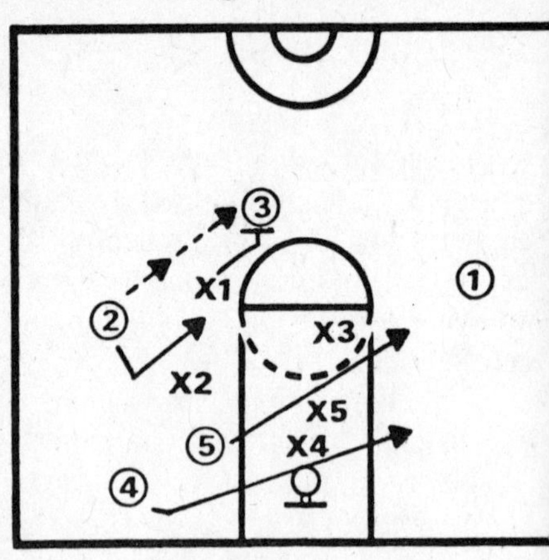

DIAGRAM 16-2

to the wing before 2 passed to 3, X3 shifted men with X1. 5 breaks to the high post, and X5 defends him man to man. X4 breaks along the baseline, and X4 defends him man to man. 2 slides into the high post opposite the overloaded side. X2 denies him, as he body-checks the movement. This triple-post offense is now ready to attack in a box overload on the right side of the court. All this movement is checked with man-to-man principles while sliding in the zone.

The primary objective of the offense is to hit the high post from the wing or initially from the point. A high-low game is run. The low defender must never allow his man to get position to receive this high-low pass from the high post.

For discussion's sake, let's let the pass go into 3 from 2 in Diagram 16-1. 3 tries to dump the ball low to 5. 5 slides across the lane if he cannot get the ball. 4 breaks to low post strongside. And 2 tries to find the hole on the strongside for the outside jumper. 1 seeks the hole on the weakside. There should be no holes and no seams if each defender has done his job. Each attacker has been defended man to man yet played a zone.

A 3-1-1 Offense Defensed

Diagrams 16-3 and 16-4 exhibit an excellent offensive continuity against the 1-2-2 zone. The offense illustrates maximum use of the dribble to force the defense into complicated slides. The offense attempts to spread the interior defense of the match-up. Your players must be well schooled so they will not over-spread, thereby weakening the defense.

X1 takes 1; X2 guards the first player left of X1, 2; X3 covers the first player right of X1, 3; X5 defends the high post, 5; and X4 denies the low post, 4. This match-up adheres perfectly with the match-up coverage rule.

1 passes to 3 and cuts, representing a pass from a point guard followed by a cut (see Chapter 15). X1 follows to the free throw line where X5 "releases" first and X4 "releases" quickly thereafter. X1 looks

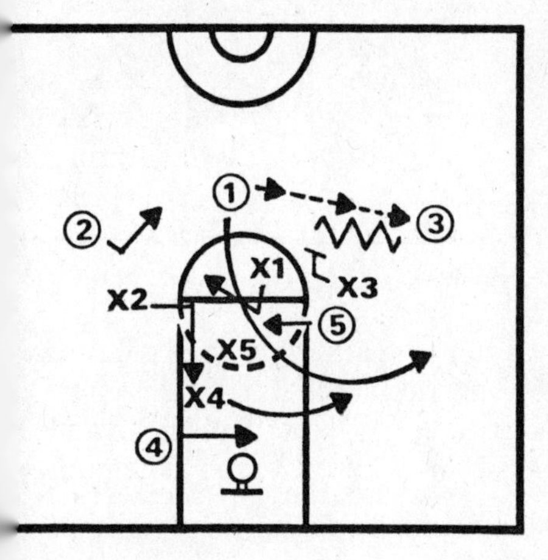

DIAGRAM 16-3

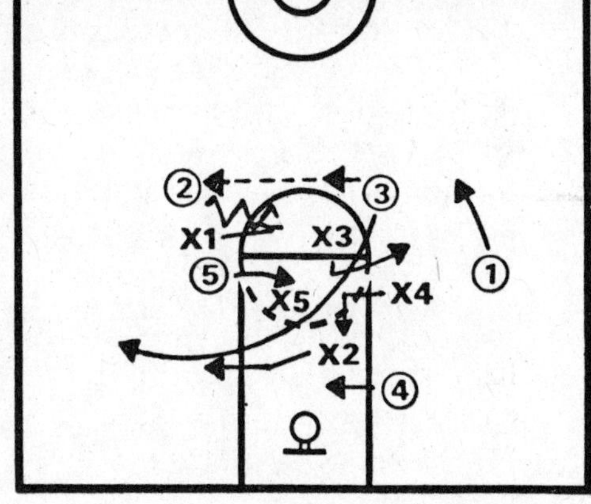

DIAGRAM 16-4

opposite the pass for his new assignment, 2. X2, who has executed his three-step drill and is playing on the plane of greatest peripheral view, drops to cover 4. X4 must let X5 know he has moved outside: "Bust out" is his call. Against the regular 1-2-2, 1 would have an easy fifteen foot jumper. Against the match-up, each attacker is covered with man-to-man principles. As 3 begins his dribble, 5 and 4 commence their cuts. X5 body checks 5, and X2 denies 4 the ball, playing on the high side. If 3 hits 5, he dumps low to 4 if 4 is open. If 3 hits 1, 5 and 4 post-up, high and low respectively. None of this should find an open seam or hole against the zone with man-to-man principles (the match-up). But this offense can destroy the basic 1-2-2 zone.

When 3 finds no opening, he passes to 2 and cuts to the strongside, and the offense continues to the left side of the court (Diagram 16-4). X3 drops to the free throw line where he hears X5 and X2 "release" him. X2 picks up 3. X4 drops to cover 4. X3 looks opposite the ball and finds his new assignment, 1. As 2 dribbles, 5 moves, facing X5's body checks. X4 covers 4 on the high side, preventing the high-low game should 5 get the ball. The offense continues until the defense makes a mistake, or the attackers lose their patience and take the bad shot. An alert match-up defense will not lose to this offense because of their man-to-man principles. A basic 1-2-2 zone defense is at the mercy of this beautiful offense.

A 2-1-2 Offense Defensed

1 passes to 2 and cuts strongside in Diagram 16-5 (see section on Weakside Guard Cut in Chapter 15). 2 passes to 4, and 3 cuts strongside, completing the box overload.

On 1's pass, X1 drops to the free throw line where he hears X3's "Release." On 2's pass to 4, X2 and X4 execute the Penn State Sliding Zone maneuver. X1 moves to cover 2 as X2 goes to guard 4. X4 drops directly to the big block, where he "releases" X3. X4 subsequently picks up 1, if 1 moves to the corner. As 1 moves to the corner, 3 cuts to the strongside low post. X3 denies this cut with body checks. X5 has the high post covered.

More offensive movement is required to break the match-up. Teams have many ways of cutting from the box overload back into their regular 2-1-2 array. During those cuts, they are trying to penetrate the holes and seams of the zone. But there are no holes or seams in a true match-up.

A 1-4 Offense Defensed

The popular catch-all 1-4 array offers no problem until cutting begins. An offense fifteen feet from the basket puts no pressure on the defense if the containment defense will not spread with the offense.

Diagram 16-6 shows a movement that destroys basic point zone defenses. Because the wing defender in the regular 1-2-2 zone must cover 2 and the two inside defenders must cover 4 and 5, there is no defender to cover 1. If 1 is an excellent outside shooter, the game is lost.

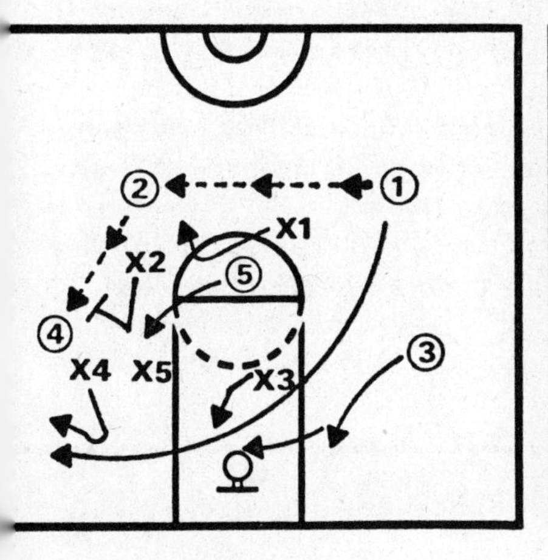

DIAGRAM 16-5

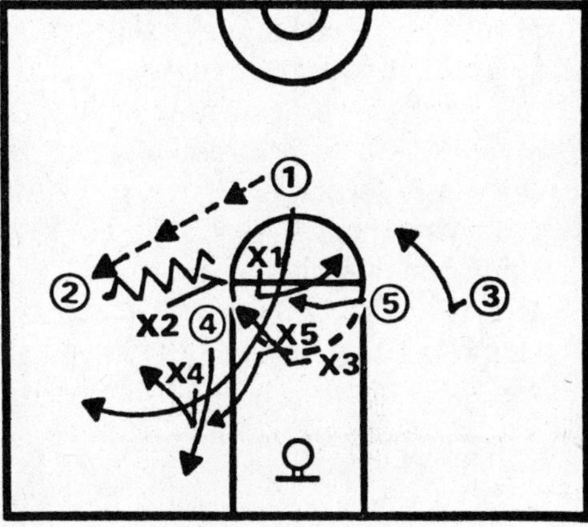

DIAGRAM 16-6

But the match-up, with its man-to-man principles, should shift into a perfect coverage. X1 would cover the point passer-cutter (see Chapter 15) to the free throw line where X5 "releases" him. 4 cuts low and 5 slides over to the high post strongside. X3 shifts onto 5. X4 and X3 body check both cuts. X4 plays high side of 4 as 4 reaches the low post. When 1 cuts out to strongside corner, X5 communicates to X4 by saying, "Bust out." This tells X4 that X5 has vacated the lane area. Now X3 has 5, X5 guards 1, X2 contains the dribbler, and X1 looks opposite to find 3, his new assignment. An excellent offense against standard zones has again been thwarted by the match-up's use of man-to-man principles.

A 1-2-2 Offense Defensed

Many coaches believe in beginning in the alignment of the zone and cutting into another array or into an overload. Diagram 16-6 could easily have begun from the 1-2-2 formation; both 4 and 5 could have started at the low post positions. 5 could cut high on the pass from 1 to 2. This would put the offense into the diamond overload of Diagram 16-6 from the 1-2-2 instead of the 1-4 beginning. The defense would have covered the cuts the same. That is another beauty of the match-up—defenders learn the rules and the fundamentals. Then, regardless of the offense they face, they apply those rules and fundamentals. Only faulty execution would defeat the well taught match-up.

A Gimmick Offense Defensed

In kindred sections in Chapters 8 and 12, we discussed pure gimmick offenses, offenses that coaches used just to beat your match-up. These offenses are rarely successful because players cannot execute to perfection special offenses that are drilled on for only a few days to beat a special but primary defense.

But there is another side of gimmick offenses: There are those coaches who begin their offenses from off-beat alignments but evolve them into formations from which they run their regular offenses. Diagrams 16-7 and 16-8 show a 1-1-3 array which evolves into the baseline shuffle or reverse action continuity made famous by Coach Pete Newell's University of California "Golden Bears." Many teams use the baseline shuffle as their primary offense against both the man-to-man and the zones.

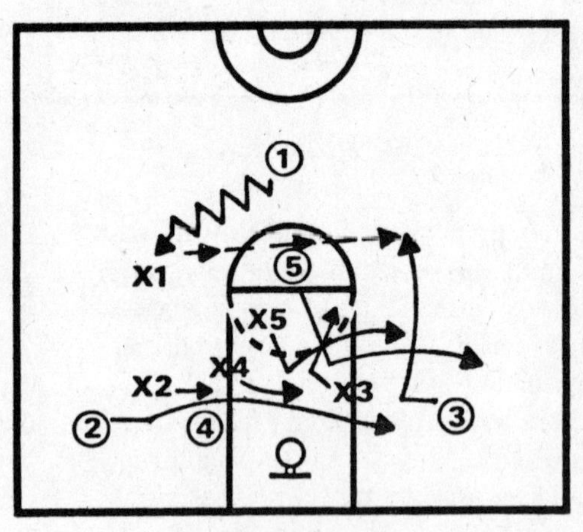

DIAGRAM 16-7

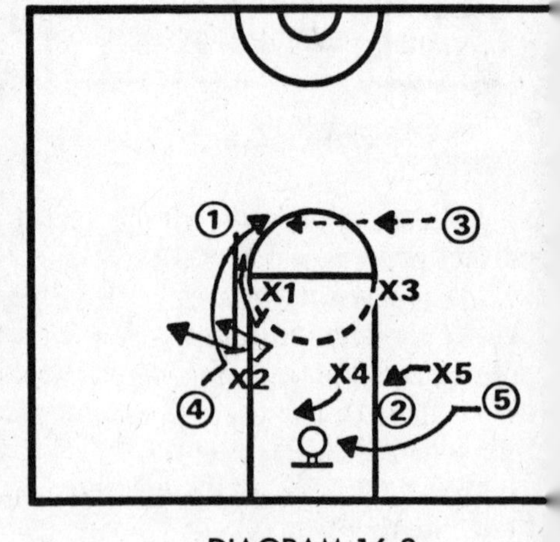

DIAGRAM 16-8

1 dribbles downcourt and drives toward one side (Diagram 16-7). This keys 5 to go screen the low post opposite. Then 5 pops to a wing. 1 passes to 3, and 2 breaks off of 4. 1 screens low for 4 to pop up to high post before 1 pops to a wing. 5 would break off of 2 and the offense continues (Diagram 16-8).

To stop this attack, you must first match the offensive array with the coverage rule. Then you defense the first few cuts before the offense begins their continuity. These beginning cuts are not as dangerous; they are for deception, sometimes put in the day before a game. They are less dangerous than the continuity cuts because they are not drilled on daily for a complete season. After matching the original alignment and stopping the decoy cuts, you must stop their basic offense. These gimmick offenses present more problems than the one-game, poorly drilled, gimmick offenses.

X1 contains 1, preventing dribbling penetration to the basket. X2 starts on 2, the first player left of X1. X3 guards 3, the first attacker right of X1. X4 has 4, the second player left of X1. And X5 defends the high post 5.

When 5 goes to screen for 3, X3 slides around the screen. X5 stays with 5. By now, X2 has sagged over 4. X4 shifts with X2 as 2 breaks by 4. When X1 screens X2, X1 shifts to 4, putting X2 on 1 as 1 pops to the wing. After the first rotation, at the end of Diagram 16-8, X1 would have 4, X3 would have 3 (first player right of X1), X2 would guard 1 (first player left of X1), X4 would cover 2 (at low post right side, therefore the second player left of X1), and X5 would cover 5 (the second player right of X1). The defense is covering the cuts with man-to-man principles yet sliding and shifting as though they were in a zone (2-3 because the offense has the appearance of a 2-3 array). The defense has the further advantage of keeping their big defenders near the basket, eliminating any possible mismatches.

Summary

In the last four chapters, you have seen the basic 1-2-2 zone grow into a match-up. Personnel types, which dictate your choice of zone, have been reviewed. The coverage rule and the cutter rule enable your defenders to match up initially and to keep that alignment while defensing cuts. Cuts from every conceivable position have been presented and defensed. All alignments and overloads have been discussed. Gaps are closed to dribbling penetrators. All that's left is for your defenders to execute the defense. And if they are drilled and drilled on the fundamentals of Chapters 1 through 4, execution should be no problem. Your containment defense, whichever zone you choose, should have reached championship caliber.

PART FIVE

ADJUSTMENTS AND PRESSURE FROM THE MATCH-UPS

17 ADJUSTMENTS FROM THE MATCH-UP

Fundamentals, properly performed at explosive rates of speed, separate the great players from the near great. Successful strategic adjustments, ordered under game duress and often at a timely juncture, differentiate the superior coach from the ordinary.

Adjustmnts can be as simple as a single personnel change, or they can be as complex as shifting the principles and objectives of a team defense or an offense. They can be subtle changes, frequently unrecognized by your opponents for several possessions. And because most games are won or lost by fewer than five points, those shrewd adaptations, unnoticed by the fan, unheeded by your opposing counterpart, and unanswered by their players, bring victory to your team.

Modifications from the most meticulous to the most substantial will receive elaboration in this chapter. Changes which involve only one defender and alterations which envelop the entire five will be presented, diagrammed, and explained. When to use them and how to teach them will occupy some of the space.

Follow First Cutter Man to Man

After your team understands your match-up and its concept thoroughly, you are ready to begin tutoring some adjustments. The easiest adaptation is to follow the first cutter through the zone man to man. This defensive adjustment may or may not confuse your opponents. When they see their cutter covered man to man, they may begin their man offense. Or they may figure it is that match-up zone with man principles. You may not want to face their man attack. Man-to-man offenses feature more player movement, and more activity can bewilder your defenders. But man-to-man attacks should not hurt zone defenses. So your first consideration becomes, do you want to face their man movement?

Many teams will run their man-to-man attacks against your match-up because they can get more player movement. When this cutting motion begins to disconcert your match-up, following the first cutter man to man can be a defensive answer.

Once you follow this initial cutter all the way through, you have three defensive options available. Any of the three can muddle the thoughts of the attacking team. And once the opposition becomes uncertain, they get flustered. Victory, then, is moments away.

After following the first cutter man to man, you could stay man to man. A clue word could key this team defensive switch. "I got the cutter" would make a good phrase. All defenders stay man to man for that possession. If your opponents should remain in their zone attack, with its minimal player movement, a bad shot could result. You could further camouflage your defensive intentions by switching on all crosses of offensive personnel. Your opponents would probably figure you were in a zone or your match-up. The worst you face is their man-to-man attack covered man to man.

Or you could stay zone after following the first cutter man to man. "Home" informs our defenders to play their basic zone, to come out of their match-up or man-to-man defenses.

This one man adjustment can be used to switch from one zone to another (Diagram 17-1). Diagram 17-1 shows X1 following 1's cut to the baseline man to man. It depicts the offense moving from a 2-3 attacking array into a 1-3-1 attack set. Many teams attack the 2-3 zone with a 1-3-1 alignment. The defense began in a 2-3 formation; but by following the first cutter man to man the defense has rotated to a 1-3-1 zone.

A third possibility exists for the team that follows the first cutter man to man. If the defender on that first cutter can accept the responsibilities of a matcher, your team can follow the first cutter man to man and then match up. In Diagram 17-1, X2 would have 2. X3 matches the first player right of X2, 3. X4 matches the first attacker left of X2, 4. X5 covers the post, 5. And X1 matches the second player left or right of X2, 1. This is the coverage rule from all the defensive formations presented in Chapters 5 through 16. From here your defense continues to accept and release cutters as they occur, per cutter rule, staying in their basic match-up zone.

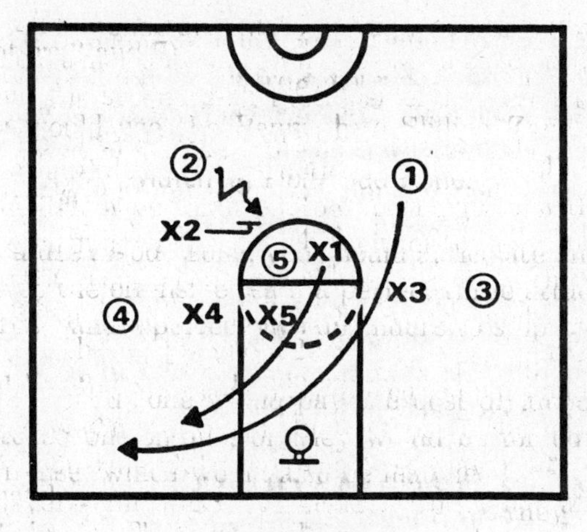

DIAGRAM 17-1

Scouting reports can help you pre-plan and pre-drill for your opponents. They aid you in deciding what adjustments you want to use against your next opponent. If the opposition is strong and you can discompose them only a possession or two each quarter, you can upset them.

Adjust from Match-Up to Basic Zone

A few times during the year, your match-up will not provide the defensive answers to the offensive probes. Perhaps you face an offense with unfamiliar cuts and your defenders misapply the coverage and cutter rules. Possibly the defenders are not alert, or are hazy or muddle-headed. Maybe the opponent's offense overpowers your match-up. Whatever the reason, you might want to stay with your basic zone. Or you might prefer to wait until halftime to discuss coverage of an opponent's surprise offense. To come out of your match-up and run your basic zone, you merely need a key word. "Home" cues our defenders to run the regular slides of our basic zone.

Adjust From Match-Up to Man

Whatever problems an offense presents to your match-up, you are only a key word away from man-to-man defensive coverage. Because your defenders have matched the array of the offense, each defender can pick up the attacker in his area man to man and stay with him man to man at least for that one possession.

This adjustment can unsettle the offensive attack. They first see the zone. They show their zone attack formation. Your defenders match up. Now each defender has a man. Your defensive quarterback, the matcher or the point guard, communicates the key word, switching your defense from the match-up to man to man. Your opponents might run their zone attack for several possessions. Remember, each possession in the Mathematical Principle of Basketball is worth four points. Just two or three indecisive offensive possessions a game can bring your club victory.

By switching on all crossing of offensive personnel, your club might convince the attackers that they are facing a zone or at least the match-up. this could add to the falsified disguise of a zone.

Adjustments are easy to practice once the team defense is thoroughly understood. Players love the mental challenge of a deception. They take pride in seeing the perplexed looks and actions of the opposition. And in a tight game, a few uncertain possessions by the opposition spell victory.

Adjust from Match-Up to Combinations

Triangle and two, box and one, and diamond and one comprise the standard combination defenses. There are many others: inverted triangle and two, the "T" and one, the inverted "T" and one, three men and a tandem, etc. Combination defenses allow man-to-man coverage on the opposition's best offensive player or players, yet have zone coverage inside. The zone defenders not only cover the areas near the basket,but they can help the man defenders when the men they are guarding move inside.

When you face a team with a great player or two, it is best to switch to the combination defense of your choice in the huddle during a time-out. This eliminates any confusion by any member of the defensive team.

But there are those coaches who drill their players to switch from the match-up to a combination while playing defense. While this certainly can bewilder any offense, it might be too great a burden on the defense. Maybe if a ball club were extremely experienced they could handle it.

While there are too many combination defenses for us to describe how you can switch from the match-up to the combination of your choice, there are certain guidelines which will help your team adapt. You can use your imagination and the formula below to synchronize the defensive movement of your alteration.

Place your man defenders in the area where their man coverage will originate. Most attackers have a favorite spot from which they begin their offense. If the great player likes to cut through the match-up, you could follow the cutter man to man, then play match-up into combination. Now your man defenders are ready to guard the great player immediately.

Place your zone defenders near the area of their assignment. This is easily done. The zone defender's slides in the combination you choose should coincide with the slides these defenders would make if they stayed matched up.

Have a definite predetermined ball position for this team defensive change to occur. Two favorite ball positions are out front in a guard or the point alley and when a teammate rotates out of a run and jump stunt (see Chapter 18). Both of these coverages allow all defenders to anticipate the impending change before it is to occur (Diagram 17-2).

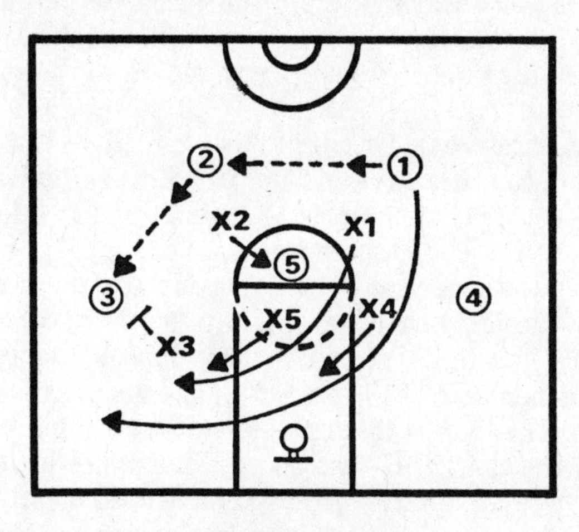

DIAGRAM 17-2

Let's use an example. Let's let X1 be the man defender of a diamond and one. Let's say you know that 1, the opponent's great player, likes to cut through to a corner against zones. You begin from your 2-1-2 match-up. 1 cuts and X1 follows. X3 slides up to a wing as does X4. X5 plays the baseline area near the basket. When 2 hits 3, X3 takes 3. X5 slides to the big block strongside, and X4 sags near the basket. X1 plays denial on 1. You are now in your diamond and one.

An advantage your defense has over playing the straight diamond and one: you have all players covered man to man for a few passes and cuts. Plus, your opponents may think you are still matching up. It can be no weaker than beginning in a diamond and one. Just be sure you drill your players until their changing defenses become automatic.

Minor Adjustments

"Minor adjustments" means that you redefine the duties of only one defender or two. You do not change the objectives or the principles of your defense. Following the first cutter man to man, the first section in this chapter, could possibly be considered a minor adjustment.

X2, in all diagrams except adjustments in this book, covers the first player left of X1. Let's say X2 is your best defender, a great defensive specialist. You naturally want him covering the area of the court where your opposition prefers to operate. Let's say they have strong tendencies to attack the left offensive side of the court. Or they have a superstar who always lines up at the left wing. X2 and X3 could exchange places and duties. This would allow X2 to take the first player right of X1, the area where their superstar always lines up, the space where the opposition likes to attack. X3 would take the first player left of X1. The objectives of the defense stayed the same, but your alteration saved your team several baskets during the game.

Your opponents have that superstar who can drive all the way to the basket or who can stop on a dime, pull up, and shoot the quick jumper off of the drive. You could put your super defender in that attacker's favorite area. You could even adjust one step further. You could have your strong defender overplay the superstar in one direction. That would allow your defender to play the jump shot better and tighter. All other defenders must know the predetermined direction: toward the middle or toward the outside. The defender nearest the offensive superstar can cheat a step or two toward the pocket where the superstar will be driving. He can close the gap or draw the charge. He can run and jump or trap (see Chapter 18). You have played the initial potential jump shot tightly. You have forced a drive in one direction. You have two men guarding that drive. The superstar gives the ball up before he gets to use all his skills. You have saved several points with your adjustment, and possibly expedited a victory.

Diagram 17-3 exhibits a favorite zone offensive technique. 1 passes to 2, and 1 exchanges positions with 3. You can allow X1 and X3 to shift on the cuts as the cutter rule of the match-up commands. Or you could adjust by letting X1 guard 1 and X3 cover 3. This is a good stratagem when you want to keep X3 on 3 or X1 on 1 because of a differential in size, speed, etc. You could also use this adaptation when you want your opponents to think you are in man to man. Your adjustment to the coverage rule would require X1 to cover the first man right of X3, and X3 to become the point defender, the man the other defenders use as their key. Of course, this alteration could be continuous if the ball were reversed and 3 exchanged with 2. Or you could stop the man coverage once X3 rotated to the point.

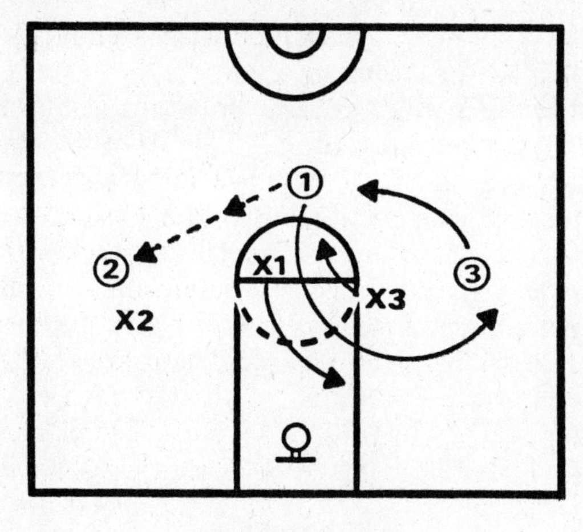

DIAGRAM 17-3

Minor adjustments are unlimited in number. These examples provide you with some thoughts. Study your opponent's plan of assault. Devise the adaptations you will need to stymie their attack, to perturb their players. Drill on those alterations until your team can execute them instinctively. Then spring those adjustments at a timely juncture during a game. And after the game listen to the fans brag about Johhny, or Paul, or Sam. But you'll know. And more importantly, so do Johnny, Paul, and Sam.

Team Adjustments Within the Match-Up

Coaches who believe in showing their zone each trip downfloor before matching up have several adjustments available to them. By showing their zone first, they will always face a regular zone attack. This eliminates the excessive player movement some coaches use against match-ups.

You can play your straight zone until the ball goes below a line tangent to the top of the foul circle. Your opponents will see your zone and set their zone offense in motion. When the ball penetrates any area within twenty-one feet of the baseline, your zone shifts into a match-up.

Or you could play straight zone until the ball goes to a corner alley. When using this variation, it is best to use Coach Charles Ward's Match-Up rules, but you can match-up using our basic rules. Counting the third and the fourth man around the perimeter becomes important so that no defender will miss his assignment.

You could deviate slightly from the above adaptation by allowing the ball to go to a corner—or by pushing it there—and then matching up when it comes back out to a wing or a guard alley. Attackers will have difficulty recognizing this alteration as a match-up. They have seen zone from the time they crossed the midcourt line. They set their offense in motion, passed to the corner while running their offense, and brought the ball back out front still seeing the basic zone defense. Your team flows gently into their match-up. When you run this adaptation, you must say "Corner," when the ball reaches the corner. All defenders respond "Corner." Now every defender knows the next pass to a wing or a guard alley will be matched. This helps eliminate defensive confusion.

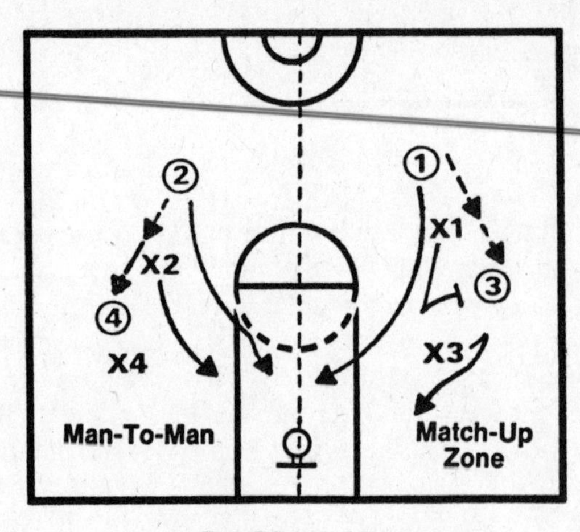

DIAGRAM 17-4

Playing the initial cut on one side man to man and on the other side your zone or match-up is a team deviation that can bewilder even the smartest offensive attack. Diagram 17-4 shows the offense making the same pass and cut on both sides of the court. On the right side, 1 passes to 3 and cuts. That move is met with the Penn State Sliding Zone maneuver of our match-up. The entire defense plays match-up zone. On the left side of the court, 2 passes to 4 and cuts. X2 follows 2 man to man and X4 covers 4. The entire defense is man to man. You let the offense call your defense by the side of the entry pass. This technique works best against regimented, patterned teams. But they must be patterned if they intend to defeat your match-up. You'll frequently be playing man defense against zone patterns and match-up zone against man-to-man patterns. The worst you get is man defense against man patterns and match-up against zone patterns. You can switch the sides of the court at half-time or the quarter breaks and further muddle the offensive thinking.

You can channel or push the offense in a predetermined direction. You can force the attack down the middle or to the outside. Or you can compel the ball to the middle on one side and to the outside on the other. Or you can give the outside to the twenty-eight foot marker and then force it inside. You can use the impelling adjustments while using any of the other adaptations. In fact, it is suicide to allow today's offenses to go where they want to go.

When playing against a team which always aligns itself in a predetermined array, and most teams do, and when you want to stay in your match-up but you want a particular defender on a specific attacker because of relative size or speed, then you can switch from our "rotation right" to "rotation left." Diagram 17-5 exhibits "rotation left."

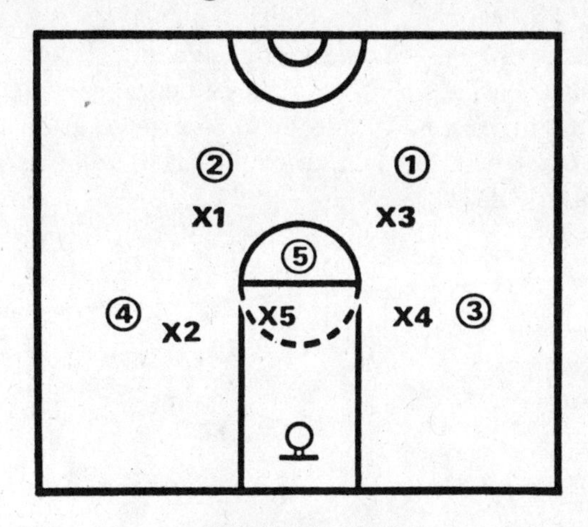

DIAGRAM 17-5

Let's say you began from a 1-3-1 zone and matched up. Most teams attack the 1-3-1 with a 2-1-2 alignment. Ordinarily, you would have X1 on 1, X2 on 2, X4 on 4, X3 on 3,and X5 on 5 because of "rotation right" and the coverage rule. But 4 is too quick for X4 and 3 is too big for X3. So you "rotate left." Instead of X1 defending the guard in the right guard alley, he picks up the guard in the left guard alley. All the other defenders use their coverage rule. X1 would pick up 2, X2 takes the first attacker around the perimeter left of X1, 4. X3 picks up the first attacker right of X1, 1. X5 guards the post, 5. X4, the matcher, defends the second player left or right of X1, 3. This is especially good strategy against the team that attacks the defensive left side of the court, and most teams do, using 3 as a strong weakside rebounder, or using 3 and 5 as strong inside attackers.

You can use your point guard to retard offensive attacks. When the opposition attacks by overloading one side of the court and passing the ball until they get it inside, your point guard can exaggerate a sink inside, helping defense the middle. But when the opposition likes excessive man movement, they usually prefer quick reversal of the ball from one side of the court to the other. In this case, your point guard can pressure the reverse passing. (For more on this see laning in Chapter 18.) This would force the offense further outside. It would slow down the reversal movement. Sometimes an interception results. Trapping, also, tends to slow down ball and player movement.

Some coaches don't like to adjust. They reason that this shows a weakness in the team defense. If you are among those coaches, don't adjust. You would betray your personality. The players would know. But then your defense will be damaged by offensive adjustments. Some easy baskets will result, baskets that could have been prevented by a wise adjustment. Changing from a man-to-man to a zone, after all, is an adjustment. And unless you have superior material, you are in for a long night, a long, long, winter.

18 TRAPPING, STUNTING, AND LANING FROM THE MATCH-UP

After teaching your players your basic zone and accompanying match-up, you study your opposition. You learn their peculiarities and preferences, their habits and customs, their individual and collective patterns. You pre-plan adjustments to counteract adaptations you judge your opponents will make in their attack.

But there is a third phase which all prominent primary defenses contain—forcing the opposition out of their game plans and/or providing a way of catching up when behind in score late late in the game. These two goals are scored for the match-up in this chapter.

Powerful defenses must provide opportunities for premeditated stunts and traps. These stunts and traps, when added to the containment half-court match-up zone defense, will give your team a thorough, time-tested championship shield, a protection that does not waver as offenses do from game to game and season to season.

Traps

Not every ball handler can be trapped, but every team can. Somewhere they have a weakest individual; and within the framework of their team pattern, they have a frail spot. As coach, you are charged with finding it.

All areas on the court are not equal for successful trapping. Some regions provide too many passing avenues of escape; other spaces reduce outlet passing lanes to three or less.

Your defense and their offense, therefore, determine the objectives of your trap. First, you decide the areas where you intend to entangle the attackers. Then you ascertain what offensive maneuvers you want to ensnare. Each section on the court will receive amplification, and offensive action peculiar to that territory will be explained and defensed. Success will come from pressure on the ball and how quickly the passing lane defenders can cover their responsibilities.

From the Corner Alley. The corner alley supplies the perfect floor position for trapping. Not only is the space for offensive maneuverability limited, but there are only three escape passing lanes available, two of which are not attacking passing lanes. Numbers are on the defensive side: two to trap and three for the three passing lanes.

Three strategies provide the best times to trap: always trap an area, and the offense will tend to never take the ball there; force the offense to an area then trap, and the defense gains a step in gambling for the steal; compel the attackers to rotate to outlet pass receiving positions, and the offense will react to the defender's dictates. All three tactics put the defense on the attack and the offense on the defensive.

There are seven attacking alleys. And when you trap in two of those alleys, the opponents will stop taking the ball there. By always trapping the corner alleys, if the offense refuses to go there, the defense only needs to defend the two wing alleys, the two guard alleys, and the point alley. A major sector of the court can be eliminated by always trapping. When you want your opponents to forget about an area, you want to safety trap. When score and time dictate a steal, you want to play all passing lanes.

Trapping the corner alleys also makes it difficult for the passer to pass to the low or high post. This is excellent strategy when a team is hurting your defense with inside passes from the corner.

There are two types of traps. You can safety trap, or you can gamble trap for a steal. Diagram 18-1 shows the safety trap. X2 and X4 trap the ball handler. X1 covers the high post passing lane, and X1 can help X2 prevent the quick jump shot on a pass back to the strongside wing position. Of course, this quick jump shot by a wing can be of great help to the defense if the defense's purpose is to speed up the opponent's attack. X5 covers the low post passing lane. X3 has weakside defensive rebounding responsibilities. X1 can alter his coverage when there are no movements into the high post lane. He can cheat into the wing passing lane when he feels that will be productive.

Diagram 18-2 depicts the gambling trap for the steal. Because the basket and bankboard prevent the ball handler from getting the ball to teammates on the weakside near the basket, the trap for steals can be effective from the corner on and off during the entire game. X2 and X4 trap the ball handler. X1 hurries out to the wing position. X3 covers the high post passing lane, and he must never allow any direct pass into that lane. A completed direct pass could give the attackers a lay-up. X5 covers the low post passing lane, and he must never allow the direct pass there.

A completed pass into X3's area should be covered by X3. X5 should move quickly to the weakside big block, and X4 should cover where X5 vacated. A completed pass into X5's area must be tightly covered by X5. X3 would race under the basket, and X1 would replace the vacated spot of X3. This coverage on completed passes to the high and low post regions eliminates the quick give-me lay in on the weakside. It forces one more move from the offense. A penetrating pass could be intercepted. A shot would come under pressure. A pass back outside allows the defense time to reset.

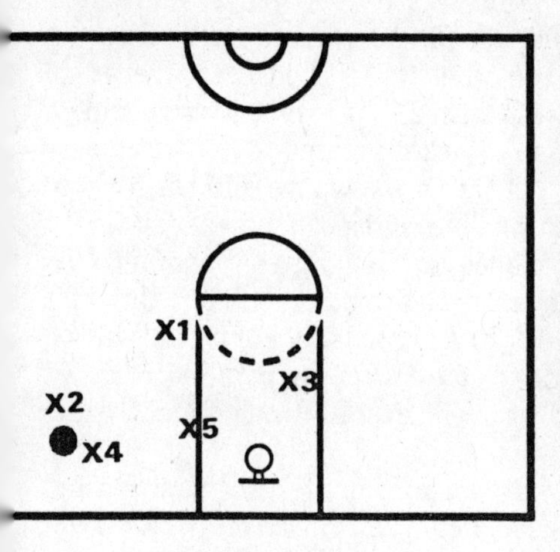

DIAGRAM 18-1

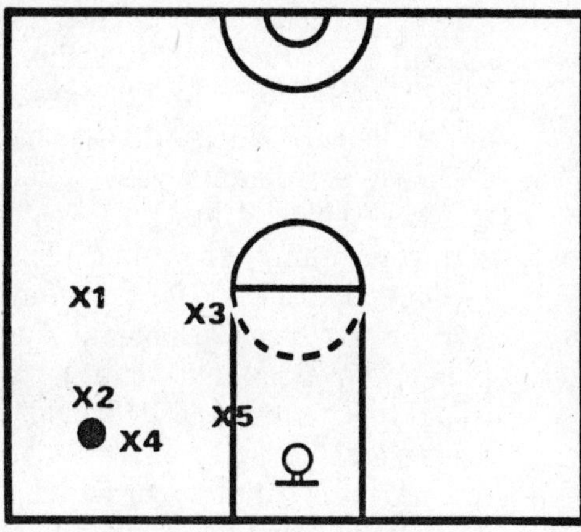

DIAGRAM 18-2

A second strategy, forcing the ball to the corner alley then trapping for a steal, usually transpires late in the game. It must occur with enough time left to allow the defense to encourage the ball into the corner alley. Without sufficient time on the clock, a smart team would not take the ball to the corner. There must be enough time left so the offense will continue attacking.

To force the ball to the corner alley, the defender in the guard alley shades the dribbler to the inside shoulder. The wing defender, if there is one, and the corner defenders sag inside and a step or two higher than their attacker. If the pass goes to the corner, the defenders trap. If the pass goes to the wing alley, the wing defender pressures the wing attacker on his high shoulder side. The corner alley defender plays his man high but sags deeply inside. The guard denies any pass back to his man. Usually, the ball follows the line of least resistance: a pass into the corner alley. Then the defenders (wing and corner) trap.

When defensive teams force the ball to a predetermined space on the court, all defenders know it. They have drilled on it. The three charged with covering the passing lanes can cheat a step or two toward those lanes. This premature cheating permits quicker coverage of the passing lanes, encourages more gambling, and brings about earlier steals.

Defensive coaches, in days past, did not have this third strategy because it was taboo for offenses to pass across a zone. Recently, however, many fine offensive coaches have taught patterns that attack the weakside of the zone by passing over it.

Diagram 18-3 depicts the 1-3-1 rotation offense that is so popular against the 2-1-2 zone. But in this option, 4 is the only player on the left side of the court after 2 cuts. 1 did not fill 2's vacated spot, choosing instead to overload the weakside. The other three offensive players also overload the weakside. X2 takes a step with 2 to prevent the give and go or middle cut. When X2 sees that no attacker rotates to an outlet pass receiving position, X2 goes to help X4 trap 4. Now it is difficult for 4 to find a receiver. 4 has been told to dribble outside if he cannot find a receiver within four seconds. This maneuver would give 4 another four seconds, time needed for the offense to rotate an outlet receiver. But X2's trap prevents the dribble. If 4 waits five seconds, a jump ball will be called. The offense must cut 1 outside to give 4 an outlet pass receiver. X2 would then take 1, and X1 would "bust over" to 3. X3 would take 2, using his "release" technique.

An alternative to corner traps: X4 can pressure tightly while X1 and X2 roam as free safeties do in football. Should X2 trap with X4, X1 could operate as a lone free safety.

From Baseline Drives. tbaseline drives are automatically trapped. A defense that can eliminate or discourage this powerful offensive maneuver has improved its chances for victory. Remember the rule: Weakside low defender stops breakaway dribblers while weakside high defenders drop to the basket area. You can alter this by allowing your center to drop to stop the driver if that suits your zone slides better.

With the ball in the corner, all weakside defenders line up even with the line through the two baskets. For discussion's sake, let's let 4 drive by X4 (Diagram 18-4). X5, the weakside low defender, recognizes the baseline drive, races over, and establishes position outside the lane if

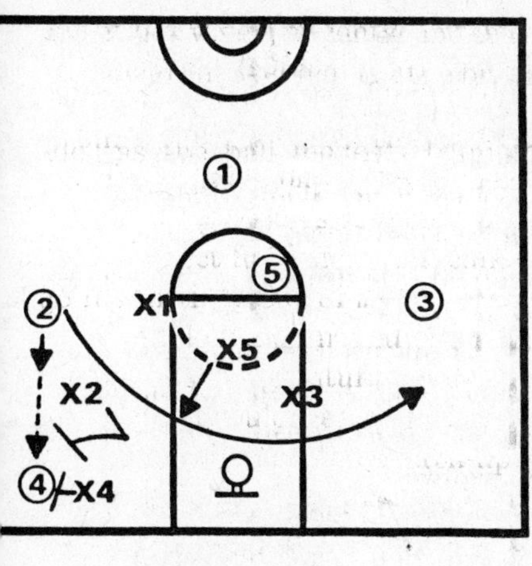

DIAGRAM 18-3

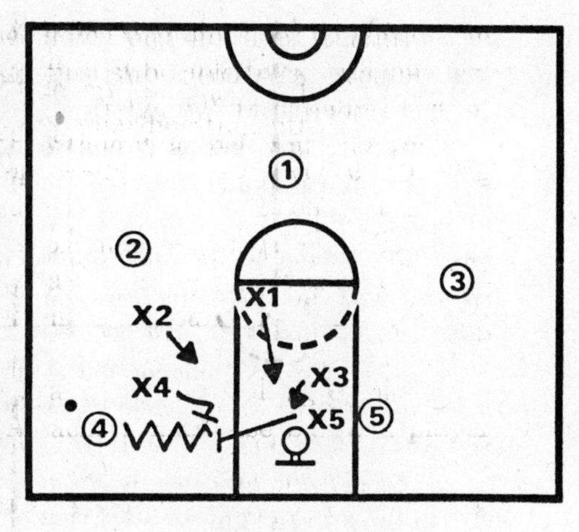

DIAGRAM 18-4

possible. X4 keeps side pressure on 4. If 4 jumps, he would probably charge into X5. X5 raises his arms but does not jump. X3 slides to the basket area. The habit pass would be from 4 to 5. X3 should steal this pass. It must be bounced, a slow pass. The bankboard prevents any lob pass. X5's body interferes with a direct chest pass. X1 covers the middle passing lane. X2 covers the passing lane that is even with 4 and parallel to the sideline. The defense can quickly regain the advantage that the offense had. A few successful baseline traps, and the offense will not drive it anymore. Or they will, during the course of the game, pay a dear price for their baseline drives.

From the Wing Alleys. The wing alleys provide the offense with five passing lanes, three of which are attacking passes. And that does not include the crosscourt lob passes. The defense does not have the numbers to trap yet fill the passing lanes. So it is defensive suicide to trap at the wings.

If it is late in the game and you must have the ball, you want to force the ball from the wing alleys. To do this, the defender need only play within six feet of the ball handler for five seconds. After five seconds of dribbling, a jump ball will be called. A player could stall twelve seconds at the most (four before dribbling, four while dribbling, and four after dribbling) in the wing alley. A pass to the corner alley or to guard alley will be trapped.

From the Guard Alleys. Guard alleys have corners where the midcourt line meets the sideline. Although these two guard corners can be trapped, they give the attackers three direct passing lanes, two of which are attacking passing lanes. So it is best to trap the guard corners under two conditions: force the ball there late in the game when time and the score demand gambling, and trap the ball as it crosses midcourt at strategic moments of the game.

Trapping the ball as it crosses midcourt requires coordination between the conventional zone traps and the match-up zone. Regardless of which array—1-3-1, 1-2-2, or 2-1-2—your conventional zone press personnel positioning as the ball crosses midcourt should look like Diagram 18-5. X1 and X2 trap the ball. X3 and X1 would trap the right guard corner. X4 covers high post left side,and X3 covers high post right side. X4 can guard the left passing lane if he feels he can intercept a pass there. X3 can jump into the crosscourt passing lane if he feels an interception can occur. X5 covers the area near the basket.

A completed pass out of the trap would bring your match-up. From the original positionings in Diagram 18-5, it is easy to get into the 2-3, the 1-3-1, or the 1-2-2 match-up. And this initial positioning prohibits any inside passing out of the trap: X3, X4 and X5 have the middle covered. Any deflection can lead to an interception. A few gambles by X4 and X3 might bring a turnover.

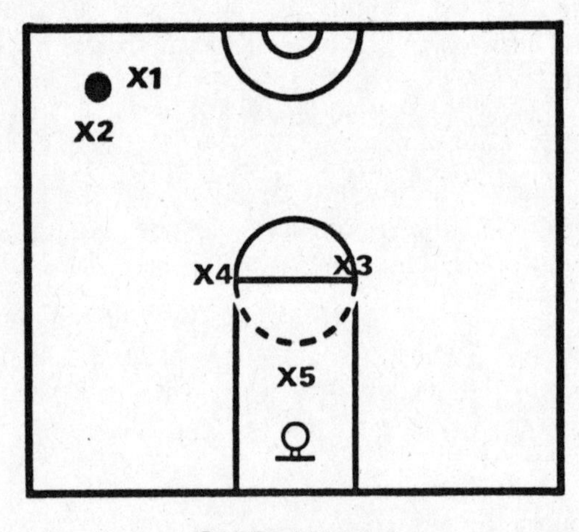

DIAGRAM 18-5

To force the ball to the guard corner late in the game requires team coordinated pressure. The wing defender pressures the wing attacker from a denial, interception stance. The defensive guards push the guard dribbles outside. The defensive center must deny the high post the ball. The other two defenders sag for help near the basket. Because there is pressure on the strongside wing and the ball is being pushed there, the strongside wing usually breaks outside toward the guard corner.When the offensive wing tries to free himself with this cut, the defensive wing trails him, hoping for the pass there, preparing to trap the completed pass with the defensive guard.

You can safety trap, as in Diagram 18-5, or you can gamble trap for steals if the score and time demand it. To trap for steals from the guard corner, extend X4 into the left passing lane and X3 into the right guard passing lane; and X5 moves up to cover the center passing lane.

Diagrams 18-1, 18-2, 18-4, and 18-5 exhibit your half court match-up zone press from each trapping position on the left side of the court. A pass to the left wing would have X4 contain him while X2 and X4 execute the Penn State Sliding Zone maneuver. Anywhere along the trap, your team can contain match-up, or you can drill the slides into a conventional half court zone trap. But make sure all team members either contain or trap. Don't have some doing one thing and the others doing another.

Stunts

Stunts are designed to throw off the execution of a well drilled offense, possibly steal a few errant passes. Offensive teams whose patience and precision bewilder your defense should face stunts, traps, and defensive ajdustments.

Two and three man run and jumps, two man run and no jumps, and the give-the-outside-then-take-it-away tactic provide the best match-up zone stunts. Each will be shown from a 2-1-2 defensive match-up array.

Two Man Run and Jump. When stunting, your defense should meet the offense at midcourt. Your defense can recover better when it is extended to midcourt, but the run and jumps can occur within scoring territory.

In Diagram 18-6, X1 cuts 2 toward X2. X2 races directly at the dribbling hand of 2. X2, your taller guard, calls, "Jump," or "Trap." "Trap" tells X1 to stay and trap with X2. "Jump" tells X1 to go cover the area X2 just vacated. It is likely that 2 will pass there. A steal results in a fast break. A completed pass allows X1 to pick up the receiver. X2 guards the first attacker around the perimeter left of X1; X3 takes the first man right of X1; etc. The defense stunted, but it remained ready to match-up, to man, or to zone. If 2 prefers to keep his dribble alive and reverse out of the "jump," X2 stays with the dribbler. When facing a dribbling guard who likes to reverse out of the run and jump, X2 should order X1 to "trap." In either case, the defense is matched up.

Diagram 18-6 initiates defensive coverage with X1 at left guard only because, after matching, it will conform to the other diagrams in the book. If both X2 and X1 can be used as keys for the match-up, either may start from the left guard position.

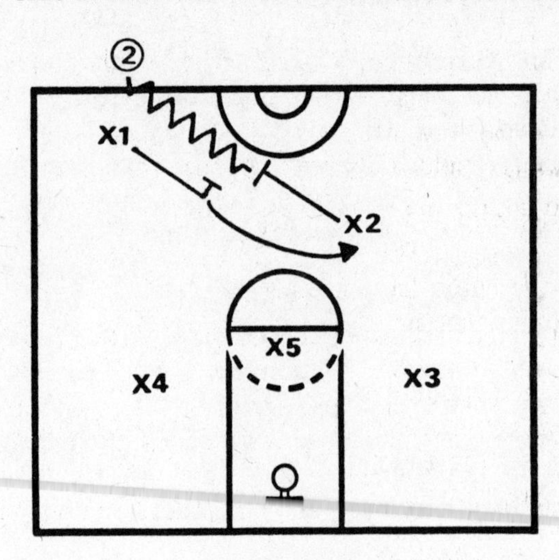

DIAGRAM 18-6

Three Man Run and Jump. When X1, X2, X3, and X4 can all play the perimeter, can all become the key man, can all provide matcher coverage, the three man run and jump will be most effective. When they all do not possess these abilities, modification must be made. For example, when only X3 can play the perimeter and X4 can only match, then you can three man run and jump from only the left side of the court. Two man run and jump would be operative from the right side.

Diagram 18-7 depicts a typical three-man run and jump. X2 races at the outside shoulder of 2, communicating "trap" or "jump" to X1. As X2 leaves, X3 begins to fill the space vacated by X2. When 2 picks up his

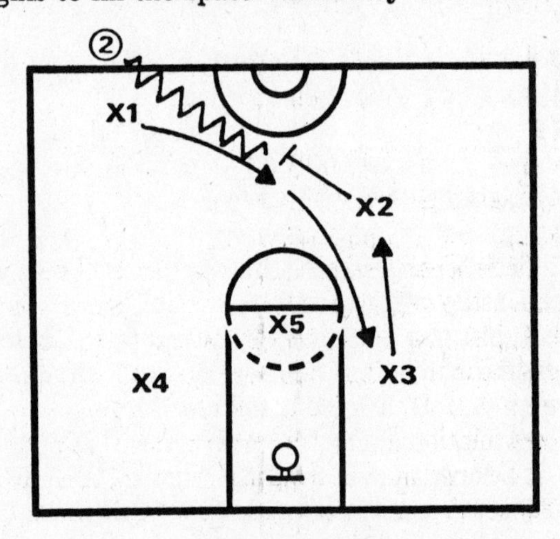

DIAGRAM 18-7

dribble, or when X1 hears "jump," X1 rotates toward X2's vacated area. But when X1 finds X3 there, X1 contiues and fills the spots X3 just vacated. Now X3 is the key. X2 has the first attacker left of X3, and X1 covers the first player right of X3. The match-up begins.

Two Man Run and No Jump. Let's use Diagram 18-6 to explain run-and-no-jump strategy. The other stunts can be automatics, or they can be called by the coach from the bench. You can develop your own cues. But this stunt must be called by the coach so all defenders will know.

You don't want 2 handling the ball inside the scoring area because of his great scoring or penetration abilities. You have X2 run but not jump. X2 stays until 2 gives the ball up, usually to the right guard alley, especially if X4 pressures the wing. This stunt also works well to force the ball down the right side of the court. You can even use this tactic to get into the box and one or diamond and one. You simply have X1 guard 2 man to man after 2 gives up the ball.

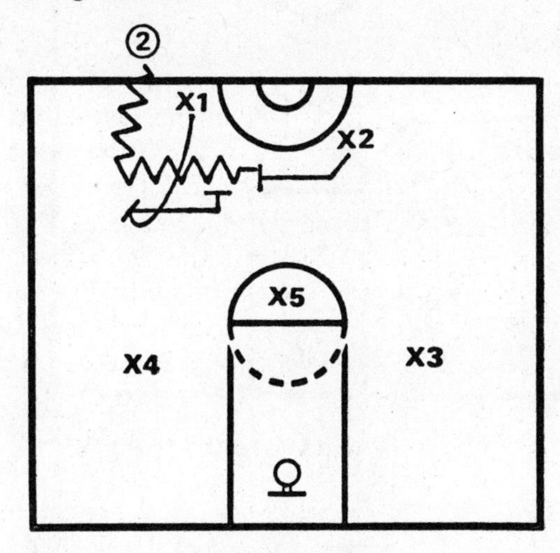

DIAGRAM 18-8

Give the Outside Then Take It Away. X1, unlike in the run and jumps, plays on the inside of 2, forcing 2 to the outside. When 2 reaches a predetermined spot, like the twenty-eight foot marker, X1 reachieves an overplay, forcing 2 to the middle. X2, knowing what stunt is called, races to double-team with X1. If X2 gets to 2 as he completes his reverse dribble, a charge or violation might occur. X2 calls, "Trap" or "Jump." X3 could even make it a three man rotation. Any steal, deflection, or jump ball helps the defense. A completed pass results in the match-up. The worst you get is harassment of the offense, forcing their smooth-working machine to make some adjustments before attacking your match-up.

Laning

Laning badgers the offenses that stress rapid player and/or ball reversals. All defenders must know when laning instead of containment has been called. Otherwise, seams open up inside and the defense fails. So the coach must call it from the bench.

In Diagram 18-9, for example, X1 stations himself in the lane between 2 and 1. X4 can lane the pass to 4, or he can sag. X1 plays the interception stance (see Chapter 3). By playing in his interception stance, X1 can steal a pass to the inside shoulder of 1, can offer moderate help if 2 tries to drive inside, and can cover any quick backdoor cut by 1. X1 gives up the high post passing lane (a seam); so the inside defender must deny all passes there.

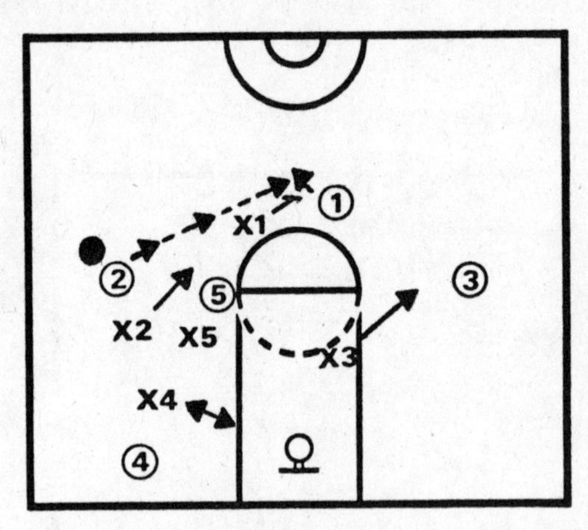

DIAGRAM 18-9

If X4 has sagged, 2 will probably pass to 4, the line of least resistance. X2 and X4 can corner trap, or X2 can lane while X1 sags his three-step drill.

Most likely, 1 will step a few steps outside and 2 will reverse the ball. Because of X1's interception stance, this pass might be stolen or deflected. To complete the pass requires more time against the laning technique. The time used slows down the effective reversals that have been hurting the defense. When 1 receives the pass, X2 and X3 would lane, using their interception stances. This continues to slow down quick ball and rapid player movements.

While outlet passing lanes are laned to slow down ball movement, the defense must be careful it does not overspread. By overextending, passing lanes to inside seams become an offensive option. The defense should be content to spread the offense, to slow down their devastating quick ball movement, yet to surrender no openings inside. If your defense wants to gamble for steals, stunts or traps—not laning—should be called.

Summary

Traps slow down ball and player movement, disrupt the timing of precision offenses, occasionally steal a pass, often compel quick, hurried, inaccurate shots, speed up any slow moving offense, and can impel an attack to spots where the defense wants it. Stunts can slow an offense, can force the offense to do what the defense wants, can distill any unpoised ball handler, and can steal an occasional errant pass. Laning forces offenses further out on the court, slows down rapid ball and player movements, defends the inside more than adequately, and intercepts babied or automatic passes.

Most stunts and traps can be automatic maneuvers, executed by your players' abilities to read; or they can be called by the bench. A mixture makes a happy blend.

Coupling traps, stunts, and laning with adjustments (Chapter 17) to your basic containment match-up gives your team all the firepower of any championship primary defense. If you plan on using the match-up, you have many decisions to make. The success or failure of your match-up depends on those choices. Chapter 19 is designed to help you make proper teaching selections.

19 DEVELOPMENTAL SCHEDULE FOR TEACHING THE MATCH-UP

No exceptional defense can become functional without intense planning, positive organization, sound teaching, and drill repetition. Translating these to your players requires a many-faceted professional.

Selling the match-up to your defenders becomes the first obstacle, the first ring from the center of treacherous concentric circles. To sell your defense, you must be firmly and thoroughly sold. You may want to re-read the material many times before you begin to peddle. Making a list of the reasons you feel you need to match up (see Chapter 1) will help you sell your match-up to your players.

After you convince yourself of the need for the match-up, you must begin making decisions which will ultimately determine the success or failure of your defense. Considerable planning and organizational ability are called for. Many out-of-season hours must be spent preparing for the actual unloading of your knowledge to your players. Be resourceful and be creative: develop your own rules and your own drills to teach those guidelines. But keep them simple and make them completely cover the subject. Leave no part to chance; bare no section to weakness; be thorough but be succinct.

Choosing the Starting Zone

Make no mistake about it, choosing the starting zone is your most important decision. Study the defensive traits of your players, their size, their speed, their quickness, their abilities of judgment. Size, speed, quickness, etc., are all relative; so you must figure your opposition's players as well. Unless you can recruit, your basic zone may change from year to year. But once you choose a zone for any particular year, stay with it. Changing it would destroy your team's confidence in your defense.

Once you have chosen your zone, several sliding possibilities might exist. You must determine which slides best suit the skills of your players, which slides they would execute at maximum efficiency. Never teach two or three different coverages: that flusters the defenders. And it's the offense that the match-up wants to confuse.

Choosing the regular zone and its accompanying slides should take place in the summer months. Your thinking should be cool, calculated, and free from the pressures of an up-coming season.

Choosing Your Coverage and Cutter Rules

You have your zone and its slides. You have drills to teach them. You know your personnel, their abilities, their strengths, and their weaknesses. From this knowledge, you can formulate your coverage and cutter rules. This, too, can be decided in the good ole summertime when leisure and not pressure can provide a cooler mental stimulus.

Teaching Basic Defensive Fundamentals: Man and Zone

Your planning has been completed. You have your zone, your guidelines, your drills. You have planned and organized; you are now ready to teach.

Your defense must stand upon the foundation of fundamentals. How well you teach the basic man fundamentals and your basic zone slides and essentials is paramount. It determines whether your defense is built on rock or on sand if the first assault wave will wash it away. Chapter 3 must be mastered, taught, drilled until it is instinctive. One week should be minimum, and two weeks would more than suffice. Constant review throughout the season is a must.

Teaching Your Zone

While you tutor your fundamentals, you should drill on the slides of your regular zone. Players must know the area they are to cover when the ball is located in the eight scoring alleys: point, right guard, left guard, right wing, left wing, right corner, left corner, and the high post lane sections. Defenders must recognize these coverage responsibilities even while playing the match-up. Twenty minutes, a day or two, should provide the proper instincts.

Teaching Coverage Rule

Floor position in relation to the ball means everything to your team zone. But each match-up defender must also know where his man is. Each defender must know where the ball is first, where his man is second. The ball scores, but the man without the ball can maneuver into a favorable position if his defender is not constantly alert.

It should take not longer than two days to have your team match up using the coverage rule. Have the offense come downcourt and line up in a regular offensive array: 1-3-1, 2-1-2, 1-2-2, 1-4, etc. Have your defenders slide, following their coverage rule, to their assigned offensive man. Scan your defender's positions to see that proper judgments have been made. Then have the offense come down the floor and line up in a typical overload alignment: box, triangular, or diamond. Study your defender's locations to determine if they have moved to the proper attacker from their zone positions.

After your defenders have matched the popular formations, you can advance to free-lance arrays or special gimmick alignments. Once this is mastered, you can allow the offense freedom to choose their stations. The defense will respond correctly. You should, all this time, monitor your players' positioning in relation to the ball handler—plane of greatest peripheral view and three-step drill. But never at this stage allow either player or ball movement.

Teaching Defense Versus Ball Movement

A week or more will be needed for this phase. If you work in a state that does not allow two weeks for preparation before your first game, you can use your man defense and your basic zone until time permits proper coaching of the match-up. Or you can double your defensive tutoring sessions from twenty to forty minutes each practice. It may even be worth trippling your defensive drill minutes. The match-up zone will equalize an opponent who has better natural talent.

Once the offense has lined up in its attacking array and your defense has matched that alignment, have the offense move the ball slowly, stopping after each pass for three or four seconds. Check each defender's assignment and positioning. Allow no cutting until the players know the coverage rules.

After you are satisfied with matching, plane of greatest peripheral view, and the three-step drill, you can begin to allow player movement, but still no cutting through the zone. At this juncture in teaching, offensive movement should be restricted to one-on-one dribbling moves, screen and roll on the perimeter, exchanging places on the perimeter but not cutting through (a guard becomes a forward and a forward rotates up to a guard, etc.), and the inside men flashing to the ball. You can even allow shots to be taken, and you can survey box-out techniques. All this time, you must correct any defender's bad judgment. You can allow the ball to be moved as slowly or as rapidly as the player's understanding permits.

Teaching Defense Versus Basic Cutters from Offenses Ordinarily Used Against Your Zone

Your zone usually determines the offensive array. For example, most 2-1-2 zones face a 1-3-1 or a 1-2-2 attack. And most attacks have pet cuts built into their formations. Each has been diagramed and explained in the chapters devoted to your zone. By drilling first against those favorite cuts, you can use your match-up earlier. Allow two days for your players to learn these.

Your match-up is almost ready. It takes about three weeks of twenty-minute daily sessions to accomplish this. But if you have more time, the next sections will solidify your defense. If you do not have more time, put the remainder in as the season progresses, or extend your twenty-minute daily practices.

Teaching Defense Versus Cutters from All Positions

Put your defenders in their zone. Begin by teaching only cutters from the strongside. Tell your players that. Take each possible cut from every strongside alley. For example, from the guard alley: have a wing pass with the guard cutting through to the strongside corner; have a wing pass with the guard cutting through to the weakside; have a guard-to-guard pass with the guard cutting through to the new strongside corner; etc. Then move to the wing alley. Then to the corner alley.

After you feel confident with these coverages, have weakside cutters come to the strongside. Drill on cuts from each weakside alley.

When all of these positions have been mastered, move to multiple cuts. First, let two attackers cut; then allow three. You keep control by designating the cutter movement. You should have drills devised, or use the ones in this book, to cover the cutters using your cutter's rule. Allow about a week for your players to absorb these coverages thoroughly. You should use both the chalk board and floor demonstrations to illustrate your meanings.

Showing Next Opponents Zone (Man) Offense

Your defense has been taught. Your players can now match any offense and any movement. To review and to familiarize your players with your next opponent, you should devise drills using your next opponent's offenses. This takes a day or two—the usual time given between games.

After teaching each basic array and overload and the offensive moves associated with them, let the players scrimmage half court. Correct each defensive mistake as it occurs. Every day or so, review the cuts from diferent popular formations, re-examine the cuts from strongside alleys one day and the weakside the next. You can use your next opponent's offense for double help: to recheck fundamentals as well as to prepare for your next game. You must astutely design drills to accomplish this.

Putting in Adjustments

You can now figure ways to bend your defense—manipulations that make the offensive attack null and void, empty. After your players know and understand the match-up, they will have little trouble responding to pre-planned, pre-drilled adjustments. Many defenders, in fact, adjust automatically. Your players get smarter, match-up wise, with each day's drilling.

After you make an offense adapt to your defensive adjustments, victory belongs to your team. The attackers are now performing part plays that they have not pre-drilled. Your defense did pre-plan, pre-drill its alterations. Your defense is now on the attack. The offense will ultimately succumb.

Putting in Pressure, Stunts, and Laning

After your containment match-up is solid, you can begin tutoring pressure maneuvers, moves designed to force the opposition out of their attack or to get the ball late in a game when score and time demand it. Pressure can be double-teaming traps with teammates covering the passing lanes, or it can be stunts designed to drive the ball to a particular area or away from a specific player.

When an opponent's offense reveals considerable player movement, you could trap. Trapping has a tendency to slow down motion.

When offenses prefer rapid reversal of the ball from one side of the court to the other, laning should be ordered. By stationing a defender between the ball and an intended receiver, you can force the speedy ball reversal to slow down, to spread, or to be intercepted.

The Final Test

In the end, ask your players to play your basic zone. Sit back several possessions during a team scrimmage and observe. If the defenders, after a few passes, automatically begin to match up, you have done your job. You are a master teacher, an expert coach. Your defenders are ready. Your match-up has come alive: a monster feared by those who must invade its lair; a demon terrorizing those who must advance against it.

INDEX

P

R

S

T

V

W

Y

Z